THE CASE FOR TENURE

The Case for Tenure

MATTHEW W. FINKIN

ILR Press
an imprint of
Cornell University Press
Ithaca and London

First published 1996 by Cornell University Press.

Library of Congress Cataloging-in-Publication Data
Finkin, Matthew W.
    The case for tenure / Matthew W. Finkin.
        p.   cm.
    Includes bibliographical references.
    ISBN 0-8014-3316-9 (cloth : alk. paper)
    1. College teachers—Tenure—United States.   I. Title.
LB2335.7.F55   1996
378.1'22—dc20   96-16788

Printed in the United States of America

This book is printed on Lyons Falls Turin Book,
a paper that is totally chlorine-free and acid-free.

[T]he concept {of tenure} is the product of historical experience and long debate. Its adoption is not merely a reflection of solicitude for the staffs of academic institutions, but of concern for the general welfare by providing for the benefits of uninhibited scholarship and its free dissemination. The security provided therefor by the consensus of learned authority should not be indifferently regarded.

—Judge Melvin P. Antell in *AAUP v. Bloomfield College*, 322 A.2d 846, 853–854 (N.J. Super. 1974)

Contents

Acknowledgments

The selections and comments in this book are my own, and I bear sole responsibility for them. But I would be remiss if I did not acknowledge the enormous educational debt I owe to my erstwhile colleagues on the staff of the American Association of University Professors (AAUP), especially Jordan E. Kurland and Bertram H. Davis; and to many of my erstwhile oarsmen and women on its Committee A on Academic Freedom and Tenure, especially Walter P. Metzger, Judith Jarvis Thomson, Peter O. Steiner, Robert K. Webb, Carol Simpson Stern, and, always, the lawyers—Clark Byse, Sanford Kadish, Ralph S. Brown, William Van Alstyne, Robert Gorman, Jesse Choper, and Robert M. O'Neil. Committee A was as fine a seminar as I ever had the pleasure to attend. It was a delight to be among a group of able academics who, though often sharply divided, shared a mutual respect; where minds changed in consequence of debate.

A word of appreciation goes to Frances Benson, editor in chief of Cornell University Press, who encouraged me, while I was in residence on the Vegetable Island *(Gemüse Insel)* of Reichenau at work on a very different project, to think about this one. And a further word of thanks goes to Linda Payne for the otherwise thankless task of reading and transcribing my handwriting.

M. W. F.

THE CASE FOR TENURE

Introduction

Tenure is today almost everywhere under assault. Legislative or governing board initiatives to limit or even to abolish tenure in public higher
education are under consideration in at least nine states. These efforts
have been stimulated or abetted by a steady polemical drumbeat in
books with provocative titles—*Profscam, Up the University, Tenured Radi-
cals;* in editorial page critiques; and in public denunciations of tenure's
evil ways by a few academic detractors who decline or "renounce" tenure. With much ballyhoo, the American Association for Higher Education announced a project to study "options to traditional tenure" to be
conducted by the co-author of an earlier effort to "slay the dragon" of
tenure.

I believe that academic tenure is good for America: that it is essential
for the protection of academic freedom, that it is necessary to attract
the intellectually gifted to the academic life and to create conditions
that allow first-rate scholarship to flourish. This is not to deny its drawbacks, both for the individual and for the institution, but it is to maintain that the system is far better for society than any substitute suggested thus far.

Moreover, I hope to persuade the reader that the stakes are too high
to permit us to sacrifice tenure on any of the altars that have been offered—seemingly of "efficiency," "accountability," and "flexibility."
But how I shall go about that task calls for a bit of explanation.

Little in the current criticism is genuinely new. Tenure was first
sought by the profession collectively in 1915 and has been the subject
of continuing scrutiny and controversy ever since. To distill the wisdom
and practical insight that have been gleaned over the years, I offer ex-
cerpts from essays, reports, judicial decisions, and the professional literature. (Some footnotes to selections have been omitted. The language
of an earlier generation, using the male pronoun for all professors, must
be retained.) These diverse sources are brought together here for the
first time and worked into a coherent picture of tenure as a whole. To

1

them I add my own comments, expanding a bit what is said, connecting it to what precedes or follows, or dealing with the salient criticism of tenure on the particular point.

The structure I have chosen does make some demands on the reader. It asks the reader simultaneously to engage with subsidiary aspects of tenure, and with sometimes nuanced argument about those aspects, while keeping an objective overview of the system as it works as a whole—from appointment to a probationary position, to the award (or denial) of tenure, to possible termination for unfitness and the elements of due process, on to the economics of tenure and tenure's relation to institutional resources, to the evaluation of the performance of tenured faculty, and, finally, to retirement—all with a fair amount of detail along the way. But I think it will pay the reader to keep these two tracks—the individual parts and the larger whole—in mind.

The contemporary attack on tenure is dealt with at the close. The "new" criticism is concerned less with arguments about economic efficiency and institutional flexibility than with the core connection of tenure to academic freedom. As will be seen, on close examination at least some of what is now claimed is not new at all; indeed, it goes back to 1915, when people who opposed the profession's claim to tenure did so because it ensured a degree of freedom that the critics were not willing to afford. Ironically, some of the "new" criticism makes the case for tenure, if unintentionally.

Ultimately, the case for tenure rests on a firm understanding of what it is and what it is not. This book is meant to illuminate that understanding. My hope is that once tenure is seen in each of its parts and as a whole, warts and all, it will need no defense.

1

The Meaning of Tenure

What is tenure? At the expiration of a period of probation, commonly not to exceed six years of full-time service, a faculty member is either to be accorded "tenure" or to be given a terminal appointment for the ensuing academic year. Thereafter, the professor can be discharged only for "just cause" or other permissible circumstance and only after a hearing before a body of his or her academic peers. What that really *means* is explained by William Van Alstyne, then Professor (now Perkins Professor) of Law at Duke University and chairman of the AAUP's Committee A on Academic Freedom and Tenure. Written with legal concision and with his customary elegance, Van Alstyne's "explanation" does more than lay out the essence of the obligation. The *reasons* for the tenure system are explored more fully in what may be the best and most comprehensive defense of tenure ever written, by the late Fritz Machlup, then Walker Professor of Economics and International Finance at Princeton and president of the AAUP. Machlup's essay draws directly upon his discipline, but it reflects the insights of a life rich in academic (and industrial) experience on two continents.

A sense of how the need for tenure draws from the realities of academic life is illuminated by two detailed case studies: one from the 1930s, when the academic community was fast coming to common ground in the need for tenure, the other from the 1990s, when tenure came once again under attack.

Tenure: A Summary, Explanation, and "Defense"

William Van Alstyne

* * *

Tenure, accurately and unequivocally defined, lays no claim whatever to a guarantee of lifetime employment. Rather, tenure provides only that no

From *AAUP Bulletin* 57 (Autumn 1971): 329–351.

person continuously retained as a full-time faculty member beyond a specified lengthy period of probationary service may thereafter be dismissed *without adequate cause*. Moreover, the particular standards of "adequate cause" to which the tenured faculty is accountable are themselves wholly within the prerogative of each university to determine through its own published rules, save only that those rules not be applied in a manner which violates the academic freedom or the ordinary personal civil liberties of the individual. An institution may provide for dismissal for "adequate cause" arising from failure to meet a specified norm of performance or productivity, as well as from specified acts of affirmative misconduct. In short, there is not now and never has been a claim that tenure insulates any faculty member from a fair accounting of his professional responsibilities within the institution which counts upon his service.

In a practical sense, tenure is translatable principally as a statement of formal assurance that thereafter the individual's professional security and academic freedom will not be placed in question without the observance of full academic due process. This accompanying complement of academic due process merely establishes that a fairly rigorous procedure will be observed whenever formal complaint is made that dismissal is justified on some stated ground of professional irresponsibility, to insure the fair determination of three facts:

1. that the stated cause is the authentic cause for dismissal, rather than a pretense or makeweight for considerations invading the academic freedom or ordinary personal civil liberties of the individual;

2. that the stated cause exists in fact;

3. that the degree of demonstrated professional irresponsibility warrants outright termination of the individual's appointment rather than some lesser sanction, even after taking into account the balance of his entire service and the personal consequences of dismissal.

* * *

Tenure may also be stated in the following way more clearly to indicate its basis and meaning. The conferral of tenure means that the institution, after utilizing a probationary period of as long as six years in which it has had ample opportunity to determine the professional competence and responsibility of its appointees, has rendered a favorable judgment establishing a rebuttable presumption of the individual's professional excellence. As the lengthy term of probationary service will have provided the institution with sufficient experience to determine whether the faculty member is worthy of a presumption of professional fitness, it has not seemed unreasonable to shift to the individual the benefit of doubt when the institution thereafter extends his service beyond the period of probation and, correspondingly, to shift to the institution the obligation fairly to show why, if at all, that faculty member should nonetheless be fired. The presumption of the tenured faculty member's professional excellence thus remains rebuttable, exactly to the extent that when it can be shown that the individual possessing tenure has nonetheless fallen short or has otherwise misconducted himself as determined according to full academic due process, the presumption is lost and the individual is subject to dismissal.

There are, moreover, certain circumstances in which tenure will not provide even this degree of professional security for faculty members of unquestioned excellence. Two of these circumstances may appropriately be specified to indicate further how utterly false is the claim that tenure would rather suffer hardship to an entire institution than hardship to any of its tenured staff. As many faculty members are painfully aware, declining student enrollments in certain academic departments not only have occurred with such suddenness as to raise a serious question of whether the decline is really a healthy turning away from less worthwhile subjects (rather than a simple turn of fashion), but have also precipitously reduced the demand for the services of some faculty members with particular skills in those departments. Nevertheless, assuming that each of the affected faculty members, even though he possesses tenure, is either unable or unwilling to retrain and equip himself to be professionally competent in some other area of the academic program with sufficient demand to sustain his employment within the institution, his services may be terminated simply by the cessation of the program itself. While the faculty appropriately must participate in any decision concerning the reduction or elimination of a given program for the same reason that it must do so when the enlargement or addition of a program may be contemplated, *viz.,* to provide some informed judgment about the educational wisdom of the proposed programmatic change, tenure provides no guarantee against becoming a casualty to institutional change.

Again, the termination of particular academic programs, not from failure of interest by students but from unavoidable conditions of financial stringency, carries with it no suggestion that the released members of the faculty have either fallen short in their duties or otherwise misconducted themselves in a manner warranting termination. Nonetheless, if there is an authentic financial emergency confronting the university, and if decisions concerning what programs must be terminated and in what order, what particular faculty members must be released and in what sequence—if these decisions are made in a nonarbitrary and reasonable way with appropriate faculty participation, then nothing at all will insulate adversely affected individuals from the hard prospect of unemployment.

Tenure, then, neither buttons up the process of institutional change nor binds the ways which each institution must consider as it copes with authentic financial distress. It is but a limited statement that each faculty member possessing it, receiving it only after a stipulated period of probationary service, is thought worthy of a rebuttable presumption of professional excellence in continuing service to the institution. Thereafter, when termination of his services is sought for any reason inconsistent with that presumption, it requires only that the burden of justification be fairly discharged under conditions of academic due process by those with whom it properly rests.

To the extent that tenure protections of full academic due process possess a marked resemblance to the procedural rights of others not involved in higher education, it is clear that tenure does contemplate an interest in professional security quite apart from its central objective to safeguard academic freedom. There is, moreover, every good reason that it should do so entirely aside from an intelligent concern to render higher education competitive with other employment opportunities by assuring that it provides at least as much job security. The more fundamental reason for the requirement of due process here as elsewhere is the desire to do justice and to avoid errors in the making of critical judgments. Even supposing that in many instances a particular charge of professional irresponsibility is neither stated in terms which anyone would claim to raise a question of academic freedom (*e.g.*, a charge that a faculty member has accepted bribes in the award of grades) nor that the charge is otherwise suspected of having been brought forward solely from an ulterior reason which itself relates to academic freedom, still the need would remain to protect the individual from unreasonable risks of error and prejudice in the resolution of that charge. The power to fire a person without a fair hearing—in this instance a hearing according to academic due process—deserves to be called "arbitrary" and to be despised, not so much on its own account as on account of its greater tendency to result in error—to yield a result utterly at odds with what we would have desired had the actual facts been known. On such a basis, we find no difficulty in understanding why an individual may not be made even to pay a fine for drunk driving in the absence of a right to fair trial which yields a civilized assurance that he did in fact violate the law. Protection of a professor from the unjust forfeiture of his position after a long period of service to the institution is surely as simple a thing to understand, and thus the appropriateness of furnishing that protection through the assurance of academic due process without regard to the nature of the charge.

Nevertheless, beyond the consideration of justice, itself, is still extremely important to understand the special relationship of tenure to academic freedom in particular. An understanding of this relationship would be worthwhile in any case, given the fact that the vast majority of contested dismissals continue to involve disputes over whether what the individual may have done is part of his academic freedom (*e.g.,* how he discharges his duties, what he has said about the college, whether his extramural utterances are defensible within his discipline), and many others have arisen under circumstances involving the suspicion of ulterior purpose in bringing the charge—a purpose itself believed to violate academic freedom. Essentially, however, the connection of tenure with academic freedom is important to understand so as to account for the particular *form* of due process to which tenure creates an entitlement, namely, full academic due process with its emphasis upon professional peer-group participation in the first instance.

The function of tenure is not only to encourage the development of specialized learning and professional expertise by providing a reasonable assurance against the dispiriting risk of summary termination; it is to maximize the freedom of the professional scholar and teacher to benefit society through the innovation and dissemination of perspectives to the conventional wisdom. The point is as old as Galileo and, indeed, as new as Arthur Jensen. An individual who is subject to termination without showing of professional irresponsibility, irrespective of the long term of his service within his discipline, will to that extent hesitate publicly to expose his own perspectives and take from all of us that which we might more usefully confront and consider. Exactly as his skill and understanding advance to a point making it more likely than before that he will contribute something to the legacy of past endeavors, exactly as he will have made an extended commitment in one given discipline diminishing his opportunities to do something else with his life or to start all over again in a wholly different kind of career, so the larger society will tend to be deprived of whatever he would have had to offer it by the very degree of chilling inhibition which it would impose through upholding institutional authority to dismiss him without full academic due process. It is the most vital function of tenure to avoid this contingency by shifting the benefit of doubt to the individual, entitling him then to full academic due process.

The shift does, indeed, do more than to provide a fair hearing in the usual sense, *i.e.*, a full hearing before disinterested parties, preceded by a statement of specific charges based upon reasonably clear standards. Rather, full academic due process locates the fulcrum of responsibility to determine in the first instance whether the tenured professor's work is professionally defensible in those with whom the risk of abuse may least dangerously be placed, namely, his professional peers.

The matter can be fairly expressed only in this way (*i.e.*, "with whom the risk of abuse may *least* dangerously be placed"), for it is true of course that there are degrees of intolerance and convention regarding the methodology and premises of "professionally responsible" utterances within academic peer groups as outside of them. Faculty committees are doubtless capable of reacting against a colleague when others would not have done so, or of favoring him when others would not have done so, and either of these may be accomplished on occasion by means against which no system can be 100 per cent foolproof. Given the necessary decision that there must be accountability somewhere, according to some standard, as initially reviewed by some group of human beings, however, the alternatives to initial peer-group hearing all seem worse where academic freedom tends so frequently to be at stake. At the same time, the entitlement of tenure to full academic due process with its emphasis upon initial peer-group hearing is not without significant checks and balances and by no means reposes final adjudicative authority within the faculty. Rather, it is characteristically hedged about the reserved authority of the university president and trustees to reverse a judgment or to modify a sanction either favoring or disfavoring the individual, for compelling reasons and following fair review with him and with the faculty committee which initially considered the case.

The sense and system of tenure, in summary, come down to this. After completing the full profile of professional preparation, an individual appointed to the faculty of an institution for the first time is neither assured of lifetime employment, nor is he assured of employment beyond the initial term on some general condition of good behavior, nor is he even presumed to be professionally excellent according to the institution's own standards of faculty excellence. Rather, the immediate premise of his appointment is extremely limited, *i.e.*, that he is appointed because he appears to be attractive and to meet certain needs better than others at the time, with only the assurance that he will not be fired without cause during the specified term of his initial appointment and that he will be given a fair chance to establish his excellence over a period of six years assuming, further, that the institution does not in the meantime find others whom it thinks may show greater promise or otherwise better meet its needs than he. If the institution so resolves its policy clearly, to "play the field" and to displace a nontenured appointee by appointing someone else it subsequently finds has become available and whom it regards as more attractive, it is free to do so at least if it has fairly articulated this prerogative and provides notice of and intention to exercise it, reasonably in advance of the end of a given probationary term.

Even assuming the necessity of this sort of rugged competition arrangement to assure each institution of flexibility of choice and an opportunity to resolve the excellence of its newer staff, however, it is surely clear that six years of experience with the faculty member's full-time professional service will provide the institution with ample opportunity to judge his fitness according to the standards and means of review it has established. The institution thus may not further postpone resolving whether that faculty member is now worthy of a conditional statement of continuing confidence, given the intrinsic unfairness of an ever-increasing degree of specialization and dependence on his part under circumstances where a qualified judgment respecting his fitness is clearly feasible and where a failure to resolve that judgment must continue to trammel both his personal security and his academic freedom.

*   *   *

In Defense of Academic Tenure

Fritz Machlup

The critics of strict tenure rules rely chiefly on three arguments: first, that rules have disadvantages for many institutions of higher education; second, that they have disadvantages for many young academic teachers and scholars; and third, that they have disadvantages even for the academic profession as a whole.

I shall argue that all these contentions are correct—but that strict tenure rules are desirable nonetheless. The point is that the tenure rules are not

From *AAUP Bulletin* 50 (Summer 1964): 112–24.

designed to be advantageous to most institutions, to most individual scholars, or to the entire profession. Their purpose is altogether different.

* * *

Four Kinds of Tenure

[After defining "tenure" as an expectation of holding one's position until separated for caused or on other adequate grounds, Machlup distinguishes four types of tenure by the grounds on which that expectation is based.]

1. Tenure by law.

2. Tenure by contract.

3. Tenure by moral commitment under a widely accepted academic code.

4. Tenure by courtesy, kindness, timidity, or inertia.

Tenure by law exists for certain state institutions. Tenure by contract exists in a good many institutions where the bylaws contain provisions about the continuity of appointments and where these bylaws are made an integral part of the contracts with the faculty members. Tenure by moral commitment, or moral code, rests on what the profession has come to regard as "acceptable academic practice," as it is, for example, spelled out in the 1940 *Statement of Principles* [on Academic Freedom and Tenure of the American Association of University Professors (AAUP) and the Association of American Colleges (AAC)]. Tenure by courtesy, kindness, timidity, or inertia is merely a *de facto* status without legal, contractual, or moral commitment.

Tenure by law and tenure by contract can be enforced by the courts. Tenure by moral code can be enforced only by the pressure of moral forces, particularly the threat of public condemnation or censure by organizations enjoying the respect of a large part of the profession and therefore expressing "professional opinion." Tenure without commitment cannot be enforced, though it is the actual state of affairs at a good many places. It may be only a tenuous tenure, but it is nevertheless real and practical: many members of the academic profession can expect to hold their positions indefinitely because the administrative officers are nice, kind, timid, or lazy. After all, it is rather unpleasant to send someone on the staff packing, and quite a bother to look for a replacement.

Tenure by courtesy has all the disadvantages which are associated with tenure of any sort without having the one advantage acceptable as a sound justification of tenure commitments. But before I can show this, I must discuss the various disadvantages. I begin with the disadvantages to the institutions.

Disadvantages to academic institutions

Of the disadvantages which strict tenure rules may inflict upon colleges or universities, the following four deserve special consideration:

1. The institution cannot get rid of deadwood and, hence, cannot within a reasonable period accomplish a desired upgrading of its faculty.

2. The institution cannot judge the qualifications of new junior faculty members in the "too short" probationary period and, hence, it either loses some "late bloomers" by letting them out before they acquire tenure, or it gets stuck with some "never bloomers" by keeping them too long.

3. The institution finds its faculty deteriorating because some professors on tenure may get lazy, stale, and dull.

4. The institution which needs a large junior faculty for elementary courses with large undergraduate enrollment, but cannot possibly grant tenure to all or most of these teachers, must terminate these junior faculty members just when they have enough experience to do a good job of teaching; the quick turnover, therefore, lowers the quality of teaching and, moreover, imposes a heavy burden of recruiting many more young teachers every year than would be necessary if they could be kept on longer.

Let us look at the four arguments in turn.

1. The problem of deadwood. This argument is only partly valid. There is no doubt that strict tenure rules make it imperative for an institution to be more careful in selecting its faculty and more courageous in sending away those who do not meet its standards. Without such care and courage, to be sure, strict tenure rules would lead to an accumulation of substandard teachers on the permanent faculty. I submit, however, that the observance of strict tenure rules will actually increase both the care and the courage of administration and senior faculty responsible for appointments and promotions, so much so that the quality of the faculty will be better under strict rules than under lax rules.

Without strict tenure rules, without severe up-or-out practice, senior faculty and administration can easily become careless and their selections for appointment may be less than satisfactory—after all, "if he does not turn out well, we can always get rid of him." Then they become dilatory—"let us try him for another year," and still "another year." And finally they find that they "cannot decently let him out," even without tenure having been granted and without giving him anything but *de facto* continuance of appointment. Personal friendships will have been formed within the academic community, and nonprofessional considerations and attachments of various sorts make it practically impossible to terminate the appointment although, from a purely professional point of view, deadwood has accumulated. Tenure by courtesy, or the absence of tenure by commitment, is responsible for this.

With strict tenure rules, implemented through a firm up-or-out practice, the risks of appointing and retaining persons not meeting the standards of the institution are too great. Consequently, administrators and senior faculty will be more alert and conscious of constant "quality control" in appointments, promotion, and retention. If in a particular institution, however, judgment and courage have been lacking, so that inadequate teacher-scholars have been kept beyond the stated probationary period, one cannot reasonably blame the accumulation of deadwood in its faculty upon its strict tenure rules. By and large, the deadwood problem seems to be more characteristic of institutions not enforcing strict limits to probationary periods than of institutions where these limits are strictly observed. I have not tested this proposition, but I believe that corroborative evidence could easily be assembled.

This does not, however, dispose of the argument. Indeed, in at least one aspect, its validity cannot be denied. I refer to the case of an institution that wants to raise its standards and improve its faculty quickly. Assume a new president takes office and finds a large part of the faculty in the category of deadwood by the higher standard of excellence. To remove the deadwood quickly would be difficult or, at least, very expensive. Some faculty members may be willing to accept premature retirement, others, large separation payments (say, three years' salary), still others, assignment to nonteaching positions at the institution. Such a program, however, may be too expensive for the institution, and without such a program the unsatisfactory professors must be retained until they retire on schedule. This involves waiting for several years, and the president, however impatient, may have to settle for a very slow improvement of the faculty. Instead of doing it in three or four years, it may take him ten years.

The case of a single department in need of improvement is more frequent than the case of an entire college or university raising its academic standards. It happens in the best of institutions: a department may be "run down" and enjoy relatively poor standing; it ought to be strengthened in the interest of the students in the particular field and the professors in other disciplines, indeed for the good of the entire institution. The existence of tenure, however, makes it difficult to replace the mediocre scholars by outstanding ones, and the only alternatives are to enlarge the department by making some good additional appointments, which is expensive, or to wait until the present senior professors retire, which takes time.

In any event, strict tenure rules are a serious handicap in upgrading the faculty, and this may be a definite disadvantage to many institutions.

2. *The judging of qualifications.* The argument that the probationary period stipulated in the 1940 *Statement* by the AAC and the AAUP is too short to allow a proper evaluation of the qualifications of a young teacher-scholar does not apply to undergraduate colleges that look chiefly for good teaching and are less concerned with productivity in research. The argument is made for universities mainly interested in published research as an evidence of originality and scholarship. Even there a distinction is usually made between fields in which the research capacity of a young man can be judged relatively quickly (as in the experimental sciences, mathematics, and economics) and other fields, in which it may take many years to complete a scholarly study (as in some of the humanities, especially English literature, classics, languages, and the descriptive social sciences).

The point, then, is that six years may not be enough to judge the capabilities of a scholar in most of the humanities and in some of the social sciences. He may have started full-time teaching two or three years before he completed his doctoral work; by the time he has recovered from his dissertation, selected a new project, and embarked on new research, another three or four years may have passed and he still has nothing published to prove his scholarly productivity. Under the strict tenure rules his university must make the decision—to let him go or to give him permanent tenure—before his eligibility for a tenure position can be appraised. If he is sent away and later develops into an outstanding scholar, the university will have lost a valuable asset. If he is kept and turns out to be a dud, the university will be saddled with an embarrassing liability. Hence, is it not perfectly reasonable for universities to oppose rules which would force them to make decisions without sufficient information? Is it not clear that strict tenure rules, requiring such decisions after six years of service, are contrary to the interests of the institution?

Even if this is granted, the situation is not quite so grave as it may sound. A university which errs on the side of caution and loses the still unproven talent, can try to bring him back as soon as he has demonstrated his scholarly productivity. To be sure, this will cost more money than if he had been kept on in the first place, but it will hardly be an excessive burden on the budget in the long run. Perhaps, though, the scholar resents not having had his promise recognized earlier, and now refuses to return to the university which let him go. The loss will then be permanent; yet, the loss to that institution will be a gain for another; even if the scholar forsakes a university career for one in government or industry, he is not lost to the nation or to mankind—and this, surely, is what matters most.

As far as the institution is concerned, however, the disadvantage which it suffers cannot be denied.

3. The growth of mediocrity. The contention that permanent tenure promotes mediocrity in the faculty must, to avoid confusion, be divided into two parts: (a) mediocrity grows if an increasing number of mediocre persons are appointed or promoted to tenure positions, and (b) mediocrity grows if able men, assured of permanent tenure, lose interest in hard work and change into mediocre persons. The two issues are different and must not be confused.

The first version of the contention is supported by a good many educators, professors as well as administrators. In the words of one professor, "Tenure provides the conditions under which bad or mediocre teaching may be perpetuated," and "Tenure . . . gives . . . the mediocre the right to continue to be mediocre."[9] This is merely another form of the deadwood argument, previously examined. There the tenure rules were said to perpetuate its poor quality and, if more mediocre teacher-scholars are added, to reduce its quality still further. This is not a tenable argument. It puts the blame on the rule book instead of on bad policies, on the rules against dismissal instead of on the practice of poor selection and evaluation of faculty. The real responsibility for accumulating mediocrity in the tenure faculty lies in poor judgment and inertia on the part of those in charge of appointments and promotions.

The second version of the mediocrity argument, on the other hand, presents a problem that cannot be blamed on poor judgment or bad policies. The problem is that some professors, secure in their position under strict tenure rules, deteriorate over the years. Perhaps they were good teachers and promising scholars at the time they were given tenure, but gradually, feeling secure in their jobs no matter how well they perform, they grow lazy, stale, and dull. They stop producing as scholars, they do not prepare new course material, they do not inspire, indeed they bore their students.

Is it really tenure, however, is it really security of continuous employment that has such sad effects on the performance of potentially good teachers and scholars? May there not be something lacking in the academic atmosphere in which they work, in the leadership of the institution

9. Charles Gordon Post, "On Relinquishing Tenure," *Vassar Alumnae Magazine,* March 1959.

which should make academic performance continuously interesting, rewarding, exciting? Is it really believable that many faculty members, once alert, ambitious, inspiring, and productive, but now lazy and dull, would still be live wires, full of spark, and constantly recharged with new learning, if only they had no assured tenure, if only they had to live in constant fear for their jobs? And what about the contrary argument that some people, especially scholars, work much better when they have no worries, no fears?

One may ask whether the doubts which I have expressed in these questions cannot be resolved by some empirical evidence. One might line up institutions with strict tenure commitments against institutions with no tenure (or only tenure by courtesy) and compare the relative number of cases of "deteriorated professors." My guess is one would find less deterioration in the institutions with the strict tenure provisions—but such comparisons would not be legitimate, because several other important variables could hide the relationship between tenure and deterioration. One might propose to confine the comparison to institutions equal in all respects except tenure commitments—if this were possible. It is not. The quality of the faculty is probably different from the outset, since institutions granting and those not granting permanent tenure are likely to attract different types of academic people. In other words, it may be impossible to devise empirical techniques which will allow to isolate the long-run effects of tenure upon performance. This difficulty of empirical testing is not exceptional, but is encountered in many or most problems in the social sciences.

My doubts about the frequency and importance of cases of faculty deterioration due to tenure must not be mistaken for a denial of their existence. Some of us know of cases of this sort. We know of professors who once were promising but have not fulfilled the promise: they have not kept up with the progress in their fields, have not done any decent research in years, do not prepare their lectures, do not carry their share of the burden in the department, are not accessible to students; but who, possibly, would still perform satisfactorily if they were not secure in their jobs, that is, if their contracts were subject to termination or renewal depending on performance. Hence, with due reservations regarding the frequency and importance of actual cases in point, it must be granted that the tenure system may contribute to some deterioration in the performance of some professors and, consequently, may harm the institutions which are stuck with the retrograde members of the faculty.

4. *The rate of turnover*. The fourth argument is both valid and important. It concerns institutions which require a large teaching staff in junior ranks

to conduct elementary courses. The shorter the probationary period, the faster will be the turnover of teaching personnel; hence, under strict tenure rules, the percentage of less experienced teachers will be greater and the quality of teaching will be poorer.

If illustrations are needed, consider Freshman English, Elementary French, American History 101, and other courses with enrollments too large to make it possible for the institution to use mainly senior faculty to teach them. For these courses large colleges and universities tend to employ fledgling instructors, often still studying towards M.A. and Ph.D. degrees, and older ones whose wings have not grown strong enough to lift them into higher ranks. The institutions do not want to grant permanent tenure to these not sufficiently scholarly but often quite effective teachers; nor do they want to send them away too quickly, because they hate to lose the most experienced of this junior faculty and to have to go to the trouble every year of recruiting replacements and administering on-the-job training to these novice teachers.

Several administrators have been concerned with this problem. It has been suggested that teachers of elementary courses in disciplines that require drill and routine work rather than a constant search for new truths would not need, and should not be granted, permanent tenure. For example, the teaching of irregular verbs in Elementary French or of remedial English composition is not so sensitive that it would require protection from interference; and hence, it is argued, it should be permissible to employ in such subjects teachers for ten, twelve, or more years without granting them permanent tenure. The same argument, however, does not apply to the teaching of literature or history, and it would surely be difficult to draw a line that would reasonably distinguish between teachers who ought to be given tenure and those who can safely do without it.

No solution has been found for this problem and we are left with the conclusion that the observance of strict tenure rules, with the agreed limits to the probationary period, increases the costs and lowers the quality of elementary instruction in certain colleges and universities.

Having evaluated the four main disadvantages which strict tenure rules impose upon institutions of higher education, I should not leave this part of our discourse without making two reservations. First, there may be still other disadvantages; and secondly, there are certainly some offsetting advantages. These advantages, however, to the extent that they are not merely part of the competition among institutions to attract and hold the best scholars, are closely connected with the one reason that outweighs all other arguments, and which I shall state and discuss after I have done full justice to the various disadvantages.

Disadvantages to individual scholars

I turn to the second of the main contentions, that tenure holds disadvantages for many individual scholars. Again, this does not mean that tenure does not also have advantages for many. The question is which are greater, the advantages or the disadvantages. Let us try to consider both.

Different types of academic persons will be impressed with different advantages and different disadvantages; the balance of advantages and disadvantages, therefore, will depend on the composition of the academic population. One may expect that the security of income which tenure affords will be appreciated less by younger men without dependents than by men in their forties, or older, with families; less by the enterprising and courageous than by the spiritless and timid; less by the self-confident than by the self-conscious; less by the professors in safe and noncontroversial subjects than by those in politically sensitive subjects; less by those satisfied with the *status quo* than by those who want to challenge tradition. Thus, in order to estimate the relative numbers of those who may personally and individually benefit from strict rules of academic tenure, one would have to estimate the sizes of the various categories enumerated. This I cannot undertake, except for one of the divisions, where the distribution is obvious without any empirical check. I refer to the fact that the teacher-scholars in safe subjects are an overwhelming majority and those in politically sensitive fields a small minority.

Apart from these general observations, I submit that for two special categories of academic teachers strict tenure rules entail distinct disadvantages. There are, first, the younger teachers in the most prestigious universities who cannot obtain promotion to tenure rank within the stipulated probationary period and thus must be "let out" under a merciless up-or-out practice. The probationary period is just a little too short for them: either they are unable to complete and publish the research that would prove their scholarly qualifications or there is at the moment no vacancy with tenure rank. In a couple of years, perhaps, a young teacher in this category might obtain his promotion, either because his eligibility as a scholar would then be established or because a tenure position at his university would then become vacant. Now, under the cruel, inflexible rules he must go.

The second category is that of the teacher who starts in a top-rank university and, unable to prove his scholarly qualifications, must be given notice at the end of his sixth year. He secures a position at another university where, still unable to meet the standards, he will be told after three years that he must leave at the end of his fourth year. (I assume the institution was careful enough to agree in writing on a new probationary period.) From now on he may have to pack and move every four years until he finds at last a position in an institution where he is able to meet standards.

The first category consists of good scholars who must move elsewhere in spite of fine qualifications; the second, of less able scholars who must move from place to place because of only-average qualifications. In both cases, the individuals concerned will resent the cost and inconvenience; indeed, sometimes the dislocation involves real hardships for them and their families.

Both types of teachers may blame the strict tenure rules for their tough luck. The top-rate scholar might have earned his permanent tenure at his first university, had he been allowed to stay for just another two years. The so-so scholar might have secured tenure by courtesy in his first or second post, what with his nice personality, sociability, and ability to make friends; only those "inhuman" rules forced him out and onto his arduous peregrination to less and less desirable academic institutions.

The disadvantages to both types of teachers are undeniable. From the point of view of academic excellence, however, one cannot complaint of an avoidable social cost or waste in these instances. In the second case, certainly, the hardships which the strict system inflicts upon the individuals are more than offset by the advantages to the institution that is saved from loading up with nice persons who do not really meet the high academic standards to which it aspires. In the first case, the hardships to the individuals might be avoided if their first university recognized their scholarly qualifications earlier, or if it created new tenure positions where none is vacant, or if it extended the probationary period beyond that provided under the strict rules. The last expedient, I submit, is the least desirable from the point of view of the entire academic community, not only because it sets a bad precedent which can undermine the system, but even from the point of view of the class of "young, promising scholars." This assertion calls for an explanation.

My category of good teacher-scholars forced out of their first position by an inflexible up-or-out practice is a class of people whose membership can be determined only *ex post*. At the time when, under the strict rule, the decision of promotion or separation must be made, it may not yet be certain that the individuals concerned really belong in this class. Can one say that individual scholars whose eligibility for a tenure position at their first university is not yet established would be better off if the decision were postponed? This is so only for those who in fact later prove their eligibility, but not for those who do not succeed. For the entire group of young scholars it is much fairer, much less embarrassing, and much more opportune if they are "left out" at the end of a fixed, short probationary period than after one extended by special consideration. If a scholar is dropped at the end of a short period, one may honestly say that "one cannot yet be sure" of his productivity; but if he is dropped after an extended period, for example, after eight or nine years, the clear implication is that "now one knows he is not good enough." This may ruin his career, for he may have to go several steps down, as far as quality and prestige of institution are concerned, to find a place for himself.

This reasonable argument will probably not convince the young scholars who are confident that, given time, they will make the grade and will be able to stay on at the institution and in the community where they have made friends. To these individuals the strict tenure rules appear disadvantageous, and we cannot prove that they are not.

Disadvantages to the profession

From the individual members, or groups of members, of the academic profession we turn now to the profession as a whole. Some of the disadvantages which strict tenure rules hold for particular institutions or for individual teachers may, of course, be also disadvantages for the profession as a whole. For example, if tenure tends to corrupt, and permanent tenure corrupts permanently, this disadvantage to the institution suffering from deteriorated faculty members is surely an injury to the entire profession. Our present task, however, is to find out whether the profession may suffer disadvantages besides those so far discussed.

Two arguments to this effect can be found, one socio-psychological, the other economic. The former is based on the generalization that a tenure system is likely to attract security-minded rather than adventurous characters, and that the academic profession would be better if it attracted fewer milksops and more fire-eaters. I am not competent to pass judgment on this hypothesis. I cannot see, however, why originality and intellectual daring should be associated with civil courage and social intrepidity; as a matter of fact, I suspect that many of the best scholars are rather timid and prefer to stay out of a hard fight. None the less, I shall not attempt to argue either for or against this thesis, and I proceed to the economic discourse, where I feel at home.

What I have to say on the economic effects of tenure rules is old hat to economists but may startle educators in other subjects. The point is that the existence of the tenure privilege tends to keep professorial salaries lower than they would be otherwise. Some noneconomists have recognized this tendency but have advanced inadequate explanations. One critic of the tenure system, for example, argued as follows:

> If I had to keep a man on for 15, 20 or 25 years—not knowing whether in the long run he would be worth it—but having to pay him month in and month out as long as he was doing a passable job, and couldn't dismiss him, my tendency would be to pay him as little as possible.[10]

To translate this hypothesis—of a tendency to pay "as little as possible"—into economic terms, one may hold that the risk of institutions getting stuck with mediocre teachers on permanent tenure reduces the demand for academic personnel.[11] This may be so, though it is not very likely under the conditions of financing our academic institutions; but what is really relevant is that the supply of teachers is increased if job security is added to pecuniary rewards offered. Even with a given demand, an increase in supply will tend to reduce the money salary on the average.[12]

The assumption that the offer of job security increases the supply of teachers is sometimes rejected on the ground that many, perhaps even most, people do not really care for tenure, and therefore would enter the academic profession regardless of tenure. This fact is beyond dispute, but of no relevance to the point. Even if the overwhelming majority of the potential supply of academic teachers did not give two hoots about tenure, it is the "margin" that counts in the determination of price. In other words,

10. Charles Gordon Post, *op. cit.* Post's explanation gets support from the analysis by a very competent economist, who stated that "the beginning [salary] rate under tenure will be lower than under non-tenure as a result of the risks of long-term contracts." Armen A. Alchian, "Private Property and the Relative Cost of Tenure," in Philip D. Bradley, ed., *The Public Stake in Union Power* (Charlottesville: University of Virginia Press, 1959), pp. 360–61.

11. Where the risks are greater, the quantity demand at any given price or the price offered for any given quantity will often be smaller. The economist, therefore, says that the demand will be smaller the greater the risk involved.

12. Some people hold that, at any one time, the amount of funds which institutions of higher education can raise for salary payments is fixed, and average money payments to teachers will then be determined by the number of teachers attracted. (Economists call this a "wages fund" theory.) The greater the number of teachers who are attracted by a package of "salary plus job security," the greater will be the number of those who compete for a share in the available funds, and the smaller will be the salary per head. This hypothesis of a fixed fund, available to the institutions for teachers' salaries, may be helpful as a first step in explaining the effect of an increased supply; but it is by no means essential. Even if the "demand curve" for teachers is "very elastic," an increase in supply will still reduce the average salary.

if only ten per cent of all teachers were attracted by the combination of salary and security, it would be this ten per cent that counts. Withdraw the security provision from the package, and these people withdraw from the academic market to other occupations, where they find higher pecuniary rewards, higher fringe benefits, more security, more prestige, or more fun.

We possess no statistical evidence to verify these relationships. Some institutions that have the best tenure practice also pay the highest salaries—so that there is no inverse correlation between pecuniary rewards and security. This is because there are still other variables involved, for example, different qualities of faculty, and good institutions compete for top-rank professors with both salary and tenure terms. But the general thesis, that tenure provisions, if they attract some people to the academic profession, tend to keep academic salaries lower, is not questioned by economists.

At least one economist has criticized tenure as a most inefficient system. Since the professors must pay for the security they purchase by accepting lower salaries, tenure, he said, "benefits the older, less able people at the expense of the younger, more able . . . individuals."[13] If teachers had a choice, the security-minded would go to institutions that offered tenure and lower salaries, while the confident would go to institutions offering higher salaries without tenure. If, however, tenure is more or less generally (though not quite voluntarily) provided by all institutions of higher education, the academic teachers have no choice and even those who do not care for tenure must buy it and pay for it by accepting lower salaries. Whether society has a right to restrict the professors' freedom of choice and to force them to buy the security of permanent tenure even if they are not interested in it—this is a question which I shall have to answer presently. At this point, I must concede that the academic profession suffers an economic, or at least pecuniary, disadvantage as a result of the existence of tenure rules.

One may look at this also from a different point of view. If it is an increase in the supply of academic teachers that tends to keep their salaries lower than they would be without tenure provisions, this same increase in supply may be credited with securing to society a larger number of teachers for a given amount of money. Assuming that the funds which society can scrape together for purposes of higher education are limited, the promise of tenure, attractive to some, makes these funds go farther and procures more teachers for the educational establishment. A greater number in the aca-

13. Alchian, *op. cit.,* p. 361.

demic profession is perhaps an advantage to society; but if it means smaller material compensation per teacher one can hardly call it an advantage for the profession.

The benefit to society

... All the disadvantages of a strict tenure system, whether they are borne by the institutions, by the individual teachers, or by the entire academic profession, are outweighed by one important advantage, accruing chiefly to society at large. This one advantage—really the only justification for the system of academic tenure—lies in the social products of academic freedom, which in many situations (more about this later) can be guaranteed only by the instrument of tenure. The various disadvantages, serious as they may be, are parts of the cost which society must incur in order to secure the great benefit of academic freedom and of the fruits it bears.

These fruits, it should be noted, accrue only in negligible part to the individual professors, their institutions, or the academic profession as a whole. That the "products" of freedom accrue chiefly to society at large explains why the academic profession would not willingly pay the cost of tenure. If individual teachers had a chance to "opt out" or "contract out" of the tenure system, too many of them would do so, would choose higher salaries without tenure. Here is an instance of what economists usually call "external benefits" or "third-party benefits." The largest part of the benefits derived from the scholars' exercise of their freedom to inquire, speak, teach, and publish accrues not to them, but to millions of their contemporaries and millions again in posterity. Only the most idealistic of the scholars would be willing to buy and pay for the tenure rights securing their unchallengeable freedom (a freedom, incidentally, which most of them find no occasion to exercise). Society, therefore, in a sort of social contract between trustees, regents, administrators, scholars, and teachers, ordains a system of strict rule of academic tenure for the entire profession.

My language here may have been somewhat fancy, using some of the economic theorist's technical jargon. This was deliberate, in order to convince some of my fellow-economists that the free competitive market for higher learning would not guarantee all the academic freedom which society ought to provide in the interest of progress; without the "interference" through the universal tenure system the degree of academic freedom would be only that which professors would be willing to pay for, and this would be much less than what is socially desirable.

Noneconomists, it seems, can assimilate these ideas, without the use of technical language. The drafters of the 1940 *Statement* were quite explicit on the conflict of interests between the individual teachers and the institutions, on the one hand, and society, on the other. This is how they expressed it:

> Institutions of higher education are conducted for the common good and not to further the interest of either the individual teacher or the institution as a whole. The common good depends upon the free search for truth and its free exposition.

* * *

The benefits of academic freedom may be either material or intangible. Materialists are chiefly impressed with technological innovations based on scientific discoveries, and it is quite proper to point out to them how scientific research is most effectively carried on in an environment of full academic freedom. Others, however, who appreciate intellectual, moral, and aesthetic values, who esteem political and social progress, and who recognize cultural advances as an important achievement of academic scholarship and higher education, will understand that the social benefits of academic freedom are of a scope much wider than that indicated by the output of goods and services entering the statistic of our gross national product.

The exercise of academic freedom has many facets; it goes far beyond the scientist's much heralded search for scientific truth. The less sublime aspects of academic freedom are not sufficiently noted and this makes it appropriate for me to attempt a catalogue.

Aspects of academic freedom

My catalogue contains six items. Five of them are so easily comprehended that one simple sentence with five brief clauses will suffice to described them: only the sixth will call for elaboration. All have in common that they imply absence of institutional sanctions for unpopular pronouncements and, consequently, a conviction on the part of teachers and scholars that they have little to fear if their words or actions are offensive to many.

We want the teacher and scholar to be uninhibited in criticizing, and in advocating changes of,

(1) accepted theories,

(2) widely held beliefs,

(3) existing social, political, and economic institutions,

(4) the policies and programs of the educational institution at which he serves, and

(5) the administration and governing board of the institution at which he serves.

(6) In addition, we want him to be uninhibited in coming to the aid of any of his colleagues whose academic freedom is in jeopardy.

The last point may need a supporting argument. All infringements of academic freedom begin with the charge that a teacher or scholar has, by his words or actions, abused his freedom. As I once wrote, "so-called abuses are the only proofs that the freedom really exists." Since the temptation to go after the "abuser" of freedom may be irresistible to the powers that be, the protection of freedom may depend on the strength of the defense. Hence we need and want teachers and scholars who would unhesitatingly come to the defense of the "odd ball," the heretic, the dissenter, the troublemaker, whose freedom to speak and to write is under some threat from colleagues, administrators, governing board, government, or pressure groups. The impulse to take up the cudgels for the "odd ball" is all too easily suppressed if unpleasant consequences must be feared by those who defend him.

It happens that some of the greatest agents of progress in human affairs and scientific knowledge about nature or society have been "troublemakers." One of the most important tasks of true, freedom-and-progress-loving scholars is to come to the aid of a troublemaker under attack, even if they disagree with what he professes and dislike him for his personal traits, manners or practices.

Tenure as an instrument of freedom

I have heard it argued that permanent tenure is not an indispensable instrument for the guarantee of academic freedom; that freedom can be safeguarded without tenure rules.

This argument is valid under two conditions: First, that all governing boards and administrators of institutions of higher education believe so strongly in academic freedom that every charge of abuse, and every suspicion of abuse, would inspire them with such a zeal to protect the offender that they would rather see the institution which they govern or administer impoverished or destroyed than allow the offender to be removed from his post. Second, that it is always possible to distinguish offenses that come under the heading of abuse of freedom from all other reasons for dispensing with the services of a teacher or scholar.

Neither of the two conditions is satisfied. The difficulty of distinguishing between different reasons for "noncontinuance" is well attested to by the experience with nonrenewals of contracts of nontenured teachers. It is rarely possible to prove that the decision not to renew a contract was influenced, let alone determined, by some offensive or embarrassing publications or utterances of the teacher concerned. As a matter of fact, the persons who make the decision may themselves not know what motivates them: do they judge him to be a poor teacher, do they dislike him as a person, or do they dislike what he wrote or said? It is probably unavoidable that ineffectiveness in teaching and lack of scholarly publications are so readily noticed in a faculty member who has taken liberties and thereby embarrassed his institution; the same defects may go unnoticed in a pleasant chap who conforms and gets along well with everybody.

To say that the first condition is not "realistic" would be the biggest understatement of the years. Without strict tenure rules, the governing boards and administrative officers of the majority of colleges and universities could not succeed in protecting a faculty member accused of having abused his freedom. Many of us can, without long deliberation, recite a list of names of well-known scholars whose survival on the faculty of their institution has been possible only thanks to the rules of tenure. The president of the institution can say to those clamoring for the dismissal of the presumed public enemy: "I am sorry, much as I should like to get rid of Professor X, we cannot do it, for he has permanent tenure."

Full efficacy of tenure as a protection of freedom requires that tenure be regarded as a genuine commitment. Tenure by courtesy, mere *de facto* tenure, is likely to break down just when it would be needed most as a protection against outside pressures. If tenure is not based on legal constraints or contractual obligations, it may be difficult for administrators or governing boards to resist a strong and vociferous public campaign for the removal of a controversial educator accused of attempts to subvert tradition or corrupt the young. Tenure based only on the recognition of a widely accepted academic code may be helpful as long as the leaders of the campaign can be convinced that violations of these moral principles would have injurious consequences for the institution. . . .

* * *

Once it is understood that academic freedom serves the purposes of society, not of individual teachers or institutions, it will also be understood that academic tenure, the safeguard of freedom, should not depend on the preferences and idiosyncrasies of particular institutions. It has been proposed that the rules of tenure be adjusted to the characteristic of each institution. Admittedly, such flexibility might alleviate some of the disadvantages which strict tenure rules hold for individual institutions. More important, however, is the danger that institutional self-determination of rules of tenure might weaken the respect for and observance of the basic principle. It would be too easy for those who want to go after some supposed "abuses" of freedom to argue that the special nature of "their" institution demanded the denial of tenure to many members of the faculty. This danger makes it imperative that we insist on national standards.

* * *

Conclusion

I shall probably be accused of having overstated my case, of having exaggerated, in particular, the dangers to which lack of tenure would expose the academic teacher or the fears and inhibitions which he would suffer, or both. If so, I may plead that exaggeration in these matters can hardly do as much harm as could underestimation. The case for tenure does not rest on the probability that a large proportion of all academic teachers and scholars would suppress some of their thoughts or sentiments in the absence of the security which tenure provides; nor does it rest on the probability that some of the suppressed thoughts or sentiments would be of extraordinary significance. It is not necessary to assume that there are several Galileos in every generation or several men who have similarly subversive ideas of similar importance to communicate. The case for tenure would be sufficiently supported by showing that a few men once in a while might feel insecure and suppress or postpone the communication of views which, true or false, wise or foolish, could inspire or provoke others to embark on or continue along lines of reasoning which may eventually lead to new insights, new judgments, or new appraisals regarding nature or society.

* * *

A Preface to the Rollins College and Bennington College Reports

Machlup's and Van Alstyne's essays are analytical; they dissect, examine, and explain, with elegance and dispassion. But the case for tenure rests equally on the realities of academic life, as it is lived. A major evidentiary source can be found in the case reports of the ad hoc committees of investigation appointed by the AAUP since its founding in 1915. As the editors of the *Harvard Law Review* explain:

> When the AAUP has been unable to bring about a satisfactory settlement of a dispute through mediation the organization's General

Secretary is authorized to appoint an ad hoc investigation committee composed of teachers from outside the university concerned. . . .
[T]he committees are given a mandate to go beyond the facts of the
particular dispute and examine the general conditions affecting academic freedom. This often results in a wide-ranging legislative inquiry into such matters as the adequacy of tenure and dismissal procedures and the overall attitude of the administration, with the
ultimate objective of the committee being the recommendation of
appropriate reforms. ["Developments in the Law—Academic Freedom," *Harvard Law Review* 81 (1968): 1109–1110 (references
omitted)]

These reports, which now number in the hundreds, are a repository
of the academic experience. The late John H. Wigmore, dean of the
Northwestern University School of Law, declared rather early on that
these reports "would do credit to any judicial court in the world." They
are, as Judge J. Skelly Wright later observed, "noted for their thorough-
ness and scrupulous care" *Browzin v. Catholic University,* 527 F.2d 843,
n. 8 at 847–848 [D.C. Cir. 1975]).

The Rollins College report details an almost paradigmatic case: an
institution facing turbulent economic times, an autocratic if often benign administration, a relatively compliant faculty, and an outspoken
faculty critic. In the more modern Bennington College case we find
some of the same features, writ larger: the governing board and president seem less benign, the college's economic situation appears more
precarious, and the divisions between administrations and faculty and
within the faculty have sharper edges. Neither institution, however,
had a system of tenure that amounted to more than a moral commitment.

Judge Wright also cautioned that the reports of these committees of
investigation are the products of an interested organization of professors alone. And that is quite right. The conclusions drawn in them are
in the nature of opinions. Thus the reader should be careful to consider
whether or not the conclusions follow from the facts.

———

Academic Freedom and Tenure: Rollins College

I. *General Background*

Rollins College [was] founded in 1885 by the Congregational churches but
[is] now undenominational. . . . During the first forty years of its history,

From *AAUP Bulletin* 19 (1933): 416–432. The ad hoc committee of inquiry consisted of
Arthur O. Lovejoy, Philosophy, Johns Hopkins University, and Austin S. Edwards, Psychology, University of Georgia.

its development was greatly hampered by inadequate endowment and by the economic vicissitudes of the State. In 1925, Dr. Hamilton Holt, distinguished as an advocate of international peace, and former editor of a weekly journal, became its president. Dr. Holt was without experience in teaching or educational administration, but dissatisfaction with the methods of instruction in vogue in his own student days and his experience in journalism had led him to form a conception of a college of a somewhat new type. He accordingly "undertook as president of Rollins to solve some of the problems of the present system of higher education in the United States. Under his leadership the faculty abolished lectures and recitations as obsolete methods of instruction and substituted therefor the Conference Plan of Study." Under this plan students were required to spend six hours daily in three two-hour sessions called "conferences," and two hours in some form of supervised exercise. This introduction into college work of the "eight-hour day" was widely advertised as a distinctive and important innovation. . . . In the selection of members of the faculty, little or no importance was attached to interest in research or to distinction in productive scholarship; the emphasis was placed upon pedagogic effectiveness in the informal method of teaching characteristic of the college. Dr. Holt not only formulated the educational plan of the institution, but also devoted much time and energy to giving it publicity throughout the country— often by ingenious methods suggested by his journalistic experience—to raising funds, and to recruiting students. In these activities, which usually entailed his absence from the College during a large part of the year, he was highly successful; approximately $2,000,000 was obtained for buildings, running expenses, and endowment, and the student enrollment was greatly increased.

It was doubtless a natural result of all this that the college became to a peculiar degree identified with the personality of its president; it was remarked by the head of a neighboring university that "Holt is Rollins and Rollins is Holt." As the originator of the general "Rollins plan" the President apparently conceived himself to be the authorized interpreter of its application in detail; and he assumed functions which not only are commonly assigned to the faculty as a body, but were specifically so assigned by the By-Laws. . . .

The faculty naturally assumed that they were to exercise the broad powers thus conferred upon them; the President, however, appears to have taken a different view. It is the understanding of the Committee that upon accepting the presidency Dr. Holt requested and was granted by the Board of Trustees exceptional and extreme power and authority, which does not seem to have then been made known by that body to the faculty. Thus the foundations of possible conflict were laid in the beginning, in the exceptional authority of the president. Appointments were made by him without consultation with faculty committees or with the departments concerned—in some cases, in the opinion of senior members of departments, unwise appointments. . . .

*   *   *

The authority thus asserted and on occasion exercised by the President appears to the Committee to have exceeded the custom of academic institutions, to have been in violation of the By-Laws, to have been used at times in a manner humiliating to the faculty, to have been incongruous with the spirit of cooperation in an educational experiment ostensibly characteristic of the College, and to have worked badly in practice. The constitution of the college, as usually interpreted by the President, has been that of an autocracy; and with this there has been, at times, an excessive demand for personal fealty to the head of the institution, as distinct from loyalty to its educational aims and principles, and the expectation of a greater degree of "harmony" and likemindedness than is ordinarily to be found—or to be desired—among any considerable body of adult persons of the intellectual type.

It is not, however, the case that the conditions outlined resulted, during the earlier years of Dr. Holt's administration, in very frequent or serious friction between president and faculty. This was in part due to the fact that the President's official conduct, in these as in other matters, was variable. His personal relations with individual members of the staff have usually been courteous, genial and kindly; his exercise of his absolute powers has, until recently, been intermittent; and his professed principles, and in many cases his practice, have been those of a believer in the liberal tradition and in the method of adjusting differences by friendly conference. . . .

II. Early Incidents of 1933

A conflict of opinion between president and faculty over a more serious issue . . . became sharply defined early in 1933. Two years before, as a sequel to a conference at the college in which a number of distinguished educational experts took part, a "New Plan" had been adopted, largely upon President Holt's initiative; and this plan presently came to seem to many of the faculty hard to reconcile with certain features of the original "Rollins Plan." . . . The "New Plan" was somewhat similar to that now in use at the

University of Chicago. The College was divided into a Lower and Upper Division, and, especially in the latter, the time-element was minimized and the role of the instructor diminished; the student was permitted and encouraged to plan his own work and proceed at his own pace, and to present himself for examination when he believed himself ready for it. Whatever the respective merits of the two plans, it is evident that the ideas underlying them were by no means identical. The old plan was not, however, abandoned at the time of the adoption of the new, but the problem of adjusting them was presently referred to the Curriculum Committee. This Committee, after much deliberation, in January, 1933, "voted against the eight-hour day as incompatible with the [new] Rollins Plan." Its report observed that that plan "is based on achievement rather than time. Its aim is to enable the individual to develop in his own way and along the line of his own interests as fast as his ability will permit. Any system or method we may authorize or suggest must be sufficiently elastic to permit (1) of more hours in class, (2) less hours in class, or (3) no hours in class, as the subject of study may require. . . . The conflict in the present anomalous situation with students under both plans should not be regarded as a weakness or failure of the New Plan."

This report, which seems to the Committee of Inquiry a well-considered one, was extremely ill-received by President Holt. He was, of course, fully entitled to form and urge his own view of it; what is pertinent to the present inquiry is the fact, established by abundant evidence, that he denied the faculty's right to do the same, and manifested great resentment over the Curriculum Committee's attitude towards the "eight-hour day" and the "two-hour conference plan." At the faculty meeting at which the report was presented his opposition was so emphatic that the report was tabled. In conversation with a member of the faculty, the latter testifies, the President said, à propos of certain members of the Committee: "There is bad blood there," and "Don't let that crowd use you." The Curriculum Committee was, shortly after, summoned to meet the President and censured by him for its report; to it, and on another occasion to the faculty, he said: "If there is as much as fifty per cent disagreement between me and any member of the faculty on what I consider a fundamental matter, either he or I should go."[1]

The position and utterances of President Holt on the occasion of the report on the eight-hour day were, in the Committee's opinion, a manifest

1. To the question of the Association's Committee whether he made this and other statements reported by faculty witnesses President Holt has declined to reply.

infringement of academic freedom, though the issue over which it took place was an educational rather than a theological, political, or economic one. The declaration that, if a teacher's view differed from the President's "as much as fifty per cent" on any matter which he might regard as "fundamental," either the teacher or the President should go, was, on its face, an official announcement that agreement with the President on questions of educational policy and methods was a requirement for continuance on the faculty—since the President did not "go" and manifestly had no intention of going. The denial of the teacher's right to adhere to his own judgment and to advocate his own views in committee and faculty meetings was the more unjustifiable because the recommendations which evoked this declaration of the President's were, as it seems to this Committee, rather obvious implications of a new plan already adopted with his approval. It was not a question of supporting or not supporting the more general and fundamental principles of the College. No teacher having a high degree of professional self-respect is, the Committee believes, likely to accept service in an institution in which freedom of individual opinion, and the exercise of professional responsibility, on educational matters is denied in the degree in which it was denied by President Holt on this occasion.

Four days after the faculty meeting at which the report of the Curriculum Committee was finally discussed, Professor Rice, a member of that Committee, was notified that his resignation was desired. . . . One or two utterances subsequent to Mr. Rice's dismissal may more appropriately be included in this section, as illustrative of the official conception of the status of members of the faculty in Rollins College. Two professors testify (with slight variations of phrasing) that Dr. Holt said to them, on separate occasions, when urged to give Mr. Rice a hearing before a faculty committee or some other body: "Why should I give him a hearing before anybody else? When you want to fire a cook, you don't go out and get a committee of the neighbors to tell you what to do, do you?" A member of the Executive Committee, the proprietor of a local department store, at a meeting of that Committee, justified the mode of government in the College and the procedure in the dismissal of professors by the analogy of his own practice in dealing with his employees. Neither President Holt nor the other members of the Executive Committee present took exception to this analogy.

III. *The Dismissal of Professor Rice*

It is necessary first to make clear the status of Mr. Rice as to tenure in February, 1933. He had been appointed to a professorship on July 12, 1930, and received from President Holt on July 13 a letter containing the following:

"I call you with the expectation that it will be permanent, but as I told you, I feel that either of us are at perfect liberty to sever the connection at the end of one or two years with or without any given reason and no hard feelings on either side." In the opinion of the Committee this was an official notification that, after two years of probation, Mr. Rice might understand his tenure to be permanent, and terminable only for "given reasons." President Holt, however, in reply to an inquiry from the Secretary of the Association wrote in April, 1933: "Automatic reappointment is assumed in the case of all associate or full professors who have served at Rollins in those ranks for three full years or more satisfactorily. The vacancy in our Classical Department has come about properly under the above provisions of the Trustees, for the incumbent had not yet completed his third year of service and a continuation of his services was not deemed best." This statement of President Holt is misleading. It is evident that a new rule adopted by the Trustees in 1932 could not abrogate a specific understanding with Mr. Rice as to the length of his probationary period, notified to him in writing in 1930. . . . The trustees' resolution of February 16, 1932, to which he refers, gave no assurance of "automatic" annual reappointment of professors and associate professors after three years of service. Its language is as follows:

> Until Rollins College achieves a greater measure of financial stability, the Trustees find it impossible to establish permanent standards for tenure of office, though the intention is to do so at the earliest possible moment. Therefore, while it is necessary to continue assistant professors and instructors on the one-year appointment basis, the Trustees are glad to assure professors and associate professors who have served in this rank for three or more years that the policy of the Trustees will be to continue their services without annual notification unless reasonable notice be given to the contrary.

The meaning of the second sentence of this resolution is manifestly determined by its final clause. While it has the appearance of giving some new assurance as to tenure of higher positions after the first three years, its only actual effect is to require the administration to give "reasonable notice" of non-reappointment and to relieve it of the obligation to send formal annual notice of reappointment in other cases. Subject to the one proviso of due notice, the unqualified right not to reappoint teachers of any grade and of any length of service is fully reserved by the resolution; and President Holt has stated to the Association's Committee that "at the present time no professor has any tenure beyond one year."

He has, however, given the Committee conflicting interpretations of the action taken with regard to Professor Rice; at times he has described it as an ordinary case of non-reappointment in accordance with the above resolution of the Trustees, at other times as a dismissal for cause, for which he recognized some obligation to give reasons; and at the time of the Committee's visit he presented his reasons with great fullness and detail, supporting them by some fifty written statements, mainly in the form of affidavits, which, in preparation for the Committee's coming, he and the Dean of the College had obtained from students and members of the administrative and teaching staff. Part of this evidence, it became clear during the hearings, was not known to the President before the dismissal. The Committee pointed out to him that any allegations not before him at that time threw no light upon the question of the grounds of dismissal, and was therefore of no interest to the Committee; but it was not found practicable to exclude from the hearings material which the Committee regarded as irrelevant.[2]

Whether there were adequate reasons for this dismissal is, however, a part of the general question on which the Committee is required to report. It is not possible in the available space, nor would it be useful, to reproduce the mass of material presented by the college officers, nor Mr. Rice's replies thereto. Much of this material relates to petty personal differences common in small communities, or to other trivialities without public interest. The significance of most of the incidents mentioned in it lay, in the view of the administration, in their cumulative effect. As to this, the Committee finds that Professor Rice had unquestionably much disturbed the harmony of the local community and had seriously offended a number of his colleagues and other persons. This was partly due to his outspoken criticism of certain features of the College life which he disapproved. He had attacked the debating system on the ground that it tends to substitute for the serious examination of public questions a form of competitive sport, and is largely a training in the sophistic art of making the worse appear the better reason. He had opposed the introduction and multiplication of fraternities and sororities as unnecessary in a small college, as a divisive influence, and as leading to an undesirable type of student politics. It was charged that he had attempted to persuade individual students to withdraw from these organizations; this charge the Committee finds to be unsubstantiated. He had attacked certain features of the athletic system and some of the methods of the department of physical culture. He had, in

2. The weight of some of the statements adverse to Mr. Rice is, in the Committee's opinion, diminished by the fact that they were given upon solicitation from administrative officers after the dismissal and also after the incidents recorded in Section IV . . . of this report.

conversation, criticized certain of the chapel services as lacking in dignity and unsuited to the edifice in which they were held. He had argued that a serious weakness in American education lay in an excessive feminization of its teaching body and had disparaged the work of women teachers. Whatever the merits of his views on these questions—on which the Committee is not called upon to pronounce—they were, of course, views which he was entitled to urge; but they drew upon him the hostility of considerable groups among students and faculty. This effect was, however, much intensified by the frequently vehement, sometimes intemperate, and in several instances discourteous language in which his criticisms were couched, and by a sometimes inopportune humor—his paradoxical or ironical expressions of ideas being taken literally by some hearers. In these respects and in certain others affecting his personal relations with a number of his colleagues and others, Mr. Rice seems to the Committee to have fallen into some serious errors of judgment and some of taste. The evidence appears to show, however, that he made every reasonable effort to restore cordial relations with those to whom he was told that he had given offense. Of those members of the teaching staff whose opinions were communicated to the Committee, approximately half disapproved of the dismissal, and most of these expressed warm esteem for Mr. Rice's personal qualities and high admiration for his abilities and his services to the College; nearly all of the latter statements contained remarks similar in substance to the two following, which the Committee thinks it only just to cite: "I think that Mr. Rice has been a great stimulation to the campus, and as a consequence a great and needed benefit. . . . He has been too outspoken against people he doesn't like both in the town and faculty, to their faces as well as behind their backs. His courage sweeps aside the value and deceit of discretion, and he says what he thinks without thought of consequence, when too emotionally roused. He has little patience with narrow-mindedness and expects that every individual in the world is bent on broadening; that, if he isn't, and Mr. Rice makes him think, he will be grateful." "Mr. Rice's indiscretions seem to be almost entirely the result of his scrupulous intellectual honesty. They are not to be attributed to fundamental ill-will, or to low motives. Mr. Rice is strongly opposed to insincerity and sham. When he found it, he did not hesitate to expose it." It was admitted by an administrative officer whose general attitude was adverse to Mr. Rice that the utterances and incidents complained of would probably have caused no serious difficulty in an institution of another type or in a larger place. With this the Committee agrees. Its concludes that a professor who had officially been given reason to suppose his tenure permanent was dismissed upon charges which, in so far as they are substantiated, would in most American institutions of higher education not be regarded as grounds for that action in such a case.

To this the Committee feels obliged in justice to add that there became apparent with the progress of its inquiry two positive reasons why it might have been expected that the retention of Mr. Rice in the faculty of Rollins College would be regarded as highly desirable. (*a*) It became evident, after interviews with students who had taken his courses, that he had shown himself an unusually stimulating and effective teacher, peculiarly adapted to the informal method of instruction in use in the College. A large proportion of those who had come for any considerable time under his instruction pronounced him either the best teacher or one of the best they had ever had. To Mr. Rice's exceptional teaching ability President Holt has borne testimony. He once describe him as "a teacher after my own heart," adding, "they didn't teach Greek that way in my time;" in April, 1933, he said to a member of the faculty that he "entirely approved of his (Mr. Rice's) teaching method, in fact he thought it the method that ought to be used;" and to the Committee he observed that Professor Rice was undeniably a "mind-quickening" teacher." (*b*) The Committee finds that the charge against Mr. Rice which President Holt has presented as "perhaps more serious" than any other is the reverse of the fact. It is to the effect that Mr. Rice's teaching was merely "upsetting" to immature minds, that "he destroyed youthful ideals without inculcating anything equally constructive or commendable in their place." What is shown by student testimony and other evidence is that he sought, in dealing with ethical and other questions in his courses and individual conferences, to bring students to substitute, in place of assumptions accepted through tradition or convention, personal convictions reached through reflection; and that he did this chiefly, not by lecturing, but by a searching and skillful use of the method of the Socratic dialogue. That some resented this method, and that others proved incapable of the effort of thought which it required and were troubled by it, is evidently true. But such results in occasional instances are manifestly inevitable incidents in any attempt to make the years of college study a period of intellectual awakening followed by a coherent reorganization of individual beliefs and standards; and to such awakening and reorganization the evidence indicates that Mr. Rice's teaching was persistently directed. The standards which he supported on ethical questions, especially those questions of personal conduct which often arise in student life, were rigorous and fundamentally conservative; and he was especially successful in steadying the minds of students who had merely impatiently broken loose from traditional codes, and in assisting them to reach an intelligent self-discipline. Evidence to this effect given by students was extremely impressive. . . . In the Committee's judgment his dismissal eliminated from the faculty a teacher who appears on the one hand to have done more than any other to provoke questioning, discussion, and the spirit of critical inquiry among his students, and on the other hand, to have aimed, with exceptional success, at constructive results both in thought and character. The presentation of the charge here in question against Mr. Rice, some of the testimony given in support of it, and other evidence, appear to the Committee to show that one of the factors in his dismissal was pressure from some members of the faculty and others, to whom his insistence upon a reflective re-examination by students of traditional ideas was fundamentally objectionable. Yet statements of the educational aims and methods of Rollins College would suggest that the first concern of its administration would be to obtain and keep teachers of this type and quality. . . .

Turning to the procedure in the case, the Committee finds that no hearing, in the sense in which the term is understood by this Association, was granted Mr. Rice before dismissal. The President asked for his resignation on February 27, assuring him that if he resigned quietly the administration would give him every assistance toward obtaining a new position. He declined to resign, and as a result of the conversation which ensued the President apparently relented and agreed to consider the matter further. A few days later he informed Mr. Rice that his decision not to reappoint was final. Nevertheless there followed a period of three weeks during which Mr. Rice and his friends were given some reason to suppose the question was still open. During this period the President consented to meet a large number of the faculty who gave testimony in Mr. Rice's behalf, but the request made by some of these that he grant a hearing in accordance with the principles approved by this Association and the Association of American Colleges was refused. At the final interview between him and Mr. Rice on March 21, he said, "I am the judge," and referred to the "stream of evidence" on which his decision was based. Mr. Rice replied, "If the 'stream of evidence' is going to tip the scale against me, I want to be told the charges and be confronted with my accusers." To this the President made no answer, and Mr. Rice received the next morning written notice of dismissal, effective at the end of the academic year. The decision was made wholly by the President—who, the Committee became convinced during its inquiry at the College, had never critically tested or weighed the evidence—and what were called "hearings" before him took place after he had twice announced his decision. . . .

* * *

[The committee then discussed a series of incidents that occurred after Professor Rice's dismissal. The most important, in the committee's view, was the president's summoning of ten faculty members and handing them a paper they were required to sign, containing a declaration that the signer agreed to accept the president's statement, made orally, of his complete authority in all matters pertaining to Rollins College. Professors Lounsbury and Georgia refused to sign, and the others present followed suit. The two were later dismissed. The committee concluded] that Professors Georgia and Lounsbury were dismissed because of their expression in faculty gatherings and in conversations with President Holt, with colleagues and friends, and with this Committee, of disagreement with certain of the President's views on college policy and of disapproval of his action with respect to Mr. Rice, and, in the case of Mr. Georgia, because of his expressed intention of continuing to advocate within the College the adoption of the principles as to tenure, grounds for and procedure in removal, and faculty participation in college government, which have been approved by this Association and other educational bodies. Dismissal for such reasons is, in the Committee's judgment, evidence of an extreme intolerance of legitimate criticism and dissent in the College. Further evidence of this is to be seen in the fact that several other teachers under suspicion were, about the same time, called before the President and asked whether they felt they could be "happy" in the College under the prevailing order of things; it was intimated that a negative answer would be inconsistent with their continuance in office. . . .

Academic Freedom and Tenure: Bennington College

* * *

I. Introduction

Bennington College is a four-year liberal arts college in southwestern Vermont on 550 acres of land in a beautiful setting at the foot of the Green

From *Academe* 81 (March–April 1995): 91–103. The ad hoc investigating committee consisted of Peter O. Steiner, Economics and Law, University of Michigan, and Dianne C. Zannoni, Economics, Trinity College, Connecticut.

Mountains. Founded in 1932 as a women's college, Bennington became coeducational in 1970. It offers undergraduate studies leading to the bachelor of arts degree in the humanities (29 percent), sciences (6 percent), social sciences (16 percent), and visual and performing arts (49 percent)—the numbers in parentheses are the rough percentage of graduates in each area during 1990 to 1992—to an undergraduate student body that in 1993 had approximately 450 students. In addition, Bennington offers several master's and postbaccalaureate certificate programs that together enroll some 80 additional students. Its tuition and fees are among the highest of any college in the United States, and its budget is dependent to a substantial degree on tuition revenue and secondarily on annual giving by alumni and friends. Since its inception Bennington has been noted for its flexible and experiential approach to education, and students are given great flexibility in the design of their programs. Relations between faculty and students and among faculty are close, intensive, and informal.

Until recently Bennington had a part- and full-time faculty of about 65, who served without academic ranks. Newly appointed faculty members generally received two three-year contracts before being reviewed in the fifth year for the acquisition of "presumptive tenure" and a five-year appointment. Their conditions of employment are spelled out in exceptional detail (including a set of guidelines for salary increases as percentage amounts over increases in the cost of living) in a *Faculty Handbook,* which the faculty regard as a description of their contractual relationship with the college. Of particular relevance to this report is the concept of presumptive tenure set forth in Section 9.43 of the handbook, which is quoted in full later in the report.

The college faculty and curriculum had been organized by divisions, of which the Division of Literature and Languages was the largest. Divisions had the autonomy and responsibility that are exercised by departments in many institutions.

The *Faculty Handbook* provided for full and active participation of the faculty in the governance of the college. Faculty control of appointments, reappointments, and curriculum had been the rule. The expectation of the faculty members had been that their determinations on virtually all academic matters would be given decisive weight by the administration and the board of trustees.

The college is governed by a self-perpetuating 34-member board of trustees (hereafter, the board), chaired by Mr. John Barr, an investment banker (and poet) who resides in New York City. Its Educational Policy Committee is chaired by Ms. Susan P. Borden, a long-time and influential member of the board. Prior to her appointment in 1987, the president of the college, Dr. Elizabeth Coleman, served as an administrative officer and faculty member at the New School for Social Research. . . .

The dean of faculty during the years 1992–94 was Ms. Susan Sgorbati, a member of the faculty since 1987. In July 1994, this deanship position was replaced by a dean of the college and was filled without prior notice or search by a physics teacher, Dr. Norman F. Derby. Ms. Sgorbati continues on the faculty as a teacher of dance.

II. Events

In a cataclysmic upheaval in June and early July 1994, the board and/or president of Bennington College:

1. revealed that the board had "determined" in January 1994 that a condition of financial exigency existed and had to be addressed through changes in educational policy embodied by a significant reorganization of instructional resources and priorities;

2. announced that a Plan had been adopted by the board in April 1994, which the president had been instructed to implement;

3. sent notices to 27 faculty members, of whom roughly two-thirds had presumptive tenure, that their services were being terminated for one of three reasons: (a) their positions were being eliminated because the subjects they taught were being eliminated in the reorganization; (b) they did not meet newly defined professional requirements defined in the Plan for positions in their subject at Bennington College; or (c) for those in the midst of normal reappointment procedures, their reappointments as recommended by the appropriate faculty committee were not approved by the president on substantive grounds. In the next weeks one of the presumptively tenured faculty members who initially had been judged not to have met the new professional standards and had been issued notice of termination was reinstated by the president after an appeal, and another faculty member whose position had been eliminated by the programmatic changes was placed in a different position. The other faculty members either have been released with a year's severance salary or are serving on terminal appointments as of this writing;

4. suspended all existing governance practices and procedures of the faculty;

5. announced a structural reorganization of the faculty, eliminating all divisions and designating a core faculty in place of a divisional structure;

6. eliminated presumptive tenure for all subsequent appointments; and

7. announced a series of new and replacement appointments to the fac-

ulty, at least some of which had been under negotiation before the termination letters had been sent.

These events were the culmination of a two-year period of extraordinary
turmoil and tension on the campus and of increasingly evident hostility
between, on one side, the board and the president, and large portions of
the faculty—including most of those actively involved in faculty governance and most members of the Division of Literature and Languages—on
the other. Events of this two-year period are the focus of this report. . . .

*   *   *

[The committee reported that the administration declined to cooperate in
the investigation, but that the information available in the documentary
record and in interviews with fifteen faculty members, about half of whom
had been terminated and half retained, was so extensive as to permit the
issues to be assessed and conclusions reached.]

A. The Prehistory

The severe financial problems of Bennington College that have played a
role in the recent events appear to have had their origins in two decisions
made in the 1970s: first, the decision to open the college to male students
and thus to increase Bennington's overall enrollment and size; and second,
the decision to undertake major new construction of facilities using com-
mercially borrowed funds. Additional operating expenses, particularly
owing to the costs of debt financing in a period of high interest rates and
rising energy costs, evidently outran tuition revenues and created operating deficits for which there were inadequate reserves. The college's endowment is very small in comparison to that of peer institutions, and efforts to
increase it by a capital campaign have been hampered by the need to use
funds contributed for that purpose to meet operating deficits.

In January 1975 the board appointed *ad hoc* subcommittee called the
Committee on Future Directions to address the emerging financial crisis.
That committee's report, issued in November 1975, recommended
changes that are similar to, though less sweeping than, those that the
board mandated in 1994. For example, the report recommended abolish-
ing presumptive tenure, discontinuing foreign language instruction, reor-
ganizing the divisions, increasing the student-faculty ratio, and permanently eliminating twelve faculty positions.

The faculty's reaction to the 1975 report was concerted and hostile.
Nearly unanimously, and led by members of the Division of Literature and

Languages, the faculty expelled the board committee from a faculty meeting called to receive its report, rejected the recommendations, and voted no confidence in the president, Dr. Gail Thain Parker. After several contentious weeks, the faculty succeeded in having the committee's recommendations withdrawn. In due course, notwithstanding an affirmation of support by the board, President Parker submitted her resignation, and it was accepted. The faculty had won a striking victory and demonstrated its power and control. It has been suggested by some of the faculty members . . . that from this date some influential members of the board became committed to challenging faculty power (and, as they saw it, arrogance). The hostility of the board toward the Division of Literature and Languages, too, is said to have its origins in the events of 1975.

Refinancing of the debt, higher enrollments, and rising tuition revenues, along with restraint in faculty and staff salary increases, seem to have temporarily alleviated the fiscal crisis, but by the mid-1980s a shortfall of tuition revenue and rising operating costs again led to the perception of an imminent budgetary crisis. The board appointed a committee that included faculty members and was chaired by the then-president, Dr. Michael Hooker. This committee was charged with eliminating eighteen of the roughly sixty-five full-time equivalent faculty positions. The committee instead persuaded the faculty to agree to a series of salary freezes and other concessions that averted the need for the faculty reductions, at least for the short run.

Faculty salaries at Bennington College never have been especially high as judged by AAUP's annual survey on the economic status of the profession. But, as a result of the concessions made by the faculty during this period, the levels of faculty compensation at Bennington appear to have lagged not only behind the formula for salary increases outlined in the *Faculty Handbook,* but also behind cost-of-living increases and behind those of comparable colleges. By 1994 compensation levels were far below those at peer institutions. Many faculty members who have the opportunity to do so engage in remunerative extracurricular activities, in part to make up for the loss of faculty compensation, but also to meet the expectations of professional involvement that are held for them.[3]

---

3. Such activities typically involve spending substantial amounts of time off campus and create a dilemma in the expectations of the board and administration, not only to have such activities, but also to encourage the faculty to be on campus full-time and available for student consultation. One distinguished writer of fiction told the investigating committee that he simply cannot afford to spend more than one term a year at Bennington if he is to have any time for his writing.

Starting in the mid-1980s, the tenuous financial balance was upset by a downward trend in tuition revenue as the number of undergraduate students declined from 600, a level consistent with budgetary balance, to 500 by 1991–92, and to 485 by 1992–93. The decline in enrollment was exacerbated by the increasing amounts of financial aid needed to help students meet the high and rising tuition and fee requirements. For a tuition-dependent institution, the crisis had re-emerged, though it had never been far beneath the surface. When Elizabeth Coleman was appointed president in 1987, despite mounting budgetary pressures she made several additional appointments and sought new programs that might enhance enrollments. These, as well as an expansion of administrative appointments, appear to have added to the operating deficits.

B. The Events of 1992

In March 1992 President Coleman received a cautionary letter from the regional accrediting institution, the New England Association of Schools and Colleges (NEASC), expressing concern about the college's declining enrollment, its deficits, and its diversion of funds intended to build endowment to meet those deficits. In April 1992 the board asserted the need to reach a steady-state enrollment of 550 undergraduates—enrollment was 485 at the time—and to make a permanent reduction of eight full-time-equivalent faculty positions. It pledged capital campaign proceeds in substantial amounts ($3.275 million) to be used over the next four or five years to facilitate a transition. To effect the faculty reduction, the board appointed a Steering Committee and issued a statement, dated April 7, 1992, which said in relevant part:

> [T]he Board looks to recommendations as to the particulars through a process that involves maximum collaboration between the duly constituted bodies of the Faculty, the Academic Council, the Academic Deans, the Student Educational Policies Committee, and Administration. . . .
>
> The Board will act on Faculty Personnel Committee recommendations involving the renewal of contractual commitments subsequent to acting on recommendations concerning the particulars of the adjustment in faculty size.

The Steering Committee effected the required position cuts without terminating the services of any faculty members involuntarily. In a resolution adopted on June 13, 1992, the board expressed its "profound appreciation" to the Steering Committee and adopted the committee's recommendations. But, foreshadowing things to come, the board went on to say:

[A] number of complex issues emerged. What, for instance, is the meaning of the "presumptive" part of presumptive tenure? Equally important: Do members of the faculty have a common understanding about professional responsibilities inside and outside the classroom? What are the Board's oversight obligations with respect to the faculty's efforts to sustain and enhance the quality of Bennington's educational life?

Over the summer, the Board will be considering ways in which it will participate with the faculty in a deeper discussion of these issues, leading to more explicit understandings and expectations.

Although those questions aroused unease, they at least suggested consultation with the faculty. From this point on, however, the situation deteriorated rapidly. A student protest—called a strike—about the proposed reductions in faculty positions included occupation of the president's office. . . . As is usually the case in time of such protests, the campus was in a state of high agitation. The board, just two weeks after its previous announcements, held a special meeting in New York City and engaged in what its chair, Mr. Barr, described as "a rare exercise of the board's authority." Expressing serious concerns about how the faculty governed and policed itself, the board:

1. asked the deans to review faculty appointment practices and responsibilities;

2. ordered a self-study by the Division of Literature and Languages, about which the board said it had "specific misgivings";

3. questioned the quality of the faculty members recommended to the board for reappointment and wondered pointedly about the rigor and integrity of the faculty review process;

4. rejected two of the eleven recommendations for reappointment made to it by the college's Faculty Personnel Committee (FPC)—all of which had been forwarded to the board with at least nominal positive recommendations from the president—on the substantive grounds that the faculty members involved did not meet threshold standards for reappointment. One of the two, Ms. Spiegel, had been reviewed and recommended by the FPC for appointment to a five-year term with presumptive tenure.

These actions, particularly the third and fourth, created a sense of outrage among the faculty and shattered whatever sense of cooperation and accommodation had seemed possible two weeks earlier. Mr. Neil Rappaport, a *de facto* leader of the faculty who had been corresponding civilly with Mr. Barr, who wrote him a long and angry letter questioning the board's "ethical right and professional capacity to judge academic merit." The promised participation of the board with the faculty in a "deeper discussion of the issues" was never to occur.

C. Events from June 1992 to April 1994

On July 16, 1992, Dean Sgorbati wrote informally to the president and the board, noting an "environment of fear, confusion, and anger" on campus. This seems to be an accurate characterization of the mood of the next two years. It was clear that a confrontation was looming between the faculty and the board and president.

In the fall of 1992 the Literature and Languages Division submitted a report in response to the instruction from the board that the division prepare a self-study. A subcommittee of the board prepared a response for the whole board that sharply criticized the division's report as being sloppy, self-serving, and arrogant.

In April 1993 the board announced that it was initiating a Symposium to generate ideas about the future of the college, and it invited participation by all constituencies. While the Symposium was to have an open-ended agenda, the board made it explicit that the process, while unequivocally inclusive, would not be consensual. The board asserted that it had, and intended to retain, the sole authority to determine policy.

In the fall of 1993 the Deans' Study was issued; it made detailed recommendations about (among other issues) changes in appointment and related procedures. If adopted, the changes would have retained most of the existing structures of faculty participation, but the changes would have substantially reduced the faculty's role by increasing at every stage the amount of decanal and presidential participation. With respect to appointments, the recommendations would have diminished the faculty's role as outlined in the *Faculty Handbook*. The faculty considered the report and adopted a resolution opposing it. The board received the report and the faculty's resolution without, so far as the investigating committee is aware, responding to the faculty. The recommendations of the report would be rendered moot by the subsequent events.

Numerous Symposium meetings were held on and off campus, with faculty becoming increasingly cynical about the sessions. Attendance at the first meeting was about 200; by the third or fourth it had dropped to fifteen. The fifth was canceled for lack of interest. The view the investigating committee heard from several faculty members was that they came to see the whole Symposium process as pretextual; that the board had determined the directions it intended to follow independent of the Symposium but was seeking legitimacy by apparently wide consultation.

Also in the fall of 1993, the faculty, hoping to increase its participation in the board's considerations of matters of central faculty concern, asked that the faculty be allowed to elect two members to the board. This proposal was promptly rejected by the board on the grounds that its membership was not constituency based.

In January 1994 the board "determined" that a state of financial exigency existed. By not sharing this determination with the faculty until June, the board effectively foreclosed discussion or debate as to whether such a determination was justified and about alternate ways of addressing the college's genuine financial problems.

On March 29, 1994, responding perhaps to insistent faculty demands for some information in a rumor-rampant atmosphere, Mr. Barr wrote a memorandum to the faculty indicating "three kinds of directions [that] could benefit now from exploration and work by others." They were, first, "several programmatic initiatives"; second, infrastructure priorities; and third, possible organizational changes "that the board is contemplating."

Eleven days later, on April 9, the board adopted the *Bennington College Plan for Changes in Educational Policy and Reorganization of Instructional Resources and Priorities* (the Plan) and instructed President Coleman to implement it. Here, as with the determination of financial exigency, the board did not make its actions known until June, when the academic year had ended and after a number of events had occurred, including a NEASC accreditation visit and the registration of continuing students for fall-term courses.

In June 1994 the board published and widely distributed the Symposium report, which sought to provide the rationale behind the Plan and its implementation, revealed the trustees' determination of financial exigency, and made public the Plan and the board's instruction to the president to implement it, which she promptly did.

D. The Plan

To understand the actions that followed in publication, the Plan needs to be read in its entirety. The text follows, excepting only Part I, which is repetitious of matters already covered in this report.

II. *PREAMBLE*

In order to re-establish the College on a viable financial footing consistent with meeting its educational responsibilities, the productivity of the College and its capacity to compete competitively in today's market must be transformed. The revenue stream of the College has declined precipitously because of an insufficient number of qualified applicants and a dramatic rise in the financial needs of those students who do enroll. If the College is to be fiscally viable, it must enroll a student body of approximately 600 students, which will require doubling its current applicant pool.

In order to increase productivity and attract applicants in these numbers, the College must pursue a plan that combines downsizing, alteration, redirection and enhancement of its programs. Downsizing alone will only make the College less competitive; it must add new programs as it reduces and transforms existing ones. In addition to attracting significantly larger numbers of students, this design must be sufficiently timely and compelling to generate philanthropic support (individual, corporate and foundation) adequate to carry it through the period of transition.

Time has shown that a continuous capacity for innovation is the lifeline of Bennington. Bennington has neither the marketplace benefits of ancient tradition (it is a very young institution in the genre of distinguished private liberal arts colleges) nor the market appeal of more vocationally defined institutions such as the community college. It is in fact precisely through its special blend of tradition and innovation that Bennington has provided a genuinely distinctive and distinguished education. If Bennington is to continue it must recover its capacity for the innovative and the distinctive; it is prudent to build that capacity into the structures that define it.

The Size and Character of the Faculty

The faculty will be reduced in overall size. There will be no academic divisions, in order to maximize the strength and importance of the faculty as a whole and to stress the necessity of collaboration across the entire spectrum rather than within sections of the faculty. With the exceptions indicated below, all of the disciplines currently offered at the College will continue to be available, with the addition of film/video and multimedia technology. Special emphasis will be given to those curricular ideas which provide an opportunity for extending beyond the confines of the disciplines as currently constituted and which are most responsive to the educational needs of our students.

The diminished size of the faculty also increases the need that it be qualitatively distinctive and increases the importance of each individual member of the faculty. Faculty members will need to be practitioner-teachers of whatever discipline or craft they teach, whose work is addressed to a wider audience than their professional colleagues. Credentials absent practice will not suffice; and such practice must take place in a public arena beyond the confines of the College, where it is subject to the evaluation of peers other than immediate colleagues. These criteria will be applied immediately in circumstances where programmatic changes dictate. Otherwise, they will be applied at times of reviews for reappointment.

Presumptively tenured faculty not affected by faculty reductions will retain presumptive tenure, but the standards for future reviews will conform to the changes in educational policy set forth in this Plan. No new presumptive tenure contracts will be offered.

Changes in Existing Programs

In order simultaneously to increase the number of languages taught and decrease the cost of such instruction, all language instruction will take place in a regional context involving the collaboration of the elementary and high schools in the area, the College, the business community, and the adult learning community. There will no longer be any faculty positions in the College for the teaching of foreign languages and literatures as such.

College faculty appointments in music will be limited to active composers whose creative work is ongoing and whose work is being currently performed for the public at large. Composition will be at the center of the curriculum. There will no longer be any faculty positions for the teaching of instruments. In order to diminish costs, increase options, and provide a basis for greater curricular coherence, the study of instruments will use resources from the community at large in the form of lessons.

Literature has always been a field of particular importance to the success of Bennington College, and it must attract significantly larger numbers of capable students interested in both the reading and the writing of literature than is currently the case. If the College is to meet its enrollment needs, reestablishment of the College's distinction in this area is critical. The teaching of literature by faculty involved primarily in academic research and scholarship will be abandoned and replaced by teachers who are themselves active and published writers of fiction, nonfiction, poetry and drama addressed to the public at large beyond professional colleagues. This will allow Bennington to reclaim a unique position in the teaching of literature that it has gradually lost. Few if any colleges in the country can offer students the opportunity to study both reading and writing with a faculty composed exclusively of published writers of the kinds of books they themselves will be studying.

The College will cease to offer the array of disciplines currently provided by the Division of Social Sciences in order to diminish costs and simultaneously to focus resources in ways that connect them more productively. Politics, economics, and sociology will be eliminated as separate disciplines and will be taught in the context of history, philosophy, anthropology, and psychology. Faculty, in addition to being active practitioners in their respective fields, will be expected to bring a breadth of perspective that connects their disciplines to diverse areas of human inquiry.

The relationship between the sciences and other areas of human inquiry will become a paramount issue. Bennington is particularly well positioned to exploit the rich educational potential of the sciences and of mathematics (and its special relation to technology) by breaking through the divides that have kept it so isolated from other intellectual enterprises. To do this, the teaching of mathematics will require particular attention, and faculty teaching mathematics will have a special interest in its pedagogy and be capable of teaching effectively at both the introductory and advanced levels.

Bennington has recently been selected as a flagship site for the New Multi-Media Program of a consortium of institutions. To strengthen the College's

competitiveness, Bennington will develop an associated program that focuses on the making of film, video, and other multi-media work.

Dance faculty will be professionally active choreographers whose creative
work is ongoing and whose work is currently being performed professionally.

The faculty position in art history will be eliminated, and the subject will
be integrated throughout appropriate curricula. Architecture will be treated
as a complex of disciplines with as many connections outside the visual arts
as within them, and its relation to technology will be expanded.

Directing will remain a priority; playwriting will be given greater importance and deeper collaborations forged with faculty whose primary focus is
the teaching of literature.

III. *FACULTY REDUCTIONS*

Financial exigency and changes in educational policy require the following faculty reductions and consolidations to effect savings and efficiencies
and to permit restructuring and enhancement of programs in order to increase competitiveness.

The faculty reduction decision is not equivalent to a termination or nonrenewal for cause and does not and should not reflect adversely on the faculty members whose positions must be eliminated.

The effective date of the elimination of all positions shall be June 30,
1994. Faculty members whose positions are eliminated shall receive either
one year's notice, or one year's pay and benefits in lieu of notice, as provided
below in Section IV.

1. All positions for the teaching of foreign languages/literatures will be
   eliminated.
2. All faculty positions for the teaching of musical instruments will be eliminated.
      All remaining music faculty will be professionally active composers
   whose creative work is ongoing and whose work is being professionally
   performed. The positions of all other music faculty will be eliminated.
3. There will be no teaching positions in politics, economics, or sociology.
   Currently presumptively tenured faculty in politics, economics, or sociology may apply for positions in history, philosophy, anthropology, or
   psychology.
4. All faculty teaching dance will be professionally active choreographers
   whose creative work is ongoing and whose work is being professionally
   performed. The positions of all other faculty teaching dance will be eliminated.
5. There will be no teaching position in art history.
      All remaining visual arts faculty will be professionally active visual
   artists whose creative work is ongoing and whose work is being professionally exhibited or commissioned. The positions of all other visual arts
   faculty will be eliminated.

6. All literature faculty will be professionally active writers of fiction, non-fiction, poetry, or drama whose creative work is ongoing, whose work is published and reviewed, and whose work is addressed to the public at large beyond professional colleagues. The positions of all other literature faculty will be eliminated.

IV. *PROCEDURES*

1. The President shall determine which faculty members' positions shall be eliminated pursuant to Section III.
2. Notices to those faculty members whose positions will be eliminated will be mailed prior to June 30, 1994.
3. (a) Each presumptively tenured faculty member whose position has been eliminated shall receive pay and benefits in lieu of notice for the period of July 1, 1994 to June 30, 1995.
   (b) Each non-presumptively tenured faculty member whose position has been eliminated shall receive one year's notice (a terminal appointment from July 1, 1994 to June 30, 1995).
   (c) A presumptively tenured faculty member whose position has been eliminated may request a terminal appointment from July 1, 1994 to June 30, 1995 instead of pay and benefits in lieu of notice for that period. Such a request must be made by the affected faculty member to the President in writing within 15 calendar days of the date of the notice to the faculty member of the elimination of the position, or, if a request for review is filed pursuant to Section V below, within 15 calendar days of the date of the President's final decision after review by the Faculty Review Committee [FRC].

V. *REVIEW PROCESS FOR FACULTY WHOSE POSITIONS ARE ELIMINATED*

1. The President shall appoint a Faculty Review Committee [FRC] to hear requests for review as described below. The Committee shall consist of three members of the faculty whose positions are not affected by the faculty reductions.
2. A request for review of the elimination of a faculty member's position may be filed by the affected faculty member. The request must be in writing and must be received by the FRC within 15 calendar days of the date of the notice to the faculty member of the elimination of the position.
3. Review shall be limited to whether the criteria stated in Part III above were properly applied in the individual case. The existence of a state of financial exigency, and the change of educational policy under which the position will be eliminated, are not subject to review.
4. Within 21 calendar days of the filing of the request for review, the FRC shall hear the faculty member. All proceedings shall be informal and conducted with dispatch. The affected faculty member shall have the burden

of producing evidence for review by the FRC. The FRC shall keep a record of its proceedings.

5. Within 14 calendar days of the proceeding, the FRC shall issue its written report to the President. The report shall state the FRC's findings on the reviewable issues raised by the faculty member. A copy of the report shall be transmitted to the faculty member.

6. Within 7 calendar days of the receipt of the written report of the FRC, the President shall review the FRC's report and make a final decision on the elimination of the position. There shall be no further review or appeal and no other body, board, or committee shall have jurisdiction in these cases.

7. Under no circumstances shall the dates specified in paragraphs 1–6 above be extended.

E. Faculty Termination Notices, June 1994, and New Appointments

The termination letters issued in mid-June 1994, to be effective June 30, 1994, were meticulously geared to the provisions of the Plan. In many cases the announced termination date would fall before the expiration of the affected faculty member's current contract. Individual letters differed only as the Plan's provisions were differently applicable. Here is one, in its entirety (save for the name of the addressee), received by a long-time, presumptively tenured member of the music faculty:

June 17, 1994

Dear [First Name]:

I regret to inform you that, pursuant to the Bennington College Plan for Changes in Educational Policy and Reorganization of Instructional Resources and Priorities, adopted by the Board of Trustees, your position is being eliminated effective June 30, 1994. A copy of the Plan is enclosed.

Pursuant to the Plan, Section III.2., all faculty positions for the teaching of musical instruments are being eliminated.

Section IV of the Plan provides that you will be entitled to pay and benefits in lieu of notice for the period July 1, 1994 to June 30, 1995. As an alternative to this provision, you may request a terminal teaching appointment for the same period. If you do wish to make such a request, you must direct it to me in writing within fifteen calendar days of the date of this letter, or, if you request a review of this decision as provided below, within fifteen calendar days of my final decision after review.

You are entitled to make a request for review of the decision to eliminate your position pursuant to the procedures set out in Section V of the Plan. Such a request must be made in writing and received by the Faculty Review Committee described in Section V within fifteen calendar days of the date of this letter. The request shall be filed with my office for forwarding to the

Review Committee, and it will be deemed received by the Committee when it has been received in my office. Pursuant to the Plan, I will be appointing three members of the faculty to serve as the Faculty Review Committee. Please carefully consult Section V of the Plan for information concerning the scope of the review and the deadlines applicable to the review process.

As stated in the Plan, elimination of faculty positions is part of a reorganization of the College directed by the Board for reasons of financial exigency and changes in educational policy. As these are not terminations or nonrenewals for cause, they do not and should not reflect adversely on the faculty members whose positions are eliminated. Faculty members whose positions are eliminated are eligible to apply for any applicable open positions at the College.

The College wishes to offer its assistance to each faculty member whose position has been eliminated in making the transition to other employment. Accordingly, I have appointed a Transition Team made up of Dave Marcell, Trudy Carter, and Gale Haas Keraga to be available to individual faculty members upon request to discuss any assistance the College might be able to provide to faculty who are in the process of obtaining new employment. If you would like to speak with the transition team, please contact Dave Marcell at Extension 269.

Sincerely, Elizabeth Coleman
President

Other members of the music faculty who were being released received similar letters, as did faculty members holding appointments in foreign languages, economics, politics, and art history—all areas where entire programs were being eliminated—with appropriate minor modifications to the second paragraph.

Faculty members in literature, dance, and visual arts received a different second paragraph—emphasizing newly defined performance criteria—of which the following is representative:

Pursuant to the Plan, Section III.6., all literature faculty will be professionally active writers of fiction, nonfiction, poetry, or drama whose creative work is ongoing, whose work is published and reviewed, and whose work is addressed to the public at large beyond professional colleagues. Based upon my review of the materials that you have on file in the Office of the Dean of Faculty, I have determined that you are not a professionally active writer of fiction, poetry, drama, or nonfiction, whose work is ongoing, is published and reviewed, and is addressed to the public at large beyond professional colleagues. Accordingly, your position is being eliminated.

Finally, some faculty members received a different letter terminating their services. Here is the first paragraph of one to a presumptively tenured mathematics instructor with nearly three decades of full-time service at the college. The letter was dated June 27. (The second paragraph is not included since it discusses alleged shortcomings of the faculty member.):

> I regret to inform you that I have decided not to recommend you to the Board of Trustees for a fifth five-year presumptive tenure appointment. Your appointment will, therefore, terminate as of June 30, 1995.

Most of those receiving termination letters sought to utilize the review (appeal) procedures specified in those letters. Since the review committee appointed by the president was permitted to consider only "whether the criteria stated in Part III [of the Plan] were properly applied in the individual case," the appeals were brief and perfunctory in cases where positions were eliminated. In two cases, however, the review committee did recommend reinstatement, and in one, that of Neil Rappaport, the president did reinstate. In the other, the president did not.

The invitation to released faculty to apply for "any applicable open position" seems to have been largely empty, since no open positions were announced or advertised, except in the case of a teacher of politics who was immediately reappointed in history.[4] Over the summer, by memorandum of July 14, 1994, President Coleman announced new appointments she had made to the faculty in literature. Language teachers who indicated to the president that they wished to be considered for the newly created position of language coordinator did not even have the opportunity to apply before learning that an appointment had been made from the outside. Some released music teachers were invited to apply for the opportunity to give music lessons with remuneration on an hourly basis.

In October 1994 an advertisement in *The Chronicle of Higher Education* invited applications for a new administrative position, Associate Dean of the College. The investigating committee does not know if any of the released faculty have been considered for this position; none were informed that the position was being created.

III. Issues

A. Tenure at Bennington College

The 1940 *Statement of Principles on Academic Freedom and Tenure* calls for a maximum period of probation not to exceed seven years, with service

---

4. Several faculty members with whom the investigating committee talked believe the provisions of the Plan in III. 3. were in fact designed to cover this individual.

beyond that period constituting continuous appointment or tenure, with requisite procedural safeguards against involuntary termination.

Until 1994 tenure at Bennington was governed by Section 9.43 of the *Faculty Handbook,* which provides as follows:

9.43   *Presumptive Tenure*

> When a faculty member is offered a first five-year presumptive tenure contract, or any subsequent five-year contract, the College thereby commits itself to offer another five-year contract at the termination of the one then being served unless it can be demonstrated by the College that the contribution to College life of the faculty member concerned has markedly deteriorated or that he/she has substantially failed to perform the terms of the contract, or unless financial exigency or a change in educational policy requires the elimination of that teaching position. A second or subsequent five-year contract will only be denied after an appropriate hearing has been held before the FPC (faculty personnel committee), at which hearing the faculty member concerned is given the opportunity to hear and challenge the arguments against reappointment.

Requiring a review every five years after the faculty member has achieved presumptive tenure status does not conform to the concept of tenure as provided under the 1940 *Statement of Principles.* Until 1992, however, presumptive tenure was *de facto* tenure at Bennington College. No presumptively tenured faculty member had ever been issued notice of termination or even recommended for termination of appointment following a five-year review, and neither faculty nor administration believed the five-year review was a serious threat to reappointment. Instead, they considered the process as providing an opportunity for constructive feedback to the faculty member. As far as the investigating committee is aware, every such five-year review led to a positive recommendation from the FPC to the president, was forwarded by the president with a positive recommendation to the trustees, and was accepted by them.

Reading Section 9.43 of the *Faculty Handbook* in light of the events of 1994 suggests how tenuous its protections were compared to those called for in the 1940 *Statement,* and how easily its provisions could be used to justify the termination of a presumptive tenured faculty member's appointment if the board should choose, unilaterally, to declare "financial exigency or a change in educational policy." But if these worries existed within the faculty prior to the 1993–94 academic year, the investigating committee is not aware of them, and there are instances where the word "tenure" is used in documents by members of the administration instead of the phrase "presumptive tenure."

* * *

In June 1994 President Coleman, following the board's mandate as expressed in the Plan, terminated the services of fifteen presumptively tenured faculty members who were found wanting in her assessment of their relative usefulness in the context of a newly defined institutional mission. Under the standards of the 1940 *Statement,* these faculty members were entitled to the safeguards of academic due process that accrue with tenure in any action to terminate their services involuntarily. These terminations occurred under the board's declaration of financial exigency and changes in educational policy that it announced at that time. Faculty members without presumptive tenure also were issued notices of termination in June 1994. Released faculty members with and without presumptive tenure were treated differently only in that the former were given the option of taking one year's salary as terminal pay in lieu of the one-year terminal appointment offered to those without the presumption of tenure. Not surprisingly, all but one of the affected faculty with presumptive tenure rejected the chance to teach at Bennington for a terminal year with no appreciable additional compensation.

While retained faculty who had achieved presumptive tenure are nominally grandfathered in that status, it can hardly be regarded as meaningful after the events of 1994. The termination of appointments of presumptively tenured faculty and the concurrent announcement that no new presumptive tenure contracts would be offered compel the investigating committee's conclusion that tenure no longer exists at Bennington College either as it is understood in the profession or as it was understood at Bennington.

B. The *Bona Fides* of Financial Exigency as Justification
   for Terminating the Appointments of Presumptively
   Tenured Faculty

* * *

[The committee considered the College's situation in light of the "financial exigency" clause (dealt with in detail in Chapter 5). It could not determine whether or not Bennington's financial condition was such as to have allowed it to terminate contracts during their term, though it entertained doubts that that was the case in light of the college's announcement that it was prepared to direct $10 million toward ensuring the success of its "transformation." The committee found] it hard to avoid the conclusion that the board's declaration of financial exigency in January 1994, rather than providing the *necessity* for abrupt and massive faculty terminations, provided the *opportunity* for them. The declaration provided the umbrella for a massive purge of the faculty and for institution of a series of educational policy changes favored by the board. The exclusion of the faculty from any role in this determination, as well as of the new directions of the college, appears to have been advertent, intended to demonstrate that the faculty's role in educational policy and indeed in faculty composition had been abrogated.

The events of June 1994 were not, in the investigating committee's view, a measured response to an imminent financial crisis, but a coup. The exclusion of faculty involvement and participation occurred despite the faculty's urgent requests to be included. In the spring of 1994, before the determination of financial exigency or the existence of the Plan had been revealed (but after they had been decided upon by the board), the faculty members asked to have a Crisis Steering Committee appointed to discuss problems and possible solutions. Their request was rejected. Members of the board, including Mr. Barr and Ms. Borden, met with members of the faculty on June 9 (*after* the relevant decisions had all been made, but before the decisions had been revealed), and answered faculty questions but, according to several participants in the meeting, made it unmistakably clear that faculty involvement in the decisions was neither needed nor welcomed.

C. Role of the Faculty in Changes of Educational Policy and Associated Terminations

* * *

An examination of the Plan, and a consideration of the presumed educational justifications for making the selective judgments that the plan did about program eliminations, faculty strengths, etc., show immediately why these judgments should have been informed by the professional insight and experience of the faculty (rather than by laypersons sitting on the board of trustees). In addition, as used by the board of Bennington College, the mere assertion of a change in educational policy can provide the requisite rationale for the elimination of any faculty position at any time. This lack of any safeguard provides no protection against the board's use of such a declaration *ad hominem* by simply describing a faculty member's position with sufficient specificity to subject it to elimination.

Several of the terminations were based on a different, arguably more remote rationale: the redefinition of the required professional activities of faculty members in choreography, the visual arts, and literature, as specified in sections III. 4., III. 5., and III. 6. of the Plan. Evidently the expectations under which the faculty members had been appointed and subsequently promoted to the status of presumptive tenure no longer applied.

D. Selection of Particular Individuals for Termination of Appointments

The investigating committee already has noted the absence of faculty participation and other safeguards in the determinations of financial exigency and changes in educational policy that are asserted as the basis for terminating the appointments of presumptively tenured members of the Bennington faculty. When those assertions have the effect of designating particular individuals for termination, they inevitably raise an additional question: To what extent was the whole structure of the Plan merely a device to purge from the faculty individuals who for one reason or another were *persona non grata* to the administration or the board?

All of the released faculty with whom the investigating committee spoke, and some of the retained faculty, stated that they believed that the basic distinction between the faculty designated for termination and those retained was opposition to or support of the president and the board. As one of them put it, "Liz Coleman demands and rewards loyalty." The faculty is small enough, with few in precisely comparable positions, that it is possible to construct a nominally abstract plan phrased in terms of principles of educational policy that has the effect of targeting specific individuals. Virtually all of those sent termination notices in June 1994 had opposed actions of the board or the president, or were members of the Division of Literature and Languages, itself long in bad repute with the board. Those serving as elected members of the committees that exercised the key elements of faculty governance were particularly hard hit. Four of the seven at-large faculty members on the Academic Council, including two of the three members of its Budget Committee; all four elected members of the FPC; and two of three members of the FPRC [Faculty Personnel Review Committee] received termination notices. Among the retained faculty, only a very small number (the committee is aware of only one) had openly opposed the president.

Statistics of this kind never can be decisive, but they raise troubling questions. Moreover, the terminations had little relation to student enrollment levels. Faculty in the Division of Literature and Languages, which offered the most popular concentrations, experienced major losses, while those in the Science Division and the former Black Music Division, two of the areas with the smallest loads judged by student concentrations, were left unscathed.

Competing hypothesis about how individuals came to be designated for termination of appointment might have been resolved by an open discussion with faculty members of the criteria and their application. Such a discussion never occurred. Instead, the board promulgated and published a Plan without faculty involvement or opportunity to comment—and without proffering any rationale for drawing the termination lines in the manner it did—and instructed the president to implement the Plan, which she did without consultation with any faculty group. The procedural safeguards against abuse were not afforded, nor were procedures for subsequent review of the decisions adequate to that purpose.

E. Manner of Termination

Neither financial exigency nor program discontinuance can account for the disrespectful, petty, indeed vindictive and inhumane, manner in which the terminations were announced and carried out. While these matters are less central to this report than other matters, they suggest something to the investigating committee about the intentions of the president and board. For example:

1. Four of the presumptively tenured faculty members who were issued notices of termination had at least twenty years of service at Bennington and were in their sixties or older. They might have been offered the opportunity to take early retirement in lieu of abrupt and immediate termination. The only one whom the investigating committee asked about this alternative indicated that he would have been more than receptive.

2. Individual termination decisions, including those based on inadequate professional activity, were made without updated resumes or complete faculty files.

3. The time interval between notification of termination and its effective date was fourteen days. Released faculty members were instructed to vacate their offices early in July. When they requested permission to retain offices until they could make other suitable arrangements, the deadline was extended to not later than July 22, a date that was described as nonnegotiable. Many had occupied those offices for more than twenty years.

4. Access to long-distance telephone service was blocked for at least

some released faculty members before the effective date of their termination.

5. Faculty members were not notified about new faculty positions even when they specifically had requested such notification, nor was any discernible effort made to place the affected individuals in other suitable positions in the college.

6. A faculty member with a book in press reports having discovered from his publisher that a representative of the administration, without revealing her identity or institutional connection, and initially presumed by the publisher to be a potential purchaser, made repeated telephone calls to find out whether a book that the faculty member had said would be published in 1994 would in fact be available before December 31. When told that the publication was slightly delayed by problems at the publishing house and would be out early in 1995, the administration claimed this as a misrepresentation on the part of the faculty member that contributed to the decision to terminate his appointment.

F. Procedures for Review of the Terminations

The procedures provided in Part V of the Plan for review of a termination decision were utilized by most of those given notice of termination. (Some faculty members did not use them, saying in effect, "Why bother?") The reviews were, by Association standards, minimal and inadequate in crucial respects. First, and perhaps most crucial, the Plan, despite a faculty member's having been granted "presumptive tenure," shifts the burden of proof by its requirement that "the affected faculty member shall have the burden of producing evidence for review by the FRC." Second, the Faculty Review Committee was appointed by the president instead of being an elected faculty body. One of its three members was the newly appointed dean of the college. Third, the key issues of the *bona fides* of financial exigency and the decisions governing program discontinuance explicitly were excluded from what the committee could review. For those whose positions had been eliminated, there was nothing to review! For those who were deemed not to have met the newly defined professional standards, there was a basis for review, and in one case, that of Mr. Rappaport, the review led to his reinstatement. Even with respect to the limited jurisdiction of the review committee, its determinations were subject to review and final decision by the president, and she rejected one of the two positive recommendations it made.

Those presumptively tenured faculty members whose services were terminated by the president, after having been recommended for reappointment by the FPC, were likewise subject to termination without further review by any faculty committee. They were permitted the opportunity to ask for reconsideration by the president, but in none of these cases did she modify her negative initial determination.

. . . The position taken by the board is that all of the procedures utilized were fully in accord with the internal regulations of Bennington College, and that nothing more was required. The board rested its interpretation on the phrase in Section 9.43 that reads "or unless financial exigency or a change of educational policy requires the elimination of that teaching position." Under this interpretation the provision, rather than affording protection to faculty members who had served beyond their probationary years and had been approved for presumptive tenure, is a license to do away with these individuals. It represents a departure not only from accepted standards of the profession with respect to academic due process, but also from the traditions of Bennington College prior to these events.

G. Governance

Although in the spring of 1992 Mr. Barr had spoken of the board's actions as "a rare exercise of the Board's authority," it is difficult in 1994 to find that description accurate.

The board's elimination of the divisional structure with which the faculty had managed both faculty appointments and curriculum, and the abrupt suspension of all practices and procedures of faculty governance, seem to the investigating committee to be wholly unrelated to changes mandated by financial exigency. They seem, rather, to be related to the changes in educational policy primarily by making it clear that faculty determinations with respect to educational matters are no longer to be invited or respected. They surely had the additional effect of preventing any coherent response by the faculty to the actions taken by the board and the president.

H. Academic Freedom at Bennington College

The *Faculty Handbook* does not include a statement on academic freedom. A faculty committee that was charged with drafting a statement on the subject in 1993–94 did so, but its report was not brought to the faculty until the fall of 1994, after the events herein described. In a divided vote, the Core Faculty, as it is now designated, did not adopt the report because, according to one member, the Core Faculty could not agree on defining the terms of academic freedom "in a manner appropriate for the college."

At least until 1992, even without such a statement, members of the Bennington faculty showed no reluctance to express their views on virtually all matters, confident that their right to do so would be protected. The events of the years since 1992 have destroyed that perception for many of the faculty. The investigating committee asked all of the faculty members it interviewed, released and retained alike, for their assessment of the current state of academic freedom in the campus. A majority of each group seemed to agree on two points.

First, they agreed that opposition to the policies and activities of the board and the president played a significant, some said decisive, role in the identification of faculty members for termination. All of the released faculty believe this. Among retained faculty, even those who agreed with the administration that a stalemate between the faculty and administration had prevented real progress in addressing the financial and admissions crisis that Bennington faces, many expressed the belief that "troublemakers" were targeted as a way to break the stalemate. While the investigating committee cannot, of course, be certain, in the absence of persuasive evidence to the contrary it cannot reject the view that the terminations in number and in designation of who was to be terminated were not the mere consequence of the implementation of an even-handed plan, but rather were intended, and served, to remove from the faculty most of those who were critical of the administration and the board.

Second, most of the faculty members interviewed agreed that the present climate at Bennington is not now conducive to the faculty's expressing strong opinions critical of the Symposium, the Plan, the board, or the president. One retained faculty member stated to the investigating committee that he is convinced that a letter he wrote protesting the termination of the appointment of one of his colleagues means that he will not be reappointed when his current contract expires, and he is already exploring alternatives.

The investigating committee does not know if these views are justified, but they are surely the common perception. While some of the retained faculty members approve of the programmatic changes that were made as essential to the survival of the college, even they have expressed concern about how the low morale and oppressive climate created by the events of June 1994.

A different view of the threat to academic freedom is strongly held and articulated by one faculty member in politics whose services were terminated. In his view the board has articulated a new orthodoxy in its educational plan and has made acceptance of its view on these matters a condition of faculty service at Bennington. In this faculty member's view, the board's position immediately removes educational policy from the possible agenda of faculty and student discussion and debate and thus critically infringes academic freedom.

In any event, the investigating committee believes that the present climate at Bennington College is tense and fragile, that the retained faculty members recognize that they are beholden to the president, and that many of them feel insecure. This is not a climate conducive to academic freedom.

* * *

A Comment on the Rollins College and Bennington College Reports

Tenure, Machlup observed, is necessary to protect an academic freedom that includes not only disciplinary debate but also uninhibited criticism of the policies and programs of the educational institution as well as of its administration and governing board, even if the professor's "words or actions are offensive to many." We need to defend "the heretic, the dissenter, the troublemaker, whose freedom to speak and to write is under some threat from colleagues, administrators, governing board, government, or pressure groups." Indeed, it was for the very connection to academic freedom that the Association of American Colleges initially opposed the idea of tenure. Trustees "must do the best they can, giving a sense of security to teachers," an AAC committee opined in 1917, but

> There are certain . . . cases which almost every institution has now and then to manage in which what a trustee of Cornell once called "vexels" or mischief-makers can break the continuity of an institution and set back for years its best interests. The very fact that "vexels" know that some excellent men in responsible positions sometimes advise that at any cost colleges get on with so-called impossible persons, is a distinct encouragement never given in a well-organized corporation to mischief-makers to retard administration processes.

To the administration of Rollins College, Professor Rice was doubtless a "troublemaker," a "mischief-maker," a "vexel." He took strenuous, tactless, and offensive issue with the debating system, the fraternity system, the athletic system, and chapel services. "He had argued that a

serious weakness in American education lay in an excessive feminization of its teaching body"—and, in a posture that would surely raise the
ire of some today—he "disparaged the work of women teachers." Not
surprisingly, his outspokenness brought Professor Rice into conflict not
only with an autocratic president but with a not insignificant number
of his colleagues. Recall, then, Machlup's admonition that tenure protects the heretic not only from the administration, the governing
board, and outside pressure groups but from colleagues as well. It is well
here to recall Kingman Brewster's observation on the role of tenure at
Yale:

> In strong universities assuring freedom from intellectual conformity
> coerced *within* the institution is even more of a concern than is the
> protection of freedom from external interference.
>   This spirit of academic freedom within the university has a value
> which goes beyond protecting the individual's broad scope of
> thought and inquiry. It bears crucially upon the distinctive quality
> of the university as a community. If a university is alive and produc-
> tive it is a place where colleagues are in constant dispute; defending
> their latest intellectual enthusiasm, attacking the contrary views of
> others. From this trial by intellectual combat emerges a sharper in-
> sight, later to be blunted by other, sharper minds. It is vital that this
> contest be uninhibited by fear of reprisal. Sides must be taken only
> on the basis of the merits of a proposition. Jockeying for favor by
> trimming the argument because some colleague or some group will
> have the power of academic life or death in some later process of
> review would falsify and subvert the whole exercise. [Yale Univer-
> sity, *Report of the President, 1971–1972*, pp. 16–17 (emphasis in orig-
> inal)]

Professor Rice apparently thought he had tenure; at least the Committee of Inquiry thought he did. But, upon review of his letter of appointment and the prevailing practices at Rollins College, it is arguable
that all he had was a presumption of annual renewal, which, if widely
observed for all others similarly situated, was only tenure as a "moral
commitment," to use Machlup's phrase; that is, there appears to have
been no provision expressly assuring him that he could be dismissed
only for good cause, and none ensuring him a fair hearing before a
dismissal could be effected. In President Holt's memorable phrase,
"When you want to fire a cook, you don't go out and get a committee
of neighbors to tell you what to do, do you?" In the event, even tenure
as a moral commitment was eradicated by the trustees' resolution of
February 16, 1932.

The events at Rollins took place many years ago, but those events—

dismissal for criticism of institution policy or of administrative behavior coupled with lack of adequate due process—have often been replayed. Such, the committee concluded, was the case at Bennington. And Bennington's trustees, too, abrogated even the "presumptive" or moral claim to periodic renewal which the college's rules had therefore afforded. The Bennington College case will be reconsidered in Chapter 5, dealing with the relation of tenure to resource allocation.

2

Probation

As Fritz Machlup pointed out, in the absence of a firm "in or out" policy after a fixed probationary period, tenure is likely to be "by courtesy," the routine renewal of the appointment of an amiable if average colleague. De jure tenure entails much greater risks, so evaluation of the candidate for tenure is correspondingly more careful. How that evaluation is carried out varies from institution to institution; but it customarily involves the participation of a variety of faculty bodies, consideration of external references, and review by administrative officers. Academics should be no strangers to the process; but to the nonacademic public the process may require a bit of elaboration. One descriptive source is the courts, for denials of tenure are not infrequently challenged and judicial opinions often engage with the process of decision making. Set out below is a description of the process of evaluation that resulted in the denial of tenure to a faculty member at the Harvard Business School, challenged unsuccessfully on grounds of sex discrimination. The purpose of laying out this part of the opinion is neither to support nor to criticize the court's finding on the statutory issue; the application of antidiscrimination law to the professoriate has been reviewed elsewhere. (See Terry L. Leap, *Tenure, Discrimination, and the Courts* [Ithaca, N.Y.: ILR Press, 1993].) Nor is it of especial relevance that the case arose at Harvard. The case is excerpted only because the court close to review in detail the procedures by which the tenure decision was made.

Jackson v. Harvard University

(United States District Court for the
District of Massachusetts, 1989)
Woodlock, J.

* * *

A. *The Plaintiff*

Barbara Jackson received her Ph.D. degree in applied mathematics from Harvard University in 1973. She joined the faculty of the Business School that year as an Assistant Professor of Business Administration. Her initial appointment was from March 1, 1973 until June 30, 1977. In 1977, she was promoted to Associate Professor and reappointed for a five-year term from July 1, 1977 to June 30, 1982.

During her first four years at the Business School, Ms. Jackson taught and conducted research in the Managerial Economics Area.[10] In 1977, she decided to change her field of specialization to Marketing, and over the course of the next two years, she gradually transferred into the Marketing Area. Broadly described, the move from Managerial Economics to Marketing was a move from theory to practice, from abstraction to application. It was a change that many others on the Business School faculty had made before her; nonetheless, it was a change that Ms. Jackson undertook with some trepidation. She was concerned that the move would place her at a disadvantage when she came up for tenure review, because she would have less time to demonstrate accomplishment and promise in her new field than would someone who had devoted his or her entire professional career to that field.

The administration of the Business School reassured Ms. Jackson that her tenure review would not be limited to her work in Marketing, but would include evaluation of her record as a whole. She was told that her work in Managerial Economics and the brevity of her exposure to Marketing would be taken into consideration in making her tenure decision. Thus reassured, Ms. Jackson completed the process of transferring to the Marketing Area in 1979. It was as a member of the Marketing Area that Ms. Jackson was reviewed for tenure in 1981 and then again in 1983.

B. *The Business School's Tenure Review Process*

An individual's candidacy for tenure at the Business School is initially reviewed by a Subcommittee of four tenured professors appointed by the

From 721 F.Supp. 1397 (D.Mass. 1989) *aff'd* 900 F.2d 464 (1st Cir.) *cert. denied* 498 U.S. 848 (1990).
10. "Area" is synonymous with "department."

Dean. The candidate does not have control over which faculty members will or will not serve on his or her Subcommittee.[11] However, candidates are routinely afforded the opportunity to inform the Dean of the names of any persons they prefer not to be on their Subcommittees, and the candidates' requests are routinely honored.[12]

The Subcommittee examines the candidate's entire academic record—including teaching, course development, and research—and solicits the confidential opinions of faculty members at the Business School, faculty at other institutions, and business practitioners, as appropriate. The Subcommittee measures the candidate's record of achievement and performance against the standards set forth in the Business School's "Policies and Procedures with Respect to Faculty Appointments and Promotions," and then writes a report of its findings. The Subcommittee's Report typically contains a recorded vote by Subcommittee members on whether the candidate has met the standards necessary for promotion with tenure, and whether the candidate should, in any event, be recommended for tenure.

The Subcommittee's Report is presented to the entire tenured faculty sitting as the Faculty Advisory Committee on Appointments ("Full Committee"). The Full Committee numbers 80 or more professors, of whom approximately 60–70 normally participate and vote. The candidate's Subcommittee Report is available to the Full Committee before, and is considered during, the deliberations of the Full Committee, along with individual faculty member opinions, assessments, and reflections about the candidate and his or her work. The Subcommittee Report plays a substantial role in framing the Full Committee's discussions, but it is not conclusive or dispositive. The recommendations of the Subcommittee may be disregarded by the Full Committee, and it is the Full Committee's vote that constitutes the faculty view concerning whether the candidate should receive tenure.

The Full Committee, with the Dean presiding, ordinarily meets twice to consider a candidate. During the first meeting, the Full Committee typically has a wide-ranging discussion of the candidate, followed by a preliminary vote in which the individual tenured faculty members vote by signed ballot. The Full Committee then adjourns and regathers within 30 days to have a second and final discussion about the candidate. At the end of this second meeting, the members once again vote by signed ballot.

11. Until 1982, the Dean appointed different subcommittees for each person who came up for tenure in a given year. Since 1982, the Dean has appointed a Standing Subcommittee, which evaluates all candidates in a given year.

12. Under the post-1982 "Standing Subcommittee" regime, the members of the Standing Subcommittee for a given year are announced before evaluations commence, and candidates are afforded the opportunity to object to individual members.

The Full Committee vote is advisory in form. The Dean is not bound by the results, and it is the Dean who determines whether to recommend to the President and governing bodies of the University that a candidate receive tenure. In making this determination, the Dean accords considerable weight to the final vote of the Full Committee. In fact, never in the history of the Business School has a candidate received less than "substantial majority" support from the Full Committee and still been recommended for tenure by the Dean. Receipt of substantial majority support is not a guarantee that the Dean will recommend tenure, but failure to receive a substantial majority insures the denial of tenure. The Dean's decision whether or not to recommend appointment with tenure is *de facto* final. Harvard's President and governing bodies have never overriden a recommendation by the Dean of the Business School that a candidate be granted tenure; and when the Dean decides against recommending tenure, with rare exceptions, no further action is taken on the candidacy.

C. *The 1981 Tenure Review*

1. The Subcommittee in 1981

Barbara Jackson first became eligible for tenure consideration in 1981. She submitted her portfolio in August 1981, and soon thereafter submitted a list of four faculty members whom she requested not be on the Subcommittee that would evaluate her work. She based her request on her impression that three of the four were biased against women and that the fourth was incompetent to judge her scholarship. Despite Ms. Jackson's request, Professor Stephen Bradley, one of the three persons she regarded as biased against women, was placed on her Subcommittee.

Ms. Jackson's Subcommittee met in the autumn of 1981 and prepared a Report on her candidacy. The Subcommittee members voted 3–1 that Ms. Jackson had met the standards necessary for promotion with tenure, and they voted 4–0 to recommend to the Full Committee that she receive tenure. Professor Bradley cast the lone vote against Ms. Jackson's qualifications, but recommended that she receive tenure as an exception to the Standards.

2. The 1977 Standards and the 1981 Standards

The "standards" against which the Subcommittee officially evaluated Ms. Jackson's work were those contained in the Revised June 1981 version of the Business School's "Policies and Procedures with Respect to Faculty

Appointments and Promotions" [hereinafter "1981 Standards"]. These 1981 Standards replaced the 1977 "Policies and Procedures with Respect to Faculty Appointments and Promotions" [hereinafter "1977 Standards"]. Although promulgated in June 1981, the 1981 Standards were not distributed to the non-tenured Business School faculty until September 15, 1981. In other words, the text of the Standards under which Barbara Jackson was evaluated for tenure was not available to her until *after* she had submitted her tenure portfolio.

Ms. Jackson maintains that the 1977 and 1981 Standards are materially different. She contends that in preparation for her 1981 tenure review she developed her portfolio of academic work with reference to the 1977 Standards, that she expected to be evaluated under those standards, that she met those standards, and, therefore, that she should have received tenure. She contends that the fact that her tenure candidacy was evaluated under Standards published after her portfolio was submitted should be considered substantial evidence that she was not given a genuine opportunity to receive tenure in 1981.

I find, however, that the differences were not material; and that, even if they were, the 1981 Standards were applied to Ms. Jackson in a way that did not prejudice her. Ms. Jackson was *formally* reviewed for tenure in 1981 under the 1981 Standards; however, she was *effectively* evaluated under the 1977 Standards.

Plaintiff maintains that the core difference between the 1977 Standards and the 1981 Standards was that under the former a Business School professor had to demonstrate excellence in *either* a) teaching and course development, *or* b) research, to be qualified for tenure, whereas under the latter the candidate was deemed unqualified unless he or she could demonstrate excellence *both* in teaching and course development *and* in research.

Dean, McArthur and Dean Gordon Donaldson[14] testified that the 1977 and 1981 Standards represented two snapshots at different times of an evolving consensus among the tenured faculty at the Business School concerning the profile future tenured faculty members should have.

14. Dean Gordon Donaldson became a tenured member of the Business School faculty in 1963. He served as faculty Appointments Coordinator from 1975 until early 1980. Shortly after John McArthur became Dean of the Business School in January 1980, Professor Donaldson was appointed Senior Associate Dean for Faculty Development, a position he held until April 1986. As Appointments Coordinator and Senior Associate Dean for Faculty Development, Professor Donaldson was the person primarily responsible for managing the entire promotions process, including the process by which associate professors at the Business School were reviewed for promotion to tenured professorships. Professor Donaldson drafted both the 1977 and 1981 Standards, and in both 1981 and 1983 he managed Barbara Jackson's tenure review process.

The policies in place at the Business School during the 1960's and early 1970's allowed professors to come up for tenure on either a teaching track or a research track. The unintended consequence of this two-track system had been the creation of a two-caste tenured faculty, one caste consisting of researchers and the other caste of teachers. This dichotomy came to be seen as not conducive to collegiality. The tenured faculty gradually decided that the way to eliminate the schism that had been created would be to require excellence in both teaching and research from future tenure candidates. This policy evolved over a two-decade period and different stages in that evolution were captured in the 1977 and 1981 written Standards.

The difference between the requirements for tenure at the Business School in the quarter century between the early 1960's when Deans McArthur and Donaldson received tenure and the requirements today may be substantial. However, the actual difference between the 1977 and 1981 Standards at issue here is not nearly as dramatic as plaintiff has maintained. Those Standards are not materially different. They represent separate points are sufficiently close together so as to be indistinguishable for purposes of this litigation.

Plaintiff alleges that the core differences between the 1977 and 1981 Standards may be seen by comparing paragraph 6 of the 1977 Standards with paragraph 5 of the 1981 Standards. Paragraph 6 of the 1977 Standards provides in relevant part:

> [F]or the large majority of its tenured Faculty, the School seeks persons who:
> a) have demonstrated effectiveness in classroom teaching and course maintenance;
> b) have demonstrated excellence in research or creative course development, or both;
> c) have demonstrated outstanding performance, overall, when teaching, research, and course development are taken together.

Paragraph 5 of the 1981 Standards provides in relevant part:

> [F]or the large majority of its tenured faculty the School seeks persons who:
> a) have demonstrated effectiveness in classroom teaching and in the normal maintenance of established course materials; and
> b) have demonstrated the excellence of their published work based on research and creative course development, the mix of which may appropriately vary widely across the pool of candidates; and
> c) have provided persuasive evidence of the capacity for intellectual leadership and for self-renewal essential to a productive tenured academic career.

These paragraphs and the provisions contained in each should not, of course, be read in isolation from the remainder of the respective Standards, which indicate that the tenure requirements in those paragraphs are not be read as setting out a rigid calculus.[15] However, even if read in isolation from the documents from which they are taken, these paragraphs establish substantially identical requirements for tenure. . . .

*   *   *

However, even if they were materially different, Barbara Jackson was effectively evaluated under the 1977 Standards. This conclusion is evidenced by the fact that Ms. Jackson's Subcommittee voted 3–1 that she had met the Standards necessary for tenure. By plaintiff's own admission, no one applying plaintiff's understanding of the 1981 Standards to plaintiff's candidacy could have found her qualified for tenure in 1981, since Ms. Jackson had not done sufficient "research." Thus, the 3–1 vote indicates that at least three of the members of plaintiff's 1981 Subcommittee mixed her research and course development together in such a way as to evaluate primarily her "creative course development," i.e., as set forth in the 1977 Standards, paragraph 6(b). The Subcommittee noted that the Standards had evolved between 1977 and 1981, but "unanimously fe[lt] the differences [we]re immaterial for purposes of this case." I agree.

My conclusion that plaintiff was effectively evaluated under the 1977 Standards is also supported by the reason Harvard has articulated as the non-discriminatory reason for denying tenure to plaintiff: plaintiff's alleged failure to demonstrate sufficient creativity. This is essentially a contention that plaintiff failed to meet the requisite for tenure set out in paragraph 6(b) of the 1977 Standards.

*   *   *

3. The Full Committee in 1981

The Subcommittee's unanimous recommendation that Ms. Jackson receive tenure was presented to the Full Committee for preliminary consideration on November 17, 1981. Sixty-three tenured faculty members were present at this preliminary meeting. Following a wide-ranging discussion

15. *See, e.g.,* 1977 Standards ¶1 ("This general statement of policy cannot be exhaustive and it should not be treated literally in all cases. The task of building a university graduate school faculty is a creative work which must call for the exercise of judgment on many considerations in a variety of combinations"); 1981 Standards ¶1 ("This general statement of policy cannot be exhaustive. The task of building a university graduate school faculty is a creative work which must call for the exercise of judgment on many considerations in a variety of combinations which cannot be detailed in advance").

of her candidacy, sixty-one members voted on the question. Forty-seven persons voted to grant tenure, seven voted to terminate her, one voted that she be reappointed without tenure, and six abstained. The sixty-one persons voting included the eight members of Ms. Jackson's department— the Marketing Area. The eight Marketing professors all voted that Ms. Jackson be promoted. It is undisputed that the level of support Ms. Jackson received on this preliminary ballot constituted the "substantial majority" required for a tenure recommendation.

Twenty-five days after the preliminary vote, the Full Committee reconvened for its final consideration of plaintiff's candidacy for tenure. When the votes were tallied at this second meeting, plaintiff's substantial majority had evaporated. Seventy-one tenured faculty members were present for the final vote, and sixty-eight voted. Twenty-nine voted to promote Ms. Jackson, twenty-seven voted to terminate her, eight voted that she be reappointed without tenure, and four abstained. Of the group of professors who had voted during the first round of voting, only twenty-five voted for promotion on the final ballot, and twenty-four voted for termination. Thus, among those who participated in both ballots, plaintiff had gone in a 25-day period from a promote to terminate ratio of 47:7 to a ratio of 25:24.

Even more remarkable than the overall dissipation of plaintiff's support was the fact that of the eight members of her own department who had voted during the preliminary round and given plaintiff their unanimous support, only four voted for tenure on the final ballot. Two who had voted for tenure on the first ballot voted to terminate; two others voted on the final ballot for reappointment without tenure. In other words, over a 25-day period, four of the professors who had worked most closely with plaintiff changed their minds on the most important question of plaintiff's academic career. Something had happened, something rather dramatic.

Unfortunately, as noted above, the parties have not introduced evidence in the case from which I can make supportable findings as to what that dramatic something may have been.

Plaintiff's support on the final ballot was still significant, but it no longer constituted a substantial majority of the Full Committee. Therefore, in accord with the normal policy of the Business School, Dean McArthur did not recommend to the President of the University that plaintiff be promoted with tenure.

4. The 1981 Reasons for Denial of Tenure

Dean McArthur articulated the reasons for Ms. Jackson's lack of promotion in 1981 in a January 15, 1982, letter to her. In that letter he indicated that she was unsuccessful in obtaining substantial support largely because she had failed to prove creative ability sufficient to satisfy a substantial majority of the tenured faculty. According to Dean McArthur, the Full Committee regarded Ms. Jackson as an outstanding teacher. It was satisfied that she was superb at taking the ideas of others and making them accessible and comprehensible to others. A substantial majority of the Full Committee was not, however, satisfied that she was able to create new ideas. In the estimation of a substantial portion of the tenured faculty, Ms. Jackson had failed to meet the standard for tenure required under paragraph 6(b) of the 1977 Standards and paragraph 5(b) of the 1981 Standards.

The Full Committee's decision was based on a review of plaintiff's overall record at the Business School. The determination that she had not demonstrated adequate creativity was based on an evaluation of her work in *both* Managerial Economics and Marketing. By evaluating her work as a whole, defendants fulfilled the promise that had been made to plaintiff when she transferred from Managerial Economics to Marketing, namely, that the transfer would not hurt her chances for tenure since it would not matter what area her work was done in, as long as the work was good. In this connection, I reject plaintiff's contention that the 1981 Full Committee unfairly focused exclusively on her Marketing work.

I recognize that Dean McArthur told plaintiff in December 1981 that he would not recommend her for tenure because she had not done enough work in Marketing per se. And I note that in the letter dated January 15, 1982, the Dean told Ms. Jackson that

> [a]s regards your work in marketing, there was unanimous agreement among both internal and external reviewers that you have not yet produced a record of outstanding course development or research in the broad field of marketing.

However, I reject plaintiff's invitation to read these isolated comments to mean that her work in Managerial Economics was not considered by the Full Committee in 1981, and that she was denied tenure because of failure to demonstrate creativity in Marketing research. When one views the Dean's remarks in context, it is clear that the Full Committee considered her Managerial Economics work alongside her Marketing work, and found the work in *both* areas to be insufficiently creative. For instance, on the same page of the January 15, 1982, letter relied upon by plaintiff for the proposition that only her Marketing work was considered, the Dean also states:

> The models work [in Managerial Economics] was constructed to be creative pedagogy, rather than creative conceptual development. Moreover, the

view that it was creative pedagogy was not unanimous. The multivariate work [in Managerial Economics] was thought to represent something between normal course maintenance and creative course development, and not, in any event, creative conceptual development.

I find, as a matter of fact, that when the 1981 Full Committee assessed plaintiff's creativity, it considered her work in both Managerial Economics and Marketing.

D. 1981–1983: Creating A Second Chance

Despite the lack of a substantial majority in the Full Committee favoring tenure, Dean McArthur decided not to follow the Business School's normal practice of giving unsuccessful tenure candidates a one-year terminal appointment for the following academic year. Rather than denying tenure to Ms. Jackson, Dean McArthur arranged to hold her tenure review process in abeyance in order to give her another opportunity to demonstrate her qualifications for tenure.

In explaining the Full Committee decision to Ms. Jackson following the final vote in December 1981, Dean McArthur told her that the reason he did not want to terminate her with the usual one-year appointment was that he believed she had the capacity to develop new ideas. He told her that he was sure that, if given additional time, plaintiff could allay the doubts of the members of the Full Committee who had not supported her promotion. Consequently, the Dean recommended to plaintiff that she meet with him and other members of the tenured faculty to devise a plan to allow her to prove her creative capacity and, thereby, qualify for tenure.

1. Establishing the Post-1981 Plan

Plaintiff agreed to meet with an informal committee, made up of Dean McArthur and several tenured faculty members from the Marketing Area, to develop a vehicle that would enable her to satisfy those who apparently did not believe she was able to create new ideas.

The informal committee met several times during the early months of 1982. As a result of these meetings, plaintiff proposed, and the informal committee agreed, that plaintiff should research and write a monograph on the subject of "account evolution paths," a subject described by plaintiff as "large, unstructured and . . . important." On March 23, 1982, following a meeting attended by plaintiff, Dean McArthur, Dean Donaldson, and several members of the Marketing Area faculty, Mr. Donaldson wrote and distributed to all attendees a memorandum containing his "understanding of the major areas of agreement at the meeting." In this memorandum, Mr. Donaldson wrote that "[t]he objective of the work Barbara Jackson is now undertaking is to establish her reputation as a respected researcher in Marketing."

Plaintiff regarded this statement of the standard against which her monograph would be evaluated as an unfair summary of the informal committee's consensus. Moreover, she regarded the as impossible to achieve for a person, such as herself, who had spent a brief time in Marketing. Plaintiff, therefore, sent a memorandum to John McArthur, Gordon Donaldson, and the other members of the informal committee summarizing *her* understanding of the results of the series of meetings that had taken place between early January and late March. In her memorandum, she explained that she understood the purpose of the monograph was to alleviate the concern "some members of the appointments committee seem to have . . . [with my] ability to create independently—and thereby to complete the evidence of my potential leadership in marketing at the School." Ms. Jackson's understanding was that she had to prove her creative potential through the monograph, and not that she had to establish herself as a complete and respected researcher in Marketing. She believed that the monograph had to prove she could create, and that it could do this without being a finished creative work in and of itself.

In a letter to Ms. Jackson dated April 14, 1982, nine days after the date of plaintiff's memorandum, Dean McArthur informed plaintiff that

> [a]fter reviewing and thinking about your memorandum and Gordon's minutes, I feel more comfortable with the draft Gordon prepared. . . . I think Gordon has captured the essence of what we discussed and tentatively agreed to at that meeting concerning your next appointment and assignment at the School. If you remain unclear or uneasy about this, I would suggest that we reconvene the group for further discussion.

Ms. Jackson discussed the differences she perceived between Dean Donaldson's memorandum and her own with Dean McArthur in his office shortly thereafter. Dean McArthur encouraged her not to draft any further memos and to get on with the project instead.

On June 9, 1982, plaintiff was reappointed as an Associate Professor of Business Administration, to serve until June 30, 1985. She was also freed from all teaching assignments so she could concentrate her energies on researching and writing her monograph.

2. Implementing the Post-1981 Plan

From early 1982 through the summer of 1983, plaintiff researched and wrote her monograph. She was in a hurry to finish because she believed that the longer the delay, the more harm would befall her reputation as an accomplished academician, which she believed to have been tarnished by the 1981 denial of tenure and by uncertainties regarding the Business School's contemporaneous search for senior faculty in the Marketing Area. By May 1983, however, certain members of the informal committee, who had continued to oversee plaintiff's progress, told Dean McArthur that they were concerned that plaintiff was rushing her work to the point of sacrificing quality for speed.

On May 5, 1983, after a meeting with plaintiff and a professor who had been reading partial drafts of plaintiff's monograph, Dean McArthur wrote to plaintiff as follows:

> The ultimate quality of the study on which you are working is much more important to us than its completion by any particular deadline prior to June 30, 1984. Therefore, rather than adhere to the deadline for appointments which are to be reviewed in the normal sequence this academic year, we will undertake to conduct your review within approximately three months of whenever you hand in your finished manuscript. Thus, so long as a reviewable manuscript is in no later than February 28, 1984, we should be able to conduct our review of your appointment prior to the end of the 1983–1984 academic year.

In addition, plaintiff knew she could have taken until as late as the summer of 1984 to submit her monograph if she wished to be reviewed in the 1984–1985 academic year.

Despite the knowledge of her actual deadlines, and despite Dean McArthur's apparent willingness to make special accommodations for her, Ms. Jackson continued her rush to judgment in the summer of 1983. She completed a draft of her monograph in July and sought professors within the Business School. In response to her solicitation she received a fair number of positive and encouraging comments, as well as several highly critical reviews.

Among plaintiff's most critical reviewers were Professors Theodore Levitt and Robert Buzzell, both tenured professors with endowed chairs in the Marketing Area. On August 4, 1983, Professor Levitt sent plaintiff a short note attached to nine pages of comments on her July draft. Professor Levitt's observations included the following:

—"I remain very uneasy about the presentation, the use of 'evidence,' and the analysis."
—"[I]t is hard for me to see how the presentation has been very substantially improved over the previous version. A lot of the redundancy is gone, but a lot remains."

—"I don't think that this manuscript really does what it says it presumes to do—namely, clinical research with analysis based on it. What I mostly see is a lot of speculation about how situations really are, with very thin evidence as to what they are, and yet pretending as if the evidence were substantial and overwhelming."

—"Opinions and conclusions parade as evidence."

—"Chapter 12 . . . is a potpourri of commonplaces, disjointed comments, and superficial factors that lead nowhere."

—"Chapter 15. . . . Very good idea, some good comments early in the chapter. The rest is superficial, sometimes gnawing, and a potpourri of stuff. It is not research. It is not analysis. It's talk. It talks of the need for more study but doesn't say how, where, nor about the specifics of the problems and issues to be studied. It looks like the author is getting sick and tired of this whole manuscript and rushing to finish—making sure to cover all tracks by saying that the examples that have been used have indeed been simple, simplified, and simplifying, and that the analysis has been somewhat superficial. Therefore there is need for more research. It looks to me just a way of covering one's tracks."

—"In summary, I say there is something in this manuscript. There are some interesting constructs. But I do not think it should parade as research or rigorous development of concepts, or rigorous theoretical analysis. It is mostly a think piece, in some places really quite insightful, but elaborated into propositions that defeat communicability and credulity. The paradigm is good to help us think, but not very good as to specific guidance for specific situations. That in itself is not bad. But it is presented to us as if it were a piece of in-depth analysis and in-depth research. Yet it's devoid of empirical richness, it's light (but long) on analysis, and thus it is not persuasive. The paradigm is a creative achievement, and often the dynamics of markets are insightful, though seldom based on the evidence the manuscript implies is there.

The whole thing leaves badly torn. It is a very neat idea. I think it is quite clever, the paradigm—but presented with lengthy analytical lightness, and with claims of validity based on data that are soft but which are asserted as being hard."

On August 16, 1983, Professor Buzzell sent plaintiff a five-page letter with his reactions to her July draft. Professor Buzzell's letter included the following comments:

—"[P]resentation seems a little self-congratulatory . . . rather pompous."

—"[R]ather pretentious effect."

—"This whole discussion strikes me as force-fitting the data to a predetermined framework."

—"[N]ot really supported by data."

—"[D]on't really support the generalization. . . . Your [sic] simply assert that this happens 'in many instances'."

—"examples are purely hypothetical."

—"conclusion . . . seem rather obvious."

—"As is Chapter VII, I don't see much connection with your field data."

—"Much of this seems to be a re-hash of general knowledge."

—"purely speculative."

—"still hard to read."

—"The biggest weakness is the sparsity of direct empirical evidence on account evolution. . . . the utility of the framework and of the quantitative model is not clearly shown."

—" 'impressionistic' use of evidence reduce[s] the credibility of the study as a whole."

—"Specifically, I would recommend: . . . Especially, presenting more evidence—if you have it—on buying patterns over time."

Plaintiff testified that she drew on what she regarded as constructive in Professors Levitt and Buzzell's criticisms and made appropriate changes in her monograph. However, she discounted much of what they wrote because she perceived them as not understanding her task, which, according to her understanding, was to produce a "think piece," not a finished product.

On August 30, 1983, plaintiff submitted her monograph on account evolution paths, and asked for a tenure decision within three months. The monograph was submitted 26 days after receiving Professor Levitt's criticisms, and just two weeks after receiving Professor Buzzell's. Plaintiff chose not to be concerned with the fact that as tenured professors in her department, Levitt and Buzzell would undoubtedly be influential in her tenure evaluation. Even though Professor Levitt had been on the informal committee established in early 1982 to formulate plaintiff's tenure project, plaintiff relied on her sense that he had misperceived the nature and scope of her charge, and effectively ignored the majority of criticisms contained in Professor Levitt's August 4th letter.

It is apparent, whatever the merits of Professors Levitt and Buzzell's criticisms may have been, that they both believed that plaintiff's work could be immeasurably improved by additional empirical research. They both believed that plaintiff's core idea was sound, interesting, and workable, and that what was needed was empirical support. In other words, their criticisms could have been addressed by additional work. However, plaintiff dismissed their central criticisms as based on a misapprehension of what she intended to be a "mere" exploratory study, and submitted her monograph six months before the deadline for tenure review during the 1983–84 academic year, and a year before what she understood to be the deadline for review in 1984–1985. At the time of the submission of the monograph, plaintiff had spent a total of 17–18 months working on it, far less than the time Harvard was willing to make available to her for the project.

E. The 1983 Tenure Review

1. The Subcommittee in 1983

In 1983, plaintiff's work was evaluated by the Business School's Standing Subcommittee. Plaintiff was aware of the identities of the Standing Subcommittee's members, and did not object to any of them.

The 1983 Subcommittee limited its evaluative focus to plaintiff's monograph. In September 1983, following plaintiff's submission of her monograph, the 1983 Subcommittee distributed it for review and comment to ten outside reviewers, consisting of eight academicians[16] and two practitioners. The Subcommittee also solicited the opinions of members of the Business School Marketing Area. It received replies from eight of the ten outside reviewers, and from seven members of the Business School faculty. The monograph was evaluated for intellectual quality, creativity, soundness of research design and execution, and potential impact.

The standard adopted by the Subcommittee for measuring the value of plaintiff's monograph was the standard stated in the Donaldson "minutes" of March 23, 1982. The 1983 Subcommittee Report states that "[t]he [Subcommittee] has undertaken an evaluation of the monograph, particularly in light of the standards given in the Donaldson memorandum." The Report framed "the issue which the [Subcommittee] was asked to address" by asking: "Does the Jackson monograph meet an appropriate standard of excellence? . . . [Does the work] '. . . establish her reputation as a respected researcher in Marketing'[?]" The Subcommittee did not consider plaintiff's perception of the intended role of her monograph, and did not inform the individual evaluators of the monograph of the dispute between the Donaldson standard and plaintiff's view of the intended role of the monograph.

The comments received by the evaluators and conclusions reached by the Subcommittee coincided with the observations plaintiff had received from Professors Levitt and Buzzell in August 1983. Many of the comments,

16. It appears that two of the eight outside academic reviewers of plaintiff's monograph were professors whom plaintiff regarded as inappropriate. Prior to the Subcommittee's solicitation of their reviews, plaintiff relayed her views about these persons to the Subcommittee through a professor who acted as her "conduit" of information into the appointments process.

There is no evidence in the record that candidates ever had any say over who the outside reviewers of their written work would be. In addition, plaintiff's reasons for not wanting the two persons at issue to evaluate her work had nothing to do with gender considerations. Accordingly, the inclusion of these two persons among the group that evaluated plaintiff's monograph is of only marginal relevance in this proceeding.

from both within and without the Business School, noted that the monograph seemed incomplete, inadequate, and hastily written. For example:

—"[I]t is not just a matter of a redraft, though that would help."
—"If Barbara had spent more time trying to pull her thinking together . . . the manuscript would have considerably more power than it does."
—"[T]he monograph is far from being complete or in a form in which it is likely to have any significant impact."
—"In my opinion, the supporting evidence would have had greater validity if she had done more in-depth and systematic interviewing at her research sites."
—"[T]he use of information from other sources . . . seems to be an opportunistic, after-the-fact force-fitting of data collected for other purposes into the framework of this study."
—"In view of the complexity of the topic she has chosen to study, it is hardly surprising that her condensed timetable has resulted in a disappointing manuscript."
—"Interesting concepts but not fully developed and an unfortunate tendency to generalize with no sufficient rationale or empirical support."
—"Some of the concepts are interesting and creative. Unfortunately they were not fully developed."
—"My sense is that the work suffers from being rushed. It is not a finished product and it is difficult to read."
—"I don't believe that the document is a completed piece of research."
—"[I]t commences in a promising manner, but does not deliver results commensurate with its promising start."
—"It is particularly disappointing to me that she had several outstanding concepts to work with, and never made them into something with the kind of impact that the ideas deserve."
—"The resulting melange is somewhat disjointed."
—"[S]he has to undertake a major revision and a serious research effort to test the hypotheses she can develop in this area."

The Subcommittee recognized that plaintiff's monograph did not receive uniformly negative reviews from all of its readers. However, the Subcommittee

consider[ed] that the negative components of the [ ] reviews [were] sufficiently strong to rule out an affirmative finding on the issue addressed. The weight of opinion . . . indicate[s] that the monograph has not "demonstrated excellence." Further, this piece of work does little ". . . to establish her reputation as a respected researcher in Marketing."

Accordingly, the 1983 Subcommittee unanimously recommended against plaintiff's promotion.

Plaintiff does not dispute the negative assessments of her monograph.

She maintains that if she had been asked to apply the specific Donaldson standard (i.e., the "establish her reputation as a respected researcher in Marketing" standard) to her monograph in the fall of 1983, she would have reached the same conclusions as the majority of her readers. However, she contends that the Donaldson standard was the wrong standard, indeed an impossible standard for her work to have met. She regards the fact that the Subcommittee applied that standard as symptomatic of the fundamental unfairness and pretextual nature of her entire tenure review. She maintains that the Donaldson standard was not only erroneous—it did not represent the consensus of the informal committee—but an impossible one for her to have met in the time allotted. In addition, she contends that her 1983 Subcommittee Report indicates that her second-round tenure decision was based solely on her monograph, whereas when males had received an extended tenure review, their ultimate tenure decisions did not stand or fall on a single written work; rather, she maintains, their receipt or denial of tenure was determined by a review of the entire corpus of their work.

I find, as a matter of fact, (1) that plaintiff was not evaluated under an unfair standard in 1983; and (2) that plaintiff's entire career was taken into consideration in the ultimate decision not to recommend her for tenure in 1983.

(1) I recognize some force to plaintiff's argument that the standard under which her monograph was evaluated in 1983 was difficult to meet. Plaintiff had not even entered the field of Marketing until 1977. Between 1977 and 1982 her written work had been devoted to course development. To have expected her to produce a completely finished research paper on a complicated problem in Marketing within a two- to three-year period would have been quite demanding; and to have expected her to produce a work of sufficient quality to establish herself as a respected researcher in Marketing would have been extraordinarily ambitious. However, this is not what defendants expected. I have concluded that the Subcommittee judged plaintiff's monograph by a standard that was no different from the standard it applied to all written work by candidates for tenure at the Business School. This conclusion is based on my assessment of Dean McArthur's and Dean Donaldson's testimony, and on the fact that the 1983 Subcommittee Report states that,

[i]n addition to evaluating the monograph in the light of the specific wording of the Donaldson memorandum, the members of the Subcommittee considered the monograph in the more general light of a piece of work by a

tenured professor. We feel that it lacks intellectual rigor, whether judged as "case-method" research or as research of some other kind. . . . The research design leaves gaps in the understanding of how this research is related to other pieces of research. Further the design as well as the execution are flawed. It follows that the work we have studied has little potential for impact. Overall this monograph does not meet a standard of excellence appropriate for tenure rank at this School.

(2) Although the 1983 Subcommittee focused its evaluation on plaintiff's 1983 monograph, plaintiff's 1983 tenure review took her entire career into consideration. As explained above, the Subcommittee evaluation and report is only one part of the Business School's tenure review process. When plaintiff's candidacy went before the Full Committee in 1983, all of her work, including her work in Managerial Economics, was taken into consideration.

2. The Full Committee in 1983

Pursuant to normal practice, the 1983 Full Committee met twice to discuss and vote on the plaintiff's candidacy for tenure. On the first ballot, following the discussion at the first meeting, the vote was 19 to promote, 18 to terminate, two to reappoint without tenure, and 13 abstentions. Following this vote, Dean McArthur asked Professor James Heskett, a strong supporter of Ms. Jackson and a member of the Full Committee, to address the Full Committee at its second meeting, and to state the case in favor of plaintiff's appointment.

At the second 1983 meeting of the Full Committee, Professor Heskett addressed the Full Committee as the Dean had requested, and other supporters of Ms. Jackson were afforded the opportunity to address the Full Committee as well. Following the discussion at the second meeting, the Full Committee voted 36 to promote and 31 to terminate, with three abstentions.

If, as plaintiff maintains, her 1983 tenure review was limited to her monograph as measured against the Donaldson standard, it would have been highly unlikely that she would have received majority support for promotion, as she did, from the Full Committee. By plaintiff's own admission, her monograph, in its fall 1983 form, did not meet the Donaldson standard. The fact that she received the extensive support that she did suggests that her tenure review process in 1983 involved consideration of far more than just her inadequate monograph.

3. The 1983 Reasons for Tenure Denial

The 36 votes for promotion which plaintiff received on the second ballot in 1983 constituted majority support. They did not, however, constitute the substantial majority required by Dean McArthur as a condition precedent to recommendation of a candidate for tenure to the President and governing bodies of the University. Accordingly, Dean McArthur did not recommend plaintiff for tenure, thus ending her candidacy.

In a letter written to plaintiff on December 16, 1983, Dean McArthur explained the decision not to recommend plaintiff for tenure as follows:

> I truly regret that it is not possible for me to recommend to the President and the Governing Boards that you be appointed to the rank of full professor with tenure.
>
> . . . As you know, and as stated in the School's "Policies and Procedures for Promotion to Tenure," demonstrated excellence in research and course development is required for appointment to tenure. Your work as reviewed in 1981 was judged not to achieve this standard. The extension of your contract at that time was to provide you with an opportunity to produce conceptual work of the required quality.
>
> In reviewing the results of your research since 1981, most internal and external reviewers and members of the Appointments Committee [Full Committee] agreed that the research and resulting manuscript does not meet our standards for demonstrated excellence in research and creative course development. The weight of opinion considered by the Committee was clearly that the work you have completed does not satisfactorily answer the questions many members had about your capacity to do creative conceptual work in Marketing.
>
> In reviewing your overall record once again, including your recent research, the members of the Appointments Committee remain roughly evenly divided in their support for your promotion. On the basis of your record and the substantial opposition to your promotion, I cannot recommend that you be given a tenured appointment at the School. In fact, it would be highly inconsistent with our past practice in promotion cases for me to recommend a tenured appointment when there is not a clear affirmation of support from, at minimum, a large majority of the Committee.

I credit this letter as a good faith and accurate explanation of the reason that plaintiff did not receive a recommendation for tenure in 1983. Plaintiff was denied tenure in 1983 because she had failed to convince a substantial majority of the tenured faculty that she possessed the level of creativity required for tenure at the Business School. Plaintiff's monograph had failed to answer the concerns identified in her 1981 tenure review. A significant percentage of the tenured faculty did not believe that plaintiff's record evidenced a capacity on her part to do creative conceptual work.

The skeptics on the tenured faculty may well have been mistaken with respect to the creative potential of plaintiff's monograph. Plaintiff turned her monograph into an article published in the November–December 1985 issue of the Harvard Business Review, and also used the monograph's materials as the basis for a book on marketing, *Winning and Keeping Industrial Customers: The Dynamics of Customer Relationships,* published in 1985 by Lexington Books. In addition, the concept of "relationship marketing" which plaintiff discussed in her monograph was cited approvingly by Professor Philip Kotler of Northwestern University in his keynote address to the 50th Anniversary Meeting of the American Marketing Association.

But the existence of differences in opinion regarding the quality of plaintiff's work does not demonstrate gender discrimination. . . .

*   *   *

A Comment on Probation

The exacting character of the procedure employed in *Jackson* is not unique. Note, for example, the description of the tenure process by the president of Colby College:

> The probationary period at Colby involves four separate, rigorous steps. First, all candidates have participated in national—and, sometimes, even international—searches involving 100 to 900 applicants. The tenure-track appointee typically has gone through interviews off campus and extensive reference checks, as well as interviews and model lectures on the campus. After that extremely competitive process, the successful candidate is normally given only a one-year contract.
>
> Mid-way through the first year, the candidate undergoes a second evaluation. Assuming sound teaching and acceptable progress in scholarship, the typical candidate receives a three-year contact renewal. If doubts arise during the first year, the person might be given only a one-year renewal and would be subjected to a further evaluation during the second year.
>
> The third evaluation is a comprehensive pre-tenure examination during the sixth semester of teaching. This involves a departmental committee of at least three members which reviews: the candidate's course syllabi, assignments, examinations and laboratory instructions; all material published or submitted by the candidate and any published reviews of that material; statements from the candidate evaluating his or her own teaching, advising, scholarship and contributions to the department, the College and the discipline; a state-

ment by the department chair evaluating the candidate's teaching as a result of departmental peer review; all evaluation forms that have been submitted by students in the candidate's courses; and statistical summaries that compare student ratings of that candidate's teaching with departmental, division and all-College averages. If the candidate passes this third review, she or he is normally granted a pre-tenure sabbatical to complete an important scholarly or creative work and is given a three-year contract extension.

The fourth review is for tenure itself. The same kinds of materials involved in the sixth-semester review are gathered for the six-year period, and the scholarship of the candidate is submitted to disinterested (non-Colby) experts for review. These materials (collectively called "the dossier") are once more examined by the departmental committee, which makes a report and recommendation to the elected, nine-person faculty Committee on Promotion and Tenure. All faculty, including those not yet tenured, are eligible to vote in the election of the committee. Once elected, faculty serve a three-year staggered term to ensure continuity and consistency over time.

The Promotion and Tenure Committee, chaired by the dean of faculty, will spend countless hours reviewing each dossier and discussing whether the candidate meets the high Colby standards for teaching, scholarship and service. Members of that committee vote individually on whether to recommend tenure, and each member submits to me a detailed evaluation of every tenure candidate in which they compare the teaching, scholarship and service of the candidate to the very best faculty tenured in recent years.

The committee, the dean and I have operated on the principle "when in doubt, don't tenure." Consequently, on average only two-thirds of those who reach the tenure decision year are recommended for tenure. Others fail to pass the first or third year reviews. In fact, some have worried that, given the rigor of our tenure policies, faculty turnover at Colby might be too high. This fear is mitigated by the fact that there is no annual tenure quota. Our procedures emphasize that "who is tenured is more important than how many." ... [William Cotter, "Why Tenure Works: The Tenure System Encourages Creativity, Ensures Stability, and Promotes Continuity," *Colby*, April 1995, p. 9]

Were the decision whether or not to reappoint for a year or two, would it consume so much time and attention of people active in their own professional lives?

At issue in the *Jackson* case was whether the Harvard Business School had unfairly applied a new (and higher) standard for achieving tenure. The court concluded that although the standard for tenure had evolved over time, it had not been unfairly applied. Subject to that caution, it seems plain that institutions are free to set new and presumably higher standards over time. As aspiring academics have been cautioned:

[T]he fact that Jones, who would not secure a favorable recommendation today, was favorably recommended only a few years ago, does
not lock the department into Jones's record as the standard of what
is to be expected of all future tenure candidates. This means, in effect, that the fact that Jones received tenure with only four published articles does not assure you of tenure if you publish six. [Mat-
thew W. Finkin, "The Tenure System," in *The Academic's Handbook*,
ed. A. Leigh De Neef and Crawford D. Goodwin, 2d ed. (Durham,
N.C.: Duke University Press, 1995), p. 144]

The Harvard Business School chose to lengthen the probationary period in respect to Professor Jackson. She should have received a terminal
appointment for 1981–82, her ninth year of service. In the event, she
was given three additional years. Would yet an additional year (or two)
thereafter have unequivocally manifested her professional excellence?
The court seemed to think that that might have been so. If so, would
the Business School have been better advised to have a system of renewable appointments instead of tenure? Recall Fritz Machlup's discussion
of the disadvantage to the individual scholar resulting from firm probationary periods and the offsetting advantage for the institution: the
people who really are better than their record establishes at the time of
decision can be determined only afterward.

A school or department might also err in declining to tenure a proba-
tioner because it doubts the worth of the work he or she is doing—not
because the work is not excellent in its frame of reference but because
the whole line of inquiry is considered professionally unprofitable.
Some people have claimed accordingly that the tenure system works an
"oppression" of those with countercultural ideas. (See, *e.g.,* Deborah
Post, "Critical Thoughts about Race, Exclusion, Oppression, and Tenure," *Pace Law Review* 15 [1994]: 69–110). (If the denial of tenure on the
ground of a genuine disciplinary disagreement about the worth of the
candidate's work is an act of "oppression," would it be curmudgeonly
to inquire what word would be reserved for detention by the secret police?) Suffice it to say, whether the department or school decided rightly
or wrongly can be known only after the fact (see Judith Jarvis Thomson,
"Ideology and Faculty Selection," in *Freedom and Tenure in the Academy,*
ed. William Van Alstyne [Durham, N.C.: Duke University Press, 1993],
pp. 155–176).

At this point the reader may be puzzled: If the primary justification
for tenure is the protection of academic freedom, how can the profession justify *any* probationary period, during which the persons who do
not have tenure can be terminated (after the expiration of their terms

of appointment) without cause as demonstrated in a hearing? Would their academic freedom not lack a critical protection? That question is dealt with by William Van Alstyne in a further portion of the essay excerpted in Chapter 1.

———

Tenure: A Summary, Explanation, and "Defense"

William Van Alstyne

*   *   *

While the need to enter a defense of tenure against the criticism that it is a shield for the incompetent and irresponsible may melt away once the actual conditions and terms of tenure have again been clarified, it may nonetheless be appropriate to . . . [an] acknowledgment of a very different kind of criticism, a criticism which finds serious fault with what is apparently the anomaly of tenure and the equal protection of academic freedom. In essence, the criticism is that insofar as the case for tenure stands or falls according to the measure of protection it yields for academic freedom, either it must be extended equally to all faculty members irrespective of their length of service, or withdrawn equally from all, (possibly then to be replaced by a uniform standard of academic due process for all, but without the invidious distinction implied by the term of "tenure" itself). If it is said that academic freedom is realistically secure for each person only to the extent that his professional status may not be placed in question without the observance of full academic due process, and if it is acknowledged that only those with tenure are entitled to full academic due process, then it necessarily follows that only those with tenure do in fact have academic freedom. On the other hand, if it is claimed that all members of a faculty are equally entitled to the free exercise of academic freedom, then it must be acknowledged either that tenure itself is not truly regarded as indispensable to the protection of that freedom or, if it is regarded as indispensable, that it must be provided for all alike. In short, the alleged equation that academic freedom = no termination without full academic due process = tenure, proves too much or too little. The anomalous combination of mutually exclusive assertions, "equal academic freedom for all, but tenure only for some," displays all the unseemliness of a motto from *Animal Farm:* all teachers are equal in their academic freedom, but some teachers are more equal than others (*viz.,* those with tenure)!

From *AAUP Bulletin* 57 (Autumn 1971): 331–333.

It will not do, as a response to this criticism, merely to point out that nontenured faculty members are equally entitled to full academic due process if sought to be dismissed within the specified term of their appointment. *I.e.,* it is not enough that newer appointees do in fact have "tenure" within their particular one-, two-, or three-year terms, and that any action to dismiss them within that term must be taken solely on the basis of adequate cause as demonstrated pursuant to full academic due process. The fact remains that the anxiety of prospective *nonrenewal* may be seen to chill the appointee's academic freedom in a manner unequaled for those members of the faculty with tenure.

Nor will it do quixotically to deny on second thought that tenure is really wholly unconcerned with academic freedom and that it is, rather, defended solely on the basis that it provides an appropriate degree of professional security for those of *demonstrated* excellence, *i.e.,* those who weathered an uncertain career (and kept their mouths shut) as probationary appointees for as long as six years and were found on the basis of experience to warrant a conditional expression of institutional confidence in their continuing excellence. Other kinds of incentives than tenure might satisfy the need for perquisites for the senior faculty, although possibly not so cheaply.

Rather, it may help to dissolve the dilemma first to note that while there is a difference in the *degree* of academic due process which tenure provides as compared with that to which a person lacking tenure is entitled when confronted with the prospect that his term appointment may not be renewed, the difference is not at all one of "full" academic due process vis-à-vis "no" academic due process. . . . The differences of degree between the two forms of academic due process are, in fact, essentially these:

1. Proceedings to dismiss one with tenure must be initiated by the employing institution, whereas proceedings to avoid termination of one lacking tenure who has received notice that nonrenewal is contemplated must be initiated by him:

2. The burden of proving the existence of adequate cause is upon the institution in proceedings to dismiss one with tenure, whereas the burden is upon the individual contesting notice of nonrenewal to establish at least a prima facie case either that reasons violative of academic freedom contributed to the proposed decision or that adequate consideration was not given to the merits of his reappointment;

3. The degree of formality in the total procedure is somewhat heavier in the case of one with tenure faced with dismissal than one without tenure faced with nonrenewal.

Recognizing then, that those in probationary service are assured of *full* academic due process against the contingency of dismissal within any term of their appointment and that they are also assured of at least minimal due process against the contingency even of nonrenewal, the disparity which remains as between themselves and those with tenure is clearly not so great as first it may have appeared. To the extent that it is nonetheless an important difference, especially as it may weigh upon the exercise of academic freedom, an explanation may rest largely in the following considerations.

First, other things being even roughly equal, the degree of hardship to one threatened with dismissal after an extended commitment to a given discipline and a longer period of service in a particular institution is likely to be greater than to a younger person subject to nonrenewal after a more tentative commitment and a briefer period of service. To the extent that the degree of due process is appropriately graduated to the degree of hardship which may result from the decision in question, it is not difficult to understand on that basis alone why dismissal proceedings are accompanied by a fuller complement of academic due process than those concerning nonrenewal. Similarly, exactly to the extent that dismissal is more portentous than nonrenewal, the chilling effect on the individual's exercise of academic freedom may itself also be greater. Correspondingly, merely to insure that the same degree of academic freedom is assured equally to the individual faced with the threat of dismissal as to the one faced with the prospect of nonrenewal, a more deliberate form of academic due process may be required in the first case than in the second.

Second, there is simply no basis to hold that the fact of one's first or second short-term appointment in teaching necessarily manifests an institutional presumption of excellence which it would thereafter be the burden of the institution to overthrow when contemplating nonrenewal at the end of the term. Surely no institution ought to be held to have made a judgment about the long-term professional excellence of a first-time appointee to its faculty in view of the fact that frequently the appointment will represent the individual's first experience in teaching and there will have been no reasonable opportunity in fact so to determine his professional fitness. It is precisely the purpose of having a probationary period to enable the institution to resolve the doubt not previously resolved by actions of the individual with whom the burden necessarily rests. To extend the presumption of professional fitness back to the point of initial appointment is to be unfair toward the institution's capacity to make a judgment on the matter so early, with all the deleterious consequences of granting "instant tenure." Similarly, to extend the assurance of full academic due process back to the time of renewal of the first appointment is functionally exactly that, *i.e.*, the establishment of instant tenure.

Third, as initial appointments are usually not made with an adequate basis for assessing the individual's long-term excellence, there is correspondingly less reason to suspect that a decision not to renew such an appointment is made on grounds unrelated to a reasonable belief about that excellence. The same obviously cannot be said of those who have been found by lengthy experience to be satisfactory, however, and correspondingly their proposed termination creates a greater suspicion that ulterior reasons (*i.e.*, reasons violative of academic freedom) are more likely to be operating, thereby providing an appropriate reason for requiring fuller academic due process as a prerequisite to their termination. Stated in another way, as between the two groups a higher rate of nonrenewal is less suspicious with respect to the first group than with respect to the second and, correspondingly, incurring the higher costs of more ponderous full academic due process is less warranted by the uniform concern for academic freedom.

Fourth, as it is normally to be expected that one may become more expert in his specialty the greater amount of time and experience he will have devoted to it, the more important it becomes not to permit the public value of his academic freedom to be circumscribed precisely as he becomes more likely to make an original contribution by what he proposes to do or to say. Correspondingly, the degree of full academic due process which protects his academic freedom is more nearly likely to be worth its cost than were it uniformly available to all irrespective of their length of experience. To this extent, the earlier suggestion that tenure does reflect an attitude that greater academic freedom is warranted for those with a longer commitment within their discipline than for those with a relatively new one, is not without a basis in fact. Some may well question whether the degree of difference is really justifiable on such a basis, of course, reasonably suggesting that what is lost to the younger teacher in lack of seasoning and familiarity with his subject is more than offset by his freshness, creativity, or lack of debilitating conventionality. Perhaps the debate may rest there, at least for the moment: not on *whether* tenure, with its assurance of full academic due process should exist at all, but rather on *when* it should appropriately be conferred!

*　　*　　*

A Comment on Probation and Sex Discrimination

Van Alstyne's concluding remark on the length of the probationary period anticipates, if tangentially, a more recent issue: the application of a firm and fixed period of probation for women faculty in their child-bearing years. Before we consider that issue, however, an earlier and grosser criticism of tenure should be noted: the claim that a cohort of senior (tenured) white males was an obstruction to the advancement of women and members of racial or ethnic minorities; in other words, that these faculty members formed a bottleneck to career advancement. The necessary corollary of the criticism is that it should be possible to dismiss white males of long service in order to free up positions for others. Assume, however, that those senior faculty had no legal claim to tenure at all—that they served at will and could be terminated on a moment's notice—and consider whether their termination toward the end sought would be morally justifiable or legally permissible. If the answer to either (or both) of those questions is no, as it is in the latter instance, then tenure becomes a nonissue.

The recent criticism, however, is more finely tuned. It is that probationary faculty labor under extraordinary pressure to prove themselves, and that that pressure is exacerbated for female faculty because the probationary period tends to coincide with their peak childbearing years. (It is argued further that the stress is especially acute in academic science, where the researcher's life is driven by research protocols that are oblivious of all personal needs.) From this premise it has been argued that tenure ought to be abandoned altogether (see Christine Anderson, "Tenure, under Fire Once Again, Still Holds Strong," *Science*, September 23, 1994), or that special accommodation should be made, allowing women a longer time span for the tenure decision (Henry Etzkowitz et al., "Barriers to Women's Participation in Academic Science and Engineering," in *Who Will Do Science? Educating the Next Generation*, ed. Willie Pearson Jr. and Alan Fechter [Baltimore: Johns Hopkins University Press, 1994], pp. 43, 51). In fact, the conflict between career and family obligations in this setting mirrors analogous conflict in the larger professional and managerial world. (See Felice Schwartz, "Management Women and the New Facts of Life," *Harvard Business Review*, January/February 1989, p. 63.) Nor is the conflict particular to the United States.

Any period of probation is stressful. The question is how long that period must be to be consistent with the institution's need adequately to ascertain the promise of professional excellence. Van Alstyne seems to suggest that six years may be too long. But the proposed response is to lengthen the probationary period a year (or possibly two) for childbearing and bonding purposes. Several institutions have done just that, either upon a showing of special need or automatically, in some cases extending the accommodation to faculty members who are adopting a child, caring for an aging parent, coping with a medical emergency in the family, or encountering other special circumstances. Suffice it to say here that in the absence of a body of experience with these various approaches, it remains to be seen who will actually avail themselves of these extensions, and, if many faculty members do take these options, men as well as women, whether they will produce a de facto lengthening of the probationary period.

3

Dismissal and Due Process

As William Van Alstyne explained at the outset, once tenure has been acquired, it cannot be divested save for adequate cause demonstrated in a hearing prior to termination; in other words, such action is subject to due process. The requirements of academic due process were refined in a joint AAUP-AAC *Statement on Procedural Standards in Faculty Dismissal Proceedings* promulgated in 1958. As Clark Byse and Louis Joughin noted, "The principle of due process and its practice are probably a good deal closer to each other in law than in nonlegal procedures" (*Tenure in American Higher Education* [Ithaca: Cornell University Press, 1959], p. 52).

In two companion cases decided in 1972 concerning faculty in public higher education—*Board of Regents v. Roth,* 408 U.S. 564 (1972), and *Perry v. Sindermann,* 408 U.S. 593 (1972)—the United States Supreme Court held that due process was constitutionally required only if the state were acting to deprive a person of life, liberty, or property. So far as one's appointment to an academic post in a public university was concerned, the Constitution required due process only if the deprivation were of a constitutionally cognizable "property" interest—that is, tenure. *What* process is due, as a constitutional matter, and *why* it is due are briefly explored here.

King v. University of Minnesota

(United States Court of Appeals for the Eighth Circuit, 1985)
Bowman, C.J.

*   *   *

I.

[George D.] King was hired by the University of Minnesota in 1970 as a full professor in the College of Liberal Arts, with a tenured appointment in the

From 774 F.2d 224 (8th Cir. 1985) *cert. denied* 475 U.S. 1095 (1986).

Department of Afro-American Studies (the Department).[2] He became the chairman of the Department in 1970 and served until 1974, when he was asked to step down as chairman by his colleagues and by the Dean.

The record reveals that from 1974 until his termination, there were complaints about King's performance by students, by colleagues, and by the successive chairmen of the Department. The complaints concerned poor teaching performance, excessive unexcused absences from class, absences from faculty meetings, low enrollment in his classes, undocumented research, and other matters.

Because of the perceived problems with his performance, King was recommended for a merit salary increase in only one year—1979. The chairman of the Department indicated that the 1979 increase was not really a merit increase, but only an acknowledgment that the problems with King had abated in that year. In other years, King was not recommended for merit increases. In 1980, for example, Geneva Southall, the chairman of the Department, gave King the following merit evaluation:

> Having therefore, continued to be only a negative to the [Department], again I must recommend that Professor King be given no merit increase with the hope that the College will in its departmental response, further emphasize to Professor King its disappointment that he has failed to be the historian/teacher that his inflated salary and professorial rank warrants. . . .

In the 1980–81 school year, the Department was under the direction of a new chairman, Earl Scott. During the course of his first year as chairman, Scott became concerned by King's numerous unexcused absences from his classes and by his lack of participation in Department governance. Scott communicated with King and with Fred Lukermann, Dean of the College of Liberal Arts, concerning King's inadequacies as a faculty member.

Concerned that the University was not addressing the Department's problems with King, in February 1982 Scott, Southall, and two other members of the Department wrote to Dean Lukermann about the Department's personnel problems and the Dean's failure to remove uncooperative and unproductive members.

Lukermann wrote to King on February 24, 1982, admonished King about his inadequate performance in teaching, research, and service, and questioned King's competence in carrying out his duties, as well as his usefulness to the Department and to the University. On the same day, Luker-

2. The Department later became the Department of Afro-American and African Studies.

mann also wrote to the chairman of the Department, with a copy to King, setting forth his dissatisfaction with King's performance and asking the Department to review these matters.

On March 12, 1982, the Department of Afro-American and African Studies met and, after a lengthy discussion with King present, voted 9–2 (with one abstention) to remove King from the Department because of his long history of disservice to the Department. Following this vote, Lukermann communicated several more times with King, but apparently was unable to satisfy himself that King was willing to improve his performance.

On February 15, 1983, Lukermann sent a letter to King initiating removal proceedings under the University of Minnesota's Regulations Concerning Faculty Tenure (Tenure Code), and giving King notice of the charges against him. In his letter Dean Lukermann referred to other communications with King that contained specific statements of dissatisfaction with King's performance as a professor.

On March 10, 1983 King requested a hearing before the Senate Judicial Committee. The Senate Judicial Committee is a group of faculty members appointed by the University of Minnesota Faculty Senate to hear faculty complaints under the Tenure Code. A panel of faculty members was appointed to hear the case in March 1983. King's counsel objected to one of the members of the panel. That member was replaced. The panel members were all tenured faculty from outside the College of Liberal Arts.

Prior to the Senate hearing, King was represented by counsel and was allowed substantial documentary discovery. King's attorney took the depositions of Lukermann, Scott, and former Dean Frank Seraph. On May 26, 1983, a prehearing conference was held at which the parties exchanged issue lists, witness lists, and exhibit lists. On May 27, 1983, the Panel issued a prehearing conference order, which specified a number of issues pertaining to the upcoming hearing. Both sides submitted objections to the prehearing conference order. The objections were ruled on by the panel prior to the hearing.

The Senate Judicial Committee hearing was held from June 4 to June 17, 1983. King was represented by counsel. King's counsel cross-examined witnesses, presented witnesses and documentary evidence on King's behalf, and made both oral and written arguments. King did not testify at the hearing. On September 15, 1983, the panel issued its Final Findings and Recommendations, in which it recommended that King be terminated for cause under the Tenure Code.[3] As provided by the Tenure Code, the find-

3. Cause for termination under the Tenure Code consists of such cause as seriously interferes with the person's capacity competently to perform his duties, or seriously interferes with his usefulness to the University. . . .

ings and recommendations were sent to the President of the University for review.

On October 27, 1983, after another round of briefing, C. Peter Magrath, President of the University, reviewed the Findings and Recommendations, and recommended to the Regents of the University of Minnesota that King be terminated.

The Regents were to consider the King matter at their December 8, 1983 meeting. Prior to the Regents' meeting, each Regent was sent the panel's findings, the President's recommendation letter, and briefs from each of the parties. The transcript of the panel hearing and the exhibits presented to the panel were available to the Regents. On December 8, 1983, the Regents heard arguments from counsel. King introduced new affidavits in support of his position and also addressed the Regents. After argument, the Regents went into closed session. The Regents adopted the findings of the Senate Judicial Committee, but did not terminate King. Instead, the Regents voted 7–2 to place King on probation for a year.

On December 14, 1984, Magrath wrote to the Regents asking them to rescind their action, claiming that the affidavits submitted by King at the Regents meeting contained misleading information, and that the decision of the Regents was contrary to the findings which were adopted. Magrath argued that this inconsistency made it difficult to ascertain or maintain any standard of performance for faculty at the University. A copy of this letter was sent to King.

The Regents indicated that a hearing would be held to consider the rescission request. Each of the parties again sent briefs to the Regents prior to the hearing. In addition, a number of faculty and community members wrote to the Regents expressing their views concerning the Regents' decision to place King on probation.

On January 12, 1984, the Regents met to consider the rescission request. They again heard arguments from counsel. King again spoke on his own behalf, as did a minister who asked the Regents not to rescind their previous action. The Regents voted in public session to rescind their previous action. The Regents then went into closed session, where they voted 8–4 to terminate King for cause.

*   *   *

[The Court's discussion of substantive due process—whether or not there was an adequate rational connection between the evidence adduced and the charges allegedly warranting Professor King's dismissal—is omitted.]

III.

King contends that he was not accorded sufficient procedural due process by the University in connection with his dismissal. In *Brouillette v. Board of Directors of Merged Area IX*, 519 F.2d 126 (8th Cir. 1975), this Court outlined the requirements of due process in a similar case:

1) clear and actual notice of the reasons for termination in sufficient detail to enable him or her to present evidence relating to them;
2) notice of both the names of those who have made allegations about the teacher and the specific nature and factual basis for the charges;
3) a reasonable time and opportunity to present testimony in his or her own defense; and
4) a hearing before an impartial board or tribunal. . . .

. . . We are satisfied that King received the process he was due.

* * *

A Comment on Due Process

The court in the *King* case explained what the procedural requirements of a dismissal proceeding are in order to ensure that so serious a decision as a dismissal is based on accurate information and that it is made fairly. *Accuracy* is advanced by a process requiring a careful winnowing and sifting of the facts alleged to support the allegations. *Fairness* requires that the judge of the allegations have no personal interest in the outcome. That requirement goes back to *Dr. Bonham's Case* (1610), at least.

As the *King* case illustrates, the precise requirements of due process are adequate notice of the grounds asserted to justify the dismissal; the right to confront one's accusers, to present evidence, to challenge the evidence presented, and to cross-examine witnesses; and the right to an impartial hearing tribunal. A good deal of case law refines these elements. Arval A. Morris, *Dismissal of Tenured Higher Education Faculty: Legal Implications of the Elimination of Mandatory Retirement* (Topeka: NOLPE, 1992), gives a comprehensive review of due process and adequate cause, but essentially they boil down to simple fairness.

Steven Uhlfelder, a particularly strident critic of tenure, asserts that because the courts have held tenure to give rise to a protectable constitutional interest, public colleges and universities have been "forced to follow a formalized system of due process that was designed to protect the professor's individual rights" (*Reform Tenure Now: Addressing Florida's Failed System,* Foundation for Florida's Future, Educational Policy

Studies Series no. 001 [August 1, 1995], p. 3). The first part of the assertion is accurate, though rather oddly put. The United States Supreme
Court held that when an institution of higher education has chosen to
grant tenure, the Constitution supplies the procedural minima that
must be observed to terminate it. As the *King* case evidences, the constitutional requirements of a hearing are not particularly exacting; nor
does Mr. Uhlfelder specify what the elements of due process are that
institutions are "forced" to observe and that he finds objectionable.
Notice of the reasons for the discharge? Opportunity to confront the
evidence? To present evidence to the contrary? An impartial hearing
body?

The second part of the assertion—that these procedures are designed
to protect individual rights—is not quite accurate insofar as it implies
that these procedures are for the individual's protection alone. Due
process is thought to inure to the benefit not of the individual alone
but to the larger community. The consequences of certain decisions
affecting individuals are such that the community requires for its own
good that they be made accurately and fairly, whether the decision is
officially to designate a membership organization as "Communist"
(*Joint Anti-Fascist Refugee Committee v. McGrath,* 341 U.S. 723 [1951]
[Frankfurter, J. concurring]) or to expel a student for misconduct (*Dixon
v. Alabama State Board of Higher Education,* 294 F.2d 150 [5th Cir.], cert.
denied, 368 U.S. 930 [1961]). The academic community and society at
large are better served when a decision as serious as the dismissal of a
professor is made by means that ensure accuracy and fairness.

A common challenge concerns the delay a hearing would require. In
Professor King's case, the proceeding from its initiation to the hearing
committee's decision took eight months. Obviously, a summary dismissal would have been faster; but by what standard are we to decide
that due process consumed an undue amount of time? According to the
most recent data compiled by the Federal Mediation and Conciliation
Service, whose administration of labor arbitration under collective bargaining agreements many observers consider a model of swift adjudication, on average the time from the filing of the grievance (most often
in cases of dismissal) to the submission of the impartial arbitrator's decision is eleven months.

4

The Economics of Tenure

It may be recalled that Fritz Machlup's argument for tenure was predicated in part on an economic analysis. Yet many economists of a neo-classical persuasion have long been critical of academic tenure: the function of a legal institution is to make the market efficient, and the most efficient labor market would be akin to a spot market, where supply and demand adjust swiftly to changing market conditions. This manner of reasoning has a hoary history. Note the famous colloquy between Professor William Graham Sumner and a student at Yale in the last quarter of the nineteenth century:

> "Professor, don't you believe in any government aid to industries?"
> "No! it's root, hog, or die."
> "Yes, but hasn't the hog got a right to root?"
> "There are no rights. The world owes nobody a living."
> "You believe then, Professor, in only one system, the contract-competitive system?"
> "That's the only sound economic system. All others are fallacies."
> "Well, suppose some professor of political economy came along and took your job away from you. Wouldn't you be sore?"
> "Any other professor is welcome to try. If he gets my job, it is my fault. My business is to teach the subject so well that no one can take the job away from me." [Quoted in Richard Hofstadter, *Social Darwinism in American Thought, 1860–1915* (Philadelphia: University of Pennsylvania Press, 1945), p. 39]

But the "labor market," Robert M. Solow reminds us, "just might be different in important ways from the market for fish" (*The Labor Market as a Social Institution* [Cambridge, Mass.: Blackwell, 1990], p. 30). And the market for academic labor—for what academics do and are trained to do—is a very special segment of the labor market. One economist, after reviewing the literature, explained the assumption underlying his modeling of academic tenure thus:

The basic idea is that the difference between a baseball team and an academic department is the way in which new members of the team are selected. In baseball, the team owners through their agents, the managers, choose who is to play. In academics this task is performed by the incumbent members of the department. In an explicit model this paper derives conditions on the reward functions of incumbents that must be satisfied if they are to be willing to hire the best candidates for jobs. Academic tenure is consistent with these conditions while the "baseball" solution is not. Loosely, tenure is necessary because without it incumbents would never be willing to hire people who might turn out to be better than themselves.

The analysis is consistent with several other aspects of the academic environment. It provides a rationale for "tenure-track" appointments and says something about the standards that can be used for tenure decisions. The job security derived here is not absolute. Incumbents can be released if they fail to meet exogenous standards of performance (i.e., engage in "gross moral turpitude") or if the separations are voluntary (contract "buy-outs" or early retirement). In times of financial crisis, when involuntary separations are inevitable, the model suggests that entire departments be eliminated. This is because the members of one department do not choose the new hires of another. [H. Lorne Carmichael, "Incentives in Academics: Why Is There Tenure?" *Journal of Political Economy* 96 (1988): 454–455]

Richard A. Posner has argued to analogous effect in *Aging and Old Age* (Chicago: University of Chicago Press, 1995). But a less mordant analysis has been provided by Michael S. McPherson and Gordon C. Winston in the piece that follows.

The Economics of Academic Tenure:
A Relational Perspective

Michael S. McPherson and Gordon C. Winston

*   *   *

From Michael S. McPherson, Morton Owen Schapiro, and Gordon C. Winston, eds., *Paying the Piper: Productivity, Incentives, and Financing in U.S. Higher Education* (Ann Arbor: University of Michigan Press, 1993), chap. 5. Copyright © by the University of Michigan 1993.

We are grateful to the Faculty Development Program at Williams College for support of this research. The views presented in this paper are those of the authors. We have been helped by comments from Richard Chait, Lee Alston, Joseph Kershaw, and members of the Williams College Economics Department. Throughout the paper we follow the convention of using the masculine pronoun to refer to both men and women.

The main argument advanced in favor of the institution of tenure is the protection it provides for academic freedom.[1] Defenders of tenure seem ready to concede its economic inefficiency but see it as a necessary price to pay to protect scholarly independence. Those who question the value of academic freedom, or see other ways to protect it, then see little to recommend the institution of tenure. Indeed, in one of the few economic articles on tenure, Armen Alchian explained its existence cynically as an expensive and wasteful luxury indulged in by a professoriate freed through the non-profit status of colleges and universities from the rigors of the competitive economy.

Such a negative view of the economic role and consequences of tenure seems to us one-sided and importantly misleading. The implicit assumption that the world outside the academy provides most workers with little effective job security is false, and the idea that colleges and universities could function efficiently by operating on the basis of personnel policies analogous to the longshoreman's shape-up is mistaken. Indeed, some of the most interesting empirical work in labor economics of late has emphasized what Robert Hall (1982) calls, in the title of one of his papers, "The Importance of Lifetime Jobs in the U.S. Economy." And much of the most exciting recent work in analytical labor economics, and in macroeconomics as well, has aimed at understanding the mutual interest workers and firms have in sustaining stable long-term employment relations and in protecting each other from the vagaries of the market.[2]

Academic tenure, of course, differs importantly from the kind of job protection seniority affords to production workers or (more to the point for comparison with academics) the kind that corporate employment policies provide to middle-level managers. But, we suggest, the difference lies less in the degree of job security afforded[3] than in the nature of the job guarantee and, surprisingly, in the explicit and risky probation that precedes obtaining the guarantee. To put the latter point somewhat polemically: the

1. A representative sample of writings is Smith 1973. Valuable material on the legal and historical aspects of academic tenure is in Keast and Macy 1973.

2. Two recent papers concerned with the academic labor market that build on this literature are Freeman 1977 and James 1980. Neither is centrally concerned with the topics of interest in this paper.

3. Legally, of course, tenure is not a job guarantee. In institutions following American Association of University Professors (AAUP) guidelines, tenured faculty are (a) appointed "without regard to term"—that is, without a specific end date—and (b) are assured of a certain formal procedure prior to dismissal. Dismissal must be for cause, but the cause quite explicitly can be incompetence or economic exigency. That few people get fired is a practical more than legal consequence of the working of these rules in an academic setting.

striking thing about the university, compared to a typical corporation, is not the number of college graduates employed there with secure jobs but the number of high-level employees who don't expect to be allowed to stay. This point is closely related to our first point, the nature of the job guarantee. For academic employees are assured not only continued employment with the "firm" but continued employment in a highly specific and well-defined position: teaching, for instance, eighteenth-century French literature. The system of rigorous probation followed by tenure is a reasonable way of solving the peculiar personnel problems that arise in employing expensively trained and narrowly specialized people to spend their lifetimes at well-defined and narrowly specialized tasks. The character of this problem, and of this solution, moreover, helps to explain a good deal about academic employment.

It is these themes that we shall develop. They will show that the tenure institution has some desirable efficiency properties that are often overlooked. This, of course, does not prove that tenure should not be reformed or abolished, especially in light of an emerging situation which may raise some of the costs of tenure. Neither does it suggest that we dismiss arguments for tenure based on academic freedom; we merely put them to one side. But we do suggest that any serious proposal for the reform of tenure has to show how alternative arrangements would solve the personnel problems tenure solves; both theory and experience suggest that the implicit alternative of providing faculty with no job guarantee does not solve these problems. Our major aim, in any event, is not to evaluate alternative policies but to contribute to understanding how tenure actually works in the context of the university.

In developing this analysis, we draw heavily on the emerging literature in a field which we call—generalizing a term of Victor Goldberg's—"relational economics." The predominant theme of this literature is that the fact of economic transactions to develop sustained relationships with one another. This perspective has been applied to good purpose in studying the economics of organizations (Arrow 1974, Williamson 1975 and 1979), the economics of law and contract (Goldberg 1980, MacNeil 1974), labor economics (Leibenstein 1976), macroeconomics (Okun 1980), and elsewhere. The analysis of tenure is only one of its many potential applications to the operation of academic institutions.

Our analysis will proceed by contrasting "stylized" or "ideal-typical" pictures of the corporation and the academic institution. Corporate employees, we will assume, are hired with an effective lifetime job guarantee, perhaps following a brief and largely perfunctory probationary period and barring gross malfeasance or severe economic hardship for the corporation (these latter qualifications corresponding to comparable limitations on the academic tenure commitment). Corporate employees are not, however, guaranteed a particular assignment, with well-defined tasks and perquisites, but rather face an array of possible career paths along which the corporation has discretion to move them at varying rates. University employees in contrast do not receive an immediate employment guarantee but face an extended and serious probation. But when they *are* guaranteed employment, it is a guarantee of employment in a specific set of tasks with well-defined perquisites.

These pictures are exaggerations but, we think, recognizable ones. The notoriety of corporation jobs that lack an implicit employment guarantee—those of CEOs or advertising executives—only stresses the contrast with the more usual case. And the narrowly defined and well-ensured tasks of the academic fit the picture of the research universities and the more prestigious colleges better than they fit other places. But we think accounting for the differences in our extreme cases will shed light on the wider range of corporate and university personnel policies encountered in the real world.

*   *   *

Job Security, Job Specificity, and Organizational Effectiveness

One of the central insights of analytical labor economics over the last decade has been the recognition that the productivity of an organization depends heavily on the character of the work environment it is able to provide. The classical picture is of the profit-maximizing firm, sensitively adjusting the wage rates of workers and hiring and firing ruthlessly to get the most out of its work force at minimum cost—such a firm turns out on a careful view of its internal requirements not to be maximizing profits at all. Most obviously, the implicit assumption of "no transactions costs" embodied in this picture of the rapidly adjusting firm is wrong. Turnover is costly to firms because of training costs and the value of accumulated information about present employees, information that cannot be cheaply or reliably purchased in the market. At the same time, mobility is expensive to workers—they value job security—because of search and relocation costs and because of information they accumulate about the firm they work for. So firms can hire a labor force of given quality more cheaply by pursuing a policy that reduces involuntary turnover of employees.[4]

4. This literature is usefully condensed and cited in Okun 1980 (chap. 3).

Within the firm, moreover, workers need to train other workers, which they will be reluctant to do if the trainee is a viable candidate for the trainer's job (Thurow 1975; Solow 1980). It is also often cheaper for employers to evaluate the performance of a team or group of workers than to judge the performance of individuals within the group, so that neither wage nor dismissal incentives may be easily targeted at individuals (Alchian and Demsetz 1972; Williamson 1975). More subtly, firms need to create an "atmosphere" (to borrow Williamson's word) within the work group that conduces to a cooperative attitude; elements of wage and employment competition within the group may poison the atmosphere and discourage workers from revealing information to higher management that might be useful in reassigning tasks, making judgments about promotions, and the like.

Williamson, Wachter, and Harris (1975) have analyzed the resulting structure of "internal" labor markets at length. Firms will maintain an active position in the "external" labor market only for a relatively few positions in the job structure: the bulk of positions in the job hierarchy will be filled by promotion from within. The wage attaching to a particular job in the hierarchy will be largely independent of who occupies it; differential success in performance will be rewarded by more rapid promotion through the hierarchy rather than by more pay for better workers within a rank. The perennial prospect of promotion provides workers with an individual incentive to stay with the firm and produce, without exacerbating the tendency toward destructive competition between workers at the same grade.

The wage and promotion structure also helps to cement the relation between the worker and the firm. The firm invests in the worker, both by training and—importantly—by accumulating information about his particular strengths and weaknesses. The worker signals his willingness to stay through and past the initial investment period by accepting a relatively low initial wage: a strategy which makes sense only if he plans to stay. He is willing to do so in part because he believes the firm will find a "slot" for him that fits his capacities and interests. Within limits, the resulting wage/promotion arrangement will be self-enforcing: the worker and the firm will have a mutual interest in getting the worker into a job where his productivity is high and where his pay is high enough both to ensure continued employment with the firm and to make other workers in the firm aspire to such high productivity jobs. The need for the firm to present itself to employment candidates as a good place to work provides it with an additional incentive for "honest" promotion and job assignment practices.

Essential to this picture, however, is the presumption that there exists in the firm a variety of jobs of varying wage and productivity which workers might be willing to accept. One might see the firm as having internalized some of the functions of a placement agency: because information about worker capabilities is a by-product of the production process, it makes sense for firms to offer to workers the service of finding the job that fits them best. Other things equal, the firm will be more attractive to workers the wider the array of potential jobs it offers.[5]

But in academic employment there is very little of this internal job mobility: it is a crucial fact that people who are hired to the faculty either stay on the faculty or are dismissed; they do not move to alternative employment within the institution, except for the relatively few who move into academic administration. And, of course, nonacademic employees are hardly ever promoted to the faculty. Reasons for this crucial fact will be discussed shortly, but first it is important to note that it radically reshapes the structure of the employment problem that colleges and universities face, compared to that of large corporations.

To the degree that firms can freely assign workers to jobs and career paths with differing wages and productivities, they can avoid the risk of radical mismatches between wage and productivity for individual workers while still avoiding the costs of high turnover. Moreover, the return on investment in information about worker performance will be increased by its dual role in the organization: the same information which is useful in monitoring the worker's performance in his present job also has value in determining when and where to reassign him.

The university, lacking this flexibility in assigning responsibilities to workers, is thus in a difficult spot. When a worker is inflexibly attached to a particular job, mismatches between wage and productivity can only be avoided by (a) adjusting wages to match individual productivities, (b) accepting the costs of higher turnover by dismissing low productivity employees, or (c) introducing more intensive and costly initial screening. Alternative (a) is of course used within limits, but unrestrained use of wage differentials is unattractive because it requires costly monitoring of the performance of every individual faculty member throughout his career and because of the disruptive and demoralizing effects of introducing large wage differentials for faculty with comparable rank and responsibilities. Freeman (1976) notes the constraints academic institutions feel in estab-

5. It might seem that all that matters is the number of "good" jobs available. But this is not so, since for workers who are uncertain about their productivity, the absence of low-productivity jobs means not assurance of a good job but a higher probability of dismissal.

lishing wage differentials between and within academic departments. (Notice that, without extensive initial screening for faculty quality, wage differentials might need to be very large indeed to reflect productivity differences. With such screen in place, the expected productivity of the monitoring needed to sustain wage differentials is lower.) Alternative (b), if seriously pursued throughout every employee's career, also requires expensive monitoring throughout the career (which itself has negative "atmospheric" effects) and introduces employment insecurity, which is costly to both workers and the firm.

Academic employers have thus settled on a version of alternative (c)—more intensive initial screening—as a central element of their personnel policies. This takes the form both of more intensive preemployment screening than corporations undertake for entry-level positions and of intensive on-the-job screening concentrated in the first few years of employment. These considerations help account for several of the key features of academic employment policy.

First, and most centrally, we can understand why such "a big deal" is made out of promotion and tenure decisions. The decision to employ a person permanently in a well-defined position is momentous both of the worker and the firm: the worker gets not merely employment security but something close to a guarantee of status and lifetime income prospects; the firm is locked into not only a stream of future wage payments but a stream of future productivity from the worker over which it will have very little control. It follows therefore that firms will invest quite heavily in the scrutiny of their nontenured employees and that workers will attach great importance to perceived fairness of the institutions for making tenure and promotion decisions. The result is a concentration of everyone's energy and attention on that single point in the career, which is quite the opposite of the more diffuse but more sustained attention to worker performance in the corporation.

The obverse of close attention to the academic worker's performance prior to tenure is the marked inattention to performance after tenure. This too can be seen as a rational response to the academic employment situation. In the corporation, with its flexible job assignment policies, a principal role for the continual monitoring of employee performance is the making of continual marginal adjustments in workers' job assignments: increasing the productivity of the existing labor force by reallocating tasks among workers. But in the university, where the tasks are final once the employment guarantee is made, monitoring performance has little value, for there is little to do with the information. To be sure, information about tenured faculty can influence the rate of wage advance to some degree and can serve as a basis for moral suasion, but the central use to which such information is put in the corporation, to shape the path of the worker's career advance, is markedly less available within an academic institution.

These considerations also help account for the existence in academia of a sharply defined "nodal point" by which time a decision of "up-or-out" on tenure must be made. Personnel decisions in the corporation are almost always taken at the margin: to hasten or delay promotion; to expand or contract the range of responsibility. In academics, the possible decisions at any time are two: the marginal one of continuing employment for another year or the dramatically non-marginal one of terminating employment. If the former decision is always available, there will be an almost inevitable tendency to evade the latter one, which is bound to be difficult and unpleasant. To force a decision by a fixed moment serves both to legitimize the harsh decision to let someone go—the option of another chance just isn't available—and provide an incentive to gather the large amounts of costly information needed to make such a weighty decision responsibly. (See Brewster 1972.)

These remarks show the fundamental differences between the personnel problems of the academic institution and the corporation that follow from the narrowness and specificity of the academic job commitment. Much more remains to be said in elaboration of the implications of these points for the operation of colleges and universities. But it is time now to examine with care the reasons for this crucial structural difference between the university and the corporation: why do universities not offer—and why do faculty not seek—the wide range of career paths offered within a typical corporation?

Sources of Job Specificity in the University

The fact that individuals are hired to do quite narrowly defined and rigidly specified jobs is central to the economics of tenure and describes the major structural contrast between university and corporate employment. The sources of this difference lie on both the production and demand sides of the market. The "organizational technology" of the university is such that it attaches relatively little value to preserving its freedom to change the job assignments of particular workers. At the same time, worker preferences are such that a faculty member would typically prefer to continue his occupation (say, teaching physics) at another institution than to stay with the "firm" in a different job. Behind these differences in organizational technology and preferences lies an important difference between the corporation and the university in the kinds of "knowledge capital" workers acquire to do their jobs. In the university, this knowledge is predominantly tied to the worker's academic subject: it is specific to the *occupation* and not to the firm. In the corporation, there is likely to be a greater premium on *firm-specific* human capital: knowledge of the particular codes, practices, and procedures of *that* corporation as opposed to others. (For the importance of firm-specific human capital in the corporation, see Arrow 1974 and Becker 1964. The distinction between occupation- and firm-specific human capital is drawn in Rosen 1977.)

This contrast is reflected in the differences in training patterns for corporate and university work. In academic employment, training is for a specific academic discipline and not for a specific employment or firm. Academic training is an extreme case of the classic "nonappropriability" of worker training—the fact that firms are reluctant to invest their resources in the training of their employees and more so the less specific is that training to that firm—the more generally valuable it is in other firms. Training for university employment is so extreme a case of nonappropriability that the firm—the hiring university—refuses to provide any training and, instead, hires its employees with virtually their full complement of training (the Ph.D.) secured elsewhere and at someone else's expense. This is understood by the curious, if familiar, fact that the new academic employee does the same thing—teaches the same sorts of classes in the same way and writes the same sorts of articles and books—as the thirty-year veteran. Quality, it is hoped, improves with maturity, but the duties of faculty members remain remarkably the same.[6]

Again, the corporation presents the antithesis in its widespread employment of individuals trained as generalists who are subsequently put through a highly firm-specific training followed by a career of additional training in different, again firm-specific, activities. The multiplicity of suitable corporate jobs with their often differentiated internal training requirements and the individual worker's multiple job assignments, seriatim, over

6. This shifting of the training function entirely out of the employing institution is especially interesting in light of the fact that the same institutions are involved in both roles, even while keeping separate. Not only does the firm have the competence to train its own workers but it is often engaged in just that activity in its own graduate schools. So the Massachusetts Institute of Technology (MIT) hires a new Stanford Ph.D. to train its Ph.D. candidates at the same time that Stanford hires a new MIT Ph.D. to train its Ph.D. candidates. Even when the formal identity of competence is not so glaring, much of the anomaly remains: when Kermit Gordon and Emile Despres were on the Williams faculty, Charles Kindleberger referred to Williams as "the best graduate school in economics in the country, only you've got to be an Assistant Professor to get in."

his career are aspects of the high degree of substitutability among those jobs. An important reason for the substitutability appears to be the absence of high levels of requisite prior training; conversely, the absence of much prior training before workers enter the firm tends to make all jobs similar for the generally talented but not specifically trained individual.

This difference in training and human capital accumulation patterns naturally shapes worker interests in the character of the job guarantee they will seek. Individual academics will typically prefer to substitute one employer for another while retaining their occupations rather than to scrap their costly training in favor of taking a different job at the same institution. Moreover, it is reasonable to expect that only workers with a relatively strong prior commitment to the occupation will undertake training in the first place, so that the commitment to the profession is a result of preferences as well as the opportunity cost of the specialized investment in training. The academic worker will thus put little value on a guarantee of employment which is not specific about the kind of employment guaranteed.[7] The new corporate employee, on the other hand, with less investment in occupation-specific training, and less knowledge about where his skills and interests lie, will care more about job security as such and may put positive value on the corporation's implicit offer to match his job assignment to his aptitudes, as information about those aptitudes emerges.

The tendency to job rigidity in the university is compounded by its objective of doing its job of education and research (producing its product) at reasonable cost. An important aspect of the technology of university production, the result of the specialized human capital possessed by academics, is that it is rarely as easy to substitute employees among jobs as it is to hire new employees from outside for those particular jobs. If the university has an opening for a worker to teach and do research in particle physics, the productivity in that job of a professor of French Literature currently employed by the university is unlikely to be nearly as high as that of a new employee trained specifically in particle physics—someone currently in graduate school or employed in the physics department of another university. The occasional Renaissance Man, of course, is the exception that proves the rule. It will similarly be unlikely that the best person for a nonacademic job opening will be a faculty member—in many cases it seems true that intense academic training does as much to *disqual-*

---

7. Presumably, he'd like to have his cake and eat it too. Both sorts of security—especially since they are rights and not obligations—are nice to have. The point here is simply that if one has to choose, the choice will typically be in favor of keeping the occupation and not the employer.

ify as to prepare people for other kinds of work. So on pure productivity grounds, too, the university will accommodate these sharp technological differences in productivity among individuals and will hire French scholars to teach French and physicists to teach physics.

The corporation, of course, shows that this employment pattern is far from inevitable. It hires the liberal arts graduate—often a history or English major—for a broadly defined "management" training program from which he or she may be assigned to a specific job in production management or financial management or sales or. . . . And even a cursory examination of corporate management careers makes it clear that once assigned to sales or production or finance, the corporate employee will often be reassigned to quite different sorts of managerial employment throughout his career with the firm. Indeed, even employees (like engineers) who may be hired for their specific skills will often, if successful, "graduate" into jobs that do not depend on those skills.

So both sides of the market lead to narrowness and rigidity of academic employment: the technology of production sharply reduces flexibility in inter-job substitution at the same time that the preferences of workers sharply reduce their willingness to change fields rather than changing firms. Neither appears dominant.[8]

It is understandable, then, in light of the important differences in the interests of work in the academic and corporate employment settings that the form of the agreements ensuring job security will differ. As Simon (1957) has stressed, the contract governing any employment relation will be importantly "incomplete," with the worker ceding an important amount of discretionary authority to the firm about exactly what activities he must undertake. In the corporate setting, the firm's authority generally extends to granting the firm considerable freedom to determine what position in the firm the worker will fill, not only to begin with but through the career. The quid pro quo is an implicit commitment by the firm to retain the employee in some capacity, barring markedly unusual circumstances. But in the university, the faculty member cedes much less authority to the "firm" to determine the content of his job. Indeed, it can be argued that this is one of the most attractive features of academic employment—the fact that workers are, to a remarkable extent, asked to do very little they

8. It is futile to ask whether it is workers' rigid preferences or universities' rigid productivity requirements that explains the job specificity and rigidity of academic employment. The more flexible, adaptable job environment into which the corporate employee is hired, too, is the result both of greater flexibility in production and greater indifference on the part of the worker whether he is assigned to one job or another within the firm.

don't choose to do. They get paid for reading, thinking, talking, and writing about those things that they find interesting and rewarding. The result, of course, is that the university has little authority to reassign workers to different work; it may make offers and suggestions, but the presumption is that an academic worker always has the right to stick to his job. An offer of tenure ensures this security in a specific job permanently. The quid pro quo is, however, a little different than in the corporate world: job security comes only following a lengthy and rigorous period of probation.

Personnel Decisions in the University

The university and the corporation, then, face sharply different sorts of personnel problems.[9] The corporation can feel relatively relaxed about the "quality" and characteristics of the persons it hires into entry-level positions and can follow an implicit policy of "instant (or almost instant) tenure" simply because it has available a wide range of job slots requiring differing capacities and offering different wages and because it retains freedom to allocate employees among those jobs, and to reallocate employees as time goes on. The essence of the corporate personnel management problem is to ensure a steady and reliable flow of information about employee performance and to maintain a responsive institutional structure to reallocate employee responsibilities on the basis of that flow of information. Economists, notably Arrow (1974) and Williamson (1975), are beginning to appreciate what a subtle and important problem this is.

The university, however, essentially *knows* what its people are going to do and, if it is to attract good employees, it cannot allow itself very much discretion about how much it will pay people to do it.[10] Its problem then is to ensure that it gets good quality workers into the "firm" and to ensure that they stay motivated in the absence of sensitive marginal incentives.

9. Many of the points in this section emerge, from a somewhat different perspective, in section 4 of James and Neuberger 1979.

10. This latter point deserves elaboration. The corporation, we assume, will fix a wage for a given job. But people's expected incomes will vary with the jobs (and career paths) they are assigned to. Why could the university not achieve a similar result by varying pay according to teacher performance? Besides the general arguments about morale implications and difficulties of productivity measurement noted earlier, there is a further problem. With a flexible array of jobs, the corporation has an interest in putting high-productivity people in high paying jobs. This tends to keep the corporation "honest," since to put a potentially high-productivity person in a low-paying job costs the firm product, as well as costing the worker income. But with the job assignment fixed, the university could save itself money by asserting falsely that a particular professor had low productivity. So there would be more ground for suspicion that the university might use its power to set wages in "unfair" ways that don't match productivity differences.

The probation-tenure system is a reasonable response to this distinctive employment problem. . . .

The Probation Period

It is possible to identify four distinct ways in which a lengthy and explicit probationary period is valuable.

(1) Performance monitoring. In any economic transaction, people need to know what they are buying. The productive organization—including the university—must have ways of knowing about the performance of its employees in doing the things that produce the firm's output. But among workers and jobs, there is very great variety in the ease with which that performance can be measured by the firm: the ditch digger quite unambiguously has or has not moved a specific amount of dirt by noon; the theoretical biologist may or may not have spent the morning in pursuit of his research objectives—he may have been daydreaming about making a killing in the stock market. Differences in the inherent measurability of different occupations are essentially technological, attaching irreducibly to the specific activity (Leibenstein 1976). Given these inherent technological measurement problems, incentives to misrepresent performance may compound the difficulties of measurement. Workers and firms may both try to give a misleading picture of what the worker is actually doing, but absent the underlying technological measurement problems in the first place, incentive distortions cannot persist: if performance can easily be monitored, there is no room for attempted misrepresentation.

The performance of the activities of academic workers—teaching and scholarship—is certainly hard to measure.[11] These activities do not produce concrete, measurable products of easily discernible quality; neither their output nor their inputs are easily observable or measurable.

It is not necessary to this analysis to assert that corporate productive activities are any easier to measure than those of academia. What counts for the present analysis in differentiating the two organizations and their

11. But not equally. There seems little doubt that teaching performance is even harder to measure than scholarship, if only because the inherent qualitative judgments made about both are made by more knowledgeable people and more publicly in the case of scholarship. Furthermore, those judgments are made by much the same people over time—there is continuity in the population of judges in the case of scholarship but a constantly changing group in the case of teaching. This difference between teaching and scholarship, while not directly relevant to the present analysis, would certainly be central in any analysis that differentiated between university and college faculties.

labor markets is, simply, that the university combines measurement difficulties *and* job-specific employment while the corporation combines its measurement difficulties with job-flexible employment: the corporation can second-guess and the university cannot.

But "hard to measure" is a bit too imprecise for our purposes. What it means is that a worker's actual job performance can be known by the firm only with the expenditure of resources—on things like record keeping but most importantly in the form of attention, time, and effort. Performance that is inherently harder to measure simply takes more of those resources. Of course, it may be both undesirable and exorbitantly expensive to try to know with certainty the quality of a performance. So what's relevant is often the achievement of a given level of confidence in that knowledge. Again, the "harder to measure," the more resources are needed to get to that level of confidence.

This applies to measurement of the performance of an individual worker at a particular point in time. There are two important additional dimensions. Spence and Williamson note the frequently greater ease—the lower cost—of measuring the performance of a *group* of workers than that of an individual worker alone. Alchian and Demsetz (1972) relied on such "non-separability" of performance measurement for their influential analysis of internal organizations—their illustration was the difficulty of the separate measurement of the work performance of two men lifting a box onto a truck. As a group, their performance is easily measured; individually it is not.

The even more relevant—and neglected—dimension of measurement is simply the duration of the period over which the performance is measured. A repetitive activity—like either teaching or scholarship—may be very costly to monitor quickly but be quite easy to judge over a longer period. So in addition to the differences among jobs in their inherent static costs of performance measurement, there will also be differences in the way performance information accumulates with the duration of observation.

The relevance of this time dimension for academic employment is obvious. Academic job performance is unusually difficult to measure quickly. The ease with which accurate judgments can be made clearly increases with a longer period of observation. While it would be very difficult to judge scholarly potential, for instance, in a week of even very intensive observation, it is easy to achieve a reasonable judgment over a five-year period. In general, a longer period of observation of any repetitive activity yields a given degree of measurement accuracy at lower total resource cost.

For these reasons, the lengthy probationary period for faculty can be a useful method of quality control.

(2) Self-selection.[12]   One hazard facing the university is analogous to the problems of moral hazard and adverse selection in the insurance industry. Given the assured status and security of the tenured academic position, there is danger of persons misrepresenting themselves—their basic attitudes, work habits, goals, etc.—in order to obtain tenure and showing their "true colors" afterwards. This problem, of course, exists for the corporation too, but it is mitigated by the fact of job flexibility. The worker who has led his superiors to overestimate his potential can be either downgraded or "kicked upstairs" in response.

The interposition of a probationary period, with relatively low pay and a relatively high dismissal probability, reduces the incentive for misrepresentation of this kind. The longer the period over which one has to "fake" desirable attitudes, the greater the cost of doing so, and since levels of performance after tenure are not so intensively monitored or enforced, there is a strong premium on granting tenure to those who genuinely enjoy their work. The longer the probationary period, the greater the tendency to screen out those who don't.

(One might add to this a point originally due to Pascal, who noted that merely acting out religious ritual may eventually produce real belief. There may be a tendency for one who tries to act the part of a well-motivated academic to actually become such eventually. Those among us who feel surprised at how hard they continue to work after receiving tenure may be cases in point.)

(3) Time to tenure as an economic variable.   With relatively rigid wages and job descriptions, the university faces a problem in adjusting the attractiveness of its employment offering to changes in market conditions. The corporation, of course, faces a comparable problem, which it solves in part by varying promotion prospects and rates of promotion in response to market conditions. The university can, in a similar way, use variations in the likelihood of promotion and in the length of the probationary period to vary the value of its employment offer as market conditions change. There is extensive empirical evidence that such variation is in fact an important feature of the academic labor market (Kuh 1977; Weiss 1981).

12. The phenomenon of self-selection in labor markets has received much attention recently. See Spence 1974, Salop and Salop 1976, and the articles referred to in Okun 1980 (chap. 3).

(4) The focusing of monitoring resources. As noted earlier, fixing a terminal point to the probationary period enforces a concentration of attention and monitoring effort that encourages careful evaluation of candidates for promotion. In the absence of such a focal point, the tendency will be to postpone the difficult decision to fire anyone and to dissipate the energies needed to stage a serious evaluation.

The Tenure Decision

While it is useful in some contexts to speak of the "university" as making decisions on tenure and job security, in fact specific individuals within the institution are charged with making them. The arrangements in the university are quite different from typical corporate arrangements, and these differences can be at least partly understood in terms of the analysis developed here.

In the corporation, decisions about promotions are typically made in a hierarchical manner, with those at higher levels in the hierarchy deciding on those lower down, and with a well-articulated structure of levels shaping the whole. In the university, however, while deans and presidents may be involved in decisions, most of the weight of the tenure decision is typically borne by those members of the discipline who have already been given tenure: peer review is the order of the day.

Several aspects of these arrangements can be addressed in our framework. Why is it disciplinary peers, rather than "higher ups" within the institution who bear the weight of the decision? Why is it peers within the institution rather than peers outside the institution who are central? And why is it tenured faculty, rather than all those in the discipline at the institution, who decide?

The rationale for peer rather than hierarchical authority is clearly linked to the specialized nature of academic job assignments: judgment of an employee's performance during the probationary period must be made by those who are competent in his field since his main productive activities are specific to that field.[13] Just as the university cannot usually hire a French professor to teach particle physics, so it cannot rely on a French professor (or a dean or president trained for that role) to judge the performance of a particle physicist. Of course, formally the role of peers may only be advisory to those with hierarchical authority, but higher-ups will rarely have

13. This is more clearly the case in scholarship than in teaching. This would lead us to hypothesize that the role of disciplinary peers in tenure decisions is stronger at schools that put more emphasis on research.

grounds to overrule strong recommendations from departments, and, if such recommendations are often overruled, the higher-ups will undermine the incentive for departments to put much effort into evaluations.

Peer judgments could, in principle, be made by committees of outsiders. Their advice is, of course, sometimes obtained but rarely given weight comparable to that of the candidate's colleagues. This is so despite the fact that it is sometimes alleged that outsiders could be more fair and objective. One reason for the importance of "locals" is that they can more cheaply be informed about aspects of a colleague's performance other than published work. Such information could only be made available to outsiders through extensive visits and observation. This fact is especially important since (as we discuss further below) an important part of the judgment is a forecast about the candidate's likely behavior *after* receiving tenure, and this requires a subtle view of the candidate's motivations, which is harder for outsiders to obtain.

Another, perhaps more important, reason for giving weight to local views concerns the motivation of the evaluators. The fact that local evaluators must live with the results of their decision and they presumably care about the reputation and quality of the department they are affiliated with gives them a stronger reason to judge with care than outsiders would have. We should add, of course, that insider evaluation is subject to abuse, for which the obtaining of outside views may be a partial corrective. The attribution of motivation may become an intrusive and arbitrary exercise, and the concern with needing to "live with" a colleague may lead to undue emphasis on traits of congeniality or even obsequiousness. But it is not clear that there is any feasible system for evaluating academic personnel which can avoid these hazards.

Last is the question why nontenured people are typically excluded from the group of peers who decide on tenure. One obvious reason is the potential conflict of interest in evaluating a potential competitor—or conversely the potential conspiracy on the part of candidates to support one another's interests. Indeed, the need for objective evaluations has been cited by some observers (we think wrongly) as the key rationale for the institution of tenure itself: without job security, faculty would be motivated to resist retaining workers superior to themselves (Freeman 1980). A separate reason for excluding nontenured personnel from tenure decisions is the relatively brief time over which they can expect to be associated with the institution, which may lead them to give undue weight to the short-term interests of the institution in making decisions.

Motivating Senior Faculty

Like universities, corporations generally avoid instituting wide merit-based pay differentials for different workers doing similar jobs: wages within grade, in fact, are closely linked to seniority (Medoff and Abraham 1981). But corporations can use promotion ladders and job reassignment as devices to continue to motivate effort among workers who are not threatened with dismissal. As we have argued, these options are much less available to universities. So the question arises, how *does* one motivate senior faculty? This is a large question, worthy of a paper (at least) in its own right, but a few observations related to the themes developed here are warranted.

First, a negative point: given the logic of the academic employment structure, it is far from obvious that intensive hierarchical efforts to evaluate and motivate senior faculty in fact make much sense. Monitoring worker performance is an expensive activity, and it may in itself have a negative impact on morale. It may be perfectly sensible, if there is little to be done with the information that is gathered anyway, to limit monitoring to what is needed to detect gross malfeasance and to the spontaneous monitoring of each colleague by his peers and to accept that a certain amount of "deadwood" is an unavoidable by-product of the system.

An interesting extension of this point has been suggested by Oliver Williamson (1975, 55–56). If, in fact, it is difficult to monitor or regulate the performance of faculty in their central activities of teaching and scholarship, it may prove *counterproductive* to monitor those ancillary activities (like use of the telephone or of paperclips) where regulation is possible. If there is no alternative but to trust faculty on important matters, it may be prudent to trust them on small matters as well, in order to make that attitude of trust as visible and pervasive as possible. More broadly, the general attitude of autonomy and mutual respect which universities try to foster among faculty can be seen as a reasonable response to their inability to monitor and regulate their central activities.

The fact that marginal incentives are hard to supply for senior faculty affects importantly the character of the screening process for nontenured faculty. It is necessary to determine not only what faculty are capable of doing but also to form a judgment about what they will be *inclined* to do, in the absence of marginal incentives. It is crucial to select for promotion faculty who have a strong "internal" motivation to perform, or, alternatively, faculty who are readily subject to "moral suasion" or "peer pressure" in regulating their performance levels. This is plainly a difficult judgment to reach, since it involves inferring by observing someone who is subject to sanctions how he will behave when he is not subject to those sanctions. The point made earlier about the self-selection function of the probationary period is relevant here, since the longer the probation, the higher the cost to the candidate of acting against his inclination. A further implication is that the need to form judgments about a candidate's inclinations and motivations argues against reducing the tenure decision to a set of purely "objectively" indicators, like number of publications. As noted, reaching judgments about motivation and about likely performance under changed conditions creates opportunities for abuse, but they seem to be unavoidable.

The discussion to this point has focused on incentives internal to the institution. It is necessary to note as well the incentive for tenured faculty to perform well in the hope of achieving a better position at another university—"better" in terms of pay, prestige, or other factors that matter to the person in question. Active markets for senior faculty only exist, however, at a relatively small number of institutions. Predictably, they are the ones where research figures and most prominently in the work of the faculty, since research performance is much easier for "outsiders" to evaluate and so to provide a basis for competing offers. At this group of universities, the external market functions as a partial substitute for the other motivating factors discussed here.

Term Contracts as an Alternative to Tenure

The logic of the present analysis may be usefully underscored by a brief comparison of tenure arrangements to the most familiar kind of employment arrangement commonly thought of as an alternative to the tenure/probation system.[14] This is the alternative of term contracts: appointing faculty to renewable contracts of relatively short (three- to five-year) duration. Under a term-contract system, faculty are offered a series of fixed-period renewable contracts. The notion is that under such a system each faculty member's performance is constantly reviewed during his career,

14. A different and in some ways rather intriguing alternative to a tenure/probation system would be the adoption of an "instant tenure" system like that of the corporation. This could only work efficiently if universities retained more discretion over the job assignments of faculty than they now do and if there were a wider range of jobs available in universities than are now. This could conceivably come about if universities were branches of multiproduct corporations. To pursue the "thought-experiment" of organizing universities in that way would take us away from the main point of this paper, but it may be worth attempting on another occasion.

with each contract renewal contingent on performance in the preceding contract period. The "naturalness" of this alternative no doubt stems from the rather odd idea—derived from taking textbook economic theory too literally—that this is how "real world" employment markets work. And indeed, judged by textbook criteria of the working of timeless markets, term contracts have a strong appeal in economic efficiency terms: "deadwood" workers are constantly being got rid of on the basis of their recent performance, and everyone is continually spurred to strong efforts by the threat of dismissal.

Our theoretical perspective, however, makes us strongly doubtful that things will work out this way in practice. Moreover, a valuable recent book on tenure by Richard Chait and Andrew Ford (1982) provides strong case-study evidence supporting our theoretical view. If the decision about contract renewal were more than nominal, it would prove very costly to universities committed to it. The resources required to evaluate everybody seriously every few years would be simply enormous. If such evaluations did not result in many dismissals, they would be largely wasted. If they did, the university would bear the costs of greater turnover. Moreover, the threat of job insecurity might make it more difficult to hire good faculty at wages comparable to those at places offering more security. And against the potential incentive advantages of more intense monitoring would have to be weighed the potential negative morale implications of that practice.

But in fact the more likely outcome is that contract renewals will become routine, and the system will approximate instant tenure. Two strong incentives contribute to such a shift from nominal job insecurity to actual job security. First, in perpetual reevaluation there is no moment of truth, no special time when the resources of the institution need be brought to bear on evaluating an employee's performance. Since that evaluation is both time and resource consuming and it risks a quite unpleasant outcome—and since another opportunity for evaluation will come along soon—the incentives are there to prevent a real and meaningful evaluation with each (or any) termination of a fixed-period contract. In a tenure decision, where the issue is a lifetime commitment, it is much more difficult to be slack and to procrastinate.

The second incentive is the simple fact of mutuality—the judges are also the judged. Since everyone on the faculty is in the same contract renewal boat, there is obvious pressure for the judges to be gentle and compassionate and not to evaluate their fellows too harshly—when one's own turn is on the horizon, only the slightest imagination is needed to see the value of such a precedent.

The schools employing term contracts that Chait and Ford examined (Hampshire College, Evergreen State College, and the University of Texas at Permian Basin) support this view of the consequences. Reappointments become routine and turnover is quite low. Chait and Ford (1982, 12) quote a Task Force established at Hampshire to review the term contract policy as asserting that "The current system also has an adverse impact on the faculty's quality by diverting inordinate faculty time away from teaching [and other work]. The involvement of so many faculty in the review of over twenty of their colleagues a year seriously drains important resources from the main educational functions of the college." The authors (p. 13) further note that the faculty, "referees today and candidates for reappointment tomorrow, fear retribution as well as strained relationships." Hampshire has since moved to create a "tenure-like" decision for a ten-year reappointment after the first two three-year appointments to create a "crunch decision" that will focus attention and resources. Evergreen has not made such a shift, but the absence of pressure for making difficult decisions seems to have been felt there too. The authors report an interview with the president of Evergreen in which he said, "Sometimes I say to myself, 'My God, we have instant tenure!' "

Instant tenure, of course, is precisely what, in our analysis, corporations have. But, to repeat our earlier point, they do not provide instant tenure to a specific job with specific responsibilities and perquisites. Universities with instant tenure are likely either to be forced toward extremely intensive screening of candidates for appointment, which is intrinsically quite difficult, since close observation of the candidate, over a long period of time, doing work like that he will be asked to, is required or else to accept a decline in quality of personnel.

One perhaps surprising point here is the potential advantage of a probation/tenure system over term contracts from the standpoint of minority employment. To the degree that term contracts amount to instant tenure, the cost to the university of making "mistakes" will rise, and there will be pressure in hiring to rely on established channels of historic reliability in locating candidates. (An illustration is the practice at Oxford, which has instant tenure through term contracts, to hire its own graduates.) To the degree that those historic channels embody past policies of discrimination, instant de facto tenure will militate against change and experiment. A similar problem arises to the degree that disadvantaged groups are victims of "statistical discrimination, "having their individual qualities discounted because of (correct or incorrect) beliefs about average characteristics of their group (characteristics which may themselves be the result of discrimination). (See Akerlof 1970; Thurow 1975.) The opportunity to observe an individual during probation will reduce the reluctance to judge the individual on his own merits rather than on group averages and may also over time lead to the undermining of the beliefs that sustain the statistical discrimination. This line of reasoning may apply not just to racially and sexually disadvantaged groups but to graduates of less prestigious universities as well.

Conclusion

The central message of this paper can be summed up as follows: the institution of tenure is not simply a constraint imposed on universities, whether to protect faculty jobs or to ensure academic freedom, but an integral part of the way universities function. The tenure/probation system is a reasonable response to the highly specialized nature of academic work and to the long training such work requires. An intelligent understanding of the operation of universities and a constructive approach to the reform of their personnel policies needs to take these realities into account.

This conclusion need not be so complacent as it may sound. One could, for example, question whether academic training needs necessarily to be so specialized as it has become. It is also true that our analysis presents a somewhat idealized picture of how tenure and promotion decisions are made, and there is room for argument about how close to these ideals various colleges and universities come in practice. Our point, however, is that criticism of the tenure system and proposals for reform must come to grips with the quite real and special academic personnel problems the tenure system responds to. Much existing criticism, by failing to understand the economic functions of tenure, fails to do that.

A further step away from complacency may be taken by recalling some of the special pressures that may arise for the tenure system in the near future. Our analysis incorporates two key assumptions about the workings of the academic labor market: one, that the typical individual will enter the academic career with a stronger commitment to the occupation than to a particular institution; the other, that the granting of tenure amounts to a lifetime employment guarantee in practice. Both these have for the most part been true over the fifty years or so that the institution of tenure has been in full force in America, but of course tenure is always granted subject to financial exigency for the institution, and people can only pursue a lifetime commitment to academic employment if jobs are available.

Many observers expect the impending decline in college age population to produce substantial strains on the academic labor market (Carter 1976; Dresch 1975; Freeman 1976; Bowen 1981; Oi 1979).[15] As the likelihood of financial crises at academic institutions rises, the value of obtaining a tenured position falls. At the same time, the familiar academic career pattern of starting out at a prestigious institution and then moving on to tenure at a less prestigious institution if necessary has ceased to be viable in many fields. For the next fifteen years, fewer people will enter academics with the expectation that it will be a lifetime career. Thus, some of the basic assumptions of our analysis will be at least partly undermined in the future. The operation of the tenure system has in the past been closely tied to the background of an expanding university and college system. A period of contraction is likely to stimulate a search for alternatives on the part of both employers and workers. Whether the pressures will be sufficient to cause such an alternative to emerge is difficult to say. But constructive thought about the form such an alternative to tenure might take, and especially analysis of its likely consequences for the performance of universities and colleges, will need to draw on the kind of functional analysis of tenure we have begun to develop here.

We would like, finally, to point toward two kinds of further work that need to be done both to extend and to strengthen the foundations of this study. First, our analysis contains a number of implications about the behavior of academic institutions which it would be desirable to test. We would expect, for example, that institutions where faculty play more specialized roles would be more likely to conform to the "ideal typical" tenure model. We would also expect that academic hiring practices in fields where there is closer substitution between academic and nonacademic employment of skills (business and medicine may be examples) will be less likely to adhere to the classic probation tenure pattern. These and other implications should be developed and tested. Second, it is possible to think of some segments of industry with labor market institutions similar to tenure (e.g., the Army's up or out policy) and also to think of occupations with similar characteristics (rigid job description and high costs of measuring performance) to academics (accounting and medicine may be examples). It would be valuable to see if there is indeed a match, as our view would suggest, between tenure-like labor market institutions and academic-like occupation characteristics.

15. For a sceptical view of these projections, see Ahlburg et al. 1981.

References

Ahlburg, Dennis, Eileen M. Crimmins, and Richard A. Easterlin. 1981. The outlook for higher education: A cohort size model of enrollment of the college age population, 1948–2000. *Review of Public Data Use* 9: 211–27.

Akerlof, George. 1970. The market for "lemons": Quality uncertainty and the market mechanism. *Quarterly Journal of Economics* 84 (Aug.): 488–500.

Alchian, Amen. N.d. Private property and the relative cost of tenure.

Alchian, Armen A., and Harold Demsetz. 1972. Production, information cost, and economic organization. *American Economic Review* 62, no. 5 (Dec.): 777–95.

Arrow, Kenneth J. 1974. *The limits of organization*. New York: W. W. Norton.

Becker, Gary S. 1964. *Human capital: A theoretical and empirical analysis, with special reference to education*. New York: National Bureau of Economic Research.

Bowen, William. 1981. Report of the President: Graduate education in the arts and sciences: Prospects for the future. Princeton University, Princeton, NJ. April.

Brewster, Kingman, Jr. 1972. On tenure. *AAUP Bulletin* 58 (Dec.): 381–83.

Carter, A. 1976. *Ph.D.'s and the academic labor market*. New York: McGraw-Hill.

Chait, Richard, and Andrew Ford. 1982. *Beyond traditional tenure*. San Francisco: Jossey-Bass.

Dresch, Stephen. 1975. Demography, technology, and higher education: Toward a formal model of educational adaptation. *Journal of Political Economy* 83 (June): 535–69.

Freeman, R. B. 1976. *The overeducated American*. New York: Academic Press.

———. 1980. The job market for college faculty. In *The demand for new faculty in science and engineering*, edited by M. McPherson, 85–134. Washington, DC: National Academy of Science.

Freeman, S. 1977. Wage trends as performance displays productive potential: A model and application to academic early retirement. *Bell Journal of Economics and Management Science* 8: 419–43.

Goldberg, Victor. 1980. Relational exchange: Economics and complex contracts. *American Behavioral Scientist* 23 (Jan./Feb.): 337–52.

Hall, Robert. 1982. The importance of lifetime jobs in the U.S. economy. *American Economic Review* 72 (March): 716–24.

James, Estelle. 1980. Job-based lending and insurance: Wage structure in tenured labor markets. Working paper no. 228. Economic Research Bureau, State University of New York at Stony Brook, Dec.

James, Estelle, and E. Neuberger. 1979. The university department as a non-profit labor cooperative. Revised version of paper presented at the U.S.-U.K. Conference on Collective Choice in Education, MA. Dec. Mimeo.

Keast, W. R., and J. W. Macy, Jr., eds. 1973. *Faculty tenure*. San Francisco: Jossey-Bass.

Kuh, Charlotte. 1977. Market conditions and tenure for Ph.D.'s in U.S. higher education. A report for the Carnegie Council on Policy Studies in Higher Education. Mimeo.

Leibenstein, Harvey. 1976. *Beyond economic man: A new foundation for micro-economics*. Cambridge, MA: Harvard University Press.

MacNeil, I. R. 1974. The many futures of contract. *Southern California Law Review* 47 (May): 691–816.

Medoff, James, and Katherine Abraham. 1981. The role of seniority at U.S. work places: A report on some new evidence. Working paper no. 618. National Bureau of Economic Research.

Oi, Walter. 1979. Academic tenure and mandatory retirement under the new law. *Science* 206 (Dec. 21): 1373–78.

Okun, Arthur. 1980. *Prices and quantities: A macroevaluation analysis.* Washington, DC: The Brookings Institution.

Rosen, Sherwin. 1977. Human capital: A survey of empirical research. In *Research in labor economics: An unusual compilation of research,* edited by R. Ehrenberg, vol. 1, 3–40. Greenwich, CT: JAI Press.

Salop, J., and S. Salop. 1976. Self-selection and turnover in the labor market. *Quarterly Journal of Economics* 90 (Nov.): 619–29.

Simon, Herbert. 1957. A formal theory of the employment relationship. In *Models of man,* 183–95. New York: Wiley.

Smith, B., ed. 1973. *The tenure debate.* San Francisco: Jossey-Bass.

Solow, Robert. 1980. On theories of unemployment. *American Economic Review* 70 (March): 1–11.

Spence, A. Michael. 1974. *Market signaling: Information transfer in hiring and related screening processes.* Cambridge, MA: Harvard University Press.

Thurow, L. C. 1975. *Generating inequality: Mechanisms of distribution in the U.S. economy.* New York: Basic Books.

Weiss, Yoram. 1981. Output variability, academic labor contracts and waiting times for promotion. Working paper no. 26-81. Foerder Institute for Economic Research, Faculty of Social Sciences, Tel Aviv University, Ramat Aviv.

Williamson, Oliver. 1975. *Market and hierarchies: Analysis and anti-trust implications.* New York: Free Press.

Williamson, Oliver E. 1979. Transaction-cost economics: The governance of contractual relations. *Journal of Law and Economics* 22: 233–61.

Williamson, Oliver E., Michael Z. Wachter, and Jeffrey E. Harris. 1975. Understanding the employment relation: The analysis of idiosyncratic exchange. *The Bell Journal of Economics* 6, no. 1 (Spring): 250–78.

A Comment on the Industrial Analogy

When the claim to tenure was first advanced in 1915, some people no doubt considered it anomalous at a time when most other employments were held "at will." Indeed, the turnover in industrial blue-collar employment at the time was enormous. (A Bureau of Labor Statistics study for 1913–14 found a "normal" annual employee turnover rate of 115 percent.) Production was often maintained by the "drive" system: by threats of summary dismissal and its exercise. To the extent that an employment analogy was debated by academics at the time, it was the tenure of office of federal judges. (See "Academic Freedom," *Nation,* December 14, 1916, pp. 561–562.)

As McPherson and Winston note, "permanent jobs" in which an incumbent employee of long service has a practical (but not legal) expectation of continued employment became a norm in many sectors of the economy in the postwar period. Recently, however, "downsizing" has brought mass layoffs of seemingly "permanent" white-collar employees. These events have been taken to argue against tenure: "[T]he very notion of economic security has become anachronistic throughout corporate America" (Richard Chait, "The Future of Academic Tenure," *AGB Priorities* [Spring 1995]: 3).

The publicity surrounding corporate "downsizing" has produced a widespread perception of greater job instability. But is it true that the very notion of economic security is an anachronism throughout corporate America? A leading student of the labor market disagrees:

> Taken as a whole, these data show that long-term employment relationships retain their centrality for men and, indeed, are of increasing importance for women. If one had to draw only one conclusion from these data, it would be that long-term relationships have an ongoing importance. The more extreme statements about . . . the substantial restructuring of career patterns are not true. [Paul S. Osterman, "Internal Labor Markets: Theory and Change," in *Labor Economics and Industrial Relations: Markets and Institutions,* ed. Clark Kerr and Paul D. Staudohar (Cambridge: Harvard University Press, 1994), p. 309]

It is not disputed, however, that most of these "lifetime" employees in corporate America are legally employed "at will"; they can be discharged on little or no notice. Thus the argument to job insecurity in other employments reverts to the earlier claim of anomaly.

Of what relevance is a comparison with employment practices in industry—in 1915, in 1940, or today? Not much, McPherson and Winston suggest; tenure is responsive to the special features of academic institutions and perhaps to a limited number of "academic-like occupations."

But there is a second and more important sense in which the industrial analogy is inapt. In industry, a premium is often placed on the subordination of the individual to the corporation, just as the AAC stressed in 1917. Consequently, corporations have exercised their prerogative to discharge employees summarily for criticizing their policies or their management, intramurally as well as publicly. The chairman of the Board of General Motors, for example, decried the "enemies of business [who] now encourage an employee to be disloyal to the enterprise. They want to create suspicion and disharmony, and pry into the proprietary interests of the business. However this is labeled—industrial espionage, whistle blowing, or professional responsibility—it is another tactic for spreading disunity and creating conflict" (quoted in *Individual Rights in the Corporation,* ed. Alan Westin and Stephan Salisbury [New York: Pantheon, 1980], pp. 92–93). Note the conflation of ethically grounded protest, of a claim of "professional responsibility," with disloyalty to the enterprise.

Institutions of higher learning, even private ones, are not "proprietary." They exist for the common good: to disseminate, test, and expand knowledge. Their work is done by highly trained and largely autonomous actors who tend to be independent-minded, one would hope creative, perhaps eccentric, sometimes tactless, and even offensive—as was John A. Rice at Rollins. The question for industry may be: What conditions best conduce to the effective realization of our corporate ends? The answer may be an exacting duty of conformity to the corporate hierarchy. But as McPherson and Winston illuminate, in higher education the question is: What conditions best conduce toward learning and research of the highest order and how shall we attract the very best talent? The Committee of Inquiry at Rollins anticipated the answer: "No teacher having a high degree of professional self-respect is, the Committee believes, likely to accept service in an institution in which freedom of individual opinion, and the exercise of professional responsibility, on educational matters is denied in the degree in which it was denied by President Holt on this occasion." This answer was more recently seconded by Howard R. Bowen and Jack H. Schuster in their *American Professors: A National Resource Imperiled* (New York: Oxford University Press, 1986), pp. 266–267.

A Comment on Coverage

Fritz Machlup observed that "if tenure is to serve freedom, it is not enough to make tenure rules inviolable or enforceable, but it is also essential to make them cover as large a proportion of the faculty as is possible without jeopardizing other equally important objectives." Upon investigating a sample of institutions in California, Illinois, and Pennsylvania in 1955, he found that the percentage of full-time faculty members with tenure was 53 percent for all institutions, varying from 52 to 65 percent, depending on the size of the institution. Data for 1961–62 indicated that at seventeen of thirty-one major universities, less than 60 percent of full-time faculty were tenured. He concluded that the former statistic revealed a coverage that was "too low," and he termed the latter "even more depressing." "In only a handful of the institutions studied did a large percentage of the faculty have tenure status."

According to data compiled more recently by the U.S. Department of

Education, the percentage of full-time faculty that had tenure (including, as did Machlup, institutions without tenure systems) was:

	Public institutions	Private institutions	All institutions
1980–81	68.0%	59.6%	64.8%
1992–93	66.3	56.1	63.4

Institutions with tenure systems may have increased since the mid-
1950s; but if so, these figures seem to reflect either the widespread use
of "revolving door" appointments or of permanent full-time but non-
tenure-track appointments. Are these data—63 percent in 1993 compared to 53 to 65 percent in 1955—significantly more encouraging?

Judith Gappa and David Leslie have attacked tenure on a different point
of coverage, from the perspective of part-time faculty. Part-timers are not
eligible for tenure and are treated (or "exploited") as contingent workers,
when in fact they often fill an important institutional niche. Their use, it
is claimed, challenges the "stranglehold" the traditional tenure system
has on the institution's ability to accommodate change. In consequence,
Gappa and Leslie question whether traditional tenure remains viable (*The
Invisible Faculty: Improving the Status of Part-Timers in Higher Education* [San
Francisco: Jossey-Bass, 1993], pp. 217–218, 228). We need not engage here
in an extended assessment of their data and arguments, for of the forty-
three recommendations they make for the better use, socialization, and
treatment of part-time faculty, only one bears upon the "stranglehold" of
tenure: "Recommended Practice 13: Provide for part-time tenure"
(p. 250).

This abbreviated reference should not be taken necessarily to disparage
the proposal out of hand. Many of the practices that Gappa and Leslie
decry concerning the use of part-timers are problematic in industry as
well. (Compare Richard S. Belous, "The Rise of the Contingent Work
Force: The Key Challenges and Opportunities," *Washington and Lee Law
Review* 52 [1995]: 863–878), with Stewart Schwab, "The Diversity of Contingent Workers and the Need for Nuanced Policy," ibid., pp. 915–936.)
Moreover, too extensive a reliance on part-time faculty may be education-
ally unsound, and their treatment may on occasion raise questions
equally applicable to full-time faculty. In fact, one of the early cases of
"political correctness" concerned a part-time faculty member. (Edward
Greeley Loring, United States Commissioner and Lecturer at the Harvard
Law School, was denied reappointment for 1854–55 by Harvard's Board

of Overseers, then elected by the Massachusetts legislature, because in his official capacity he had enforced the Fugitive Slave Act.) But reference to the recommendation is made merely to question the claim that the use of part-time faculty poses a challenge to tenure's "stranglehold." Inasmuch as more than 35 percent of the professoriate are now such contingent (non–tenure track) faculty, how much of an obstacle to institutional "flexibility" can tenure be?

5

Tenure and Resource Allocation

The award of tenure implicates a long-term financial commitment. As Ralph Brown and Jordan Kurland note, "If we assume a thirty-five year duration of tenure until a normal retirement age, with annual compensation starting at $40,000 (and sure to increase with time and inflation), the employing institution incurs a commitment that will doubtless reach two million dollars" ("Academic Tenure and Academic Freedom," in *Freedom and Tenure in the Academy,* ed. William Van Alstyne [Durham, N.C.: Duke University Press, 1993], p. 331). This is one reason why the tenure decision in such an exacting one. See Chapter 2. If, however, a university were free to reallocate resources at will—to terminate a tenured professor of classics in order to hire a professor of accounting, to build a bigger athletic facility, or merely to reduce operating costs—then the "tenure" accorded would be no tenure at all: it would be a claim to one's position only for so long as the institution was willing to allocate the funds to maintain it. Under such a system, evaluation of performance and the prospect of professional excellence need not be especially exacting, and academic freedom would lack protection.

The relation of tenure to the allocation of the institution's resources has been explored by the profession and by the courts in two situations: (1) an alleged "financial exigency," a condition that is claimed to necessitate the termination of tenured appointments; and (2) the termination of entire schools, departments, or programs of instruction, not necessarily for financial reasons. Both situations are discussed in this chapter.

The academic community has striven to reach a balance between financial responsibility (short of bankruptcy) and the protection of tenure. The joint 1925 *Conference Statement,* forerunner of the 1940 *Statement,* provided:

> Termination of permanent or long-term appointments because of financial exigencies should be sought only as a last resort, after every

effort has been made to meet the need in other ways and to find for the teacher other employment in the institution. Situations which make drastic retrenchment of this sort necessary should preclude expansions of the staff at other points at the same time, except in extraordinary circumstances.

It anticipated the "financial exigency" clause of the joint 1940 *Statement,* a product of the Great Depression.

The idea of financial exigency—a condition that would permit an institution the drastic act of abrogating a tenure commitment—drew upon two notions. One, a threat to the institution as a whole, had more relevance to private than to public institutions, which are more likely to be under a legislatively imposed budgetary reduction than to face extinction. The other, relevant in both the private and public settings, is the idea that the abrogation of tenure must be a genuine last resort, employed after all other responsible means of adjusting to the condition have been exhausted. As Judge J. Skelly Wright observed, "[T]he obvious danger remains that 'financial exigency' can become too easy an excuse for dismissing a teacher who is merely unpopular or controversial or misunderstood—a way for the university to rid itself of an unwanted teacher but without according him his important procedural rights" (*Browzin v. Catholic University,* 527 F.2d 843, 847 [D.C. Cir. 1975], citing *AAUP v. Bloomfield College,* 322 A.2d 846 [N.J. Super. 1974], aff'd, 346 A.2d 615 [App. Div. 1975]).

A difficulty in illuminating the condition and its consequences is that it cannot be dealt with in the abstract: an assessment requires all the facts that permit an appreciation of the precise financial situation of the institution. And in presenting those facts, one runs the risk of causing the reader's eyes to glaze. At that risk, however, excerpted below is a report concerning San Diego State University. This case study was chosen for three reasons. First, it was a nationally prominent event involving the potential of wholesale dismissals. Second, because the dismissals were eventually rescinded, the investigation was undertaken for an avowedly educational purpose, "to examine the relationship of faculty government, tenure, due process, and academic freedom to financially-driven decisions." Third, the case has been characterized by a critic of tenure as one of entrenched faculty resistance, in the cause of job security, "forcing" a retreat from an impliedly justified layoff (Richard Chait, "The Future of Academic Tenure," *AGB Priorities* 1 [Spring 1995]: 3). The reader is urged to consider whether or not tenure (and the tenured faculty) were culprits in the case.

San Diego State University:
An Administration's Response
to Financial Stress

I. Introduction

By letters dated June 9, 1992, one hundred and eleven tenured professors and thirty-five probationary faculty members at San Diego State University (SDSU) were informed by Dr. Thomas B. Day, president of the university, that, "[b]ecause of lack of funds or lack of work" they would be laid off from their positions effective October 7. These letters were preceded and followed by faculty protests, student demonstrations, and expressions of concern by outside parties, the latter including the Washington Office of the American Association of University Professors. On June 26, Associate General Secretary Jordan E. Kurland wrote to President Day in pertinent part:

> The more we learn of the magnitude of the current assault on the tenured faculty of San Diego State University, the more troublesome we find it. You indicated in your letter of May 26 that "catastrophic cuts" were in prospect not merely at SDSU but at virtually all California State University campuses, that the University of California system was "threatened with a disaster," and that other states appeared to be "facing the same or similar problems." Information that we received just a few days ago, however, indicates that within the CSU system the overwhelming majority of terminations of tenured faculty appointments are occurring at SDSU. . . .

. . . On August 27, a general faculty meeting urged the recission of the layoff notices by vote of 580 to 102 (twenty-four abstaining), and the removal of the president, by vote of 486 to 370 (sixteen abstaining). Chancellor Barry Munitz of the California State University system stated at a meeting on September 11 that all outstanding notices within CSU were being rescinded, and notices of recission at San Diego State went out by certified mail on September 18.

Because the effort to terminate the appointments of tenured faculty on such a scale is historically unprecedented, because these events illuminate the significance of tenure—and of sound academic government—in a time

From *Academe* 79 (March–April 1993): 94–115. The ad hoc investigating committee consisted of Matthew Finkin (Law, University of Illinois), Sanford Jacoby (Industrial Relations, UCLA), and Karen Lindenberg (Political Science, Eastern Michigan University).

of financial stress, and because many of the institutional concerns which gave rise to the decisions at San Diego State remained, the general secretary authorized an investigation. . . .

II. *The Institutional Setting*

* * *

The CSU system is currently composed of twenty campuses; it enrolls more than 350,000 students, who are taught by over 20,000 faculty members. San Diego State enrolls approximately 30,000 students; it offers bachelor degrees in seventy-six areas, masters in fifty-four, and doctorates in eight— several of the doctoral programs as joint degrees with the University of California, San Diego.

Since 1983, the instructional personnel of the system have been represented under the California Higher Education Employer-Employee Relations Act by the California Faculty Association (CFA) in a single system-wide collective bargaining unit. The CFA is in turn affiliated with the National Education Association and its state affiliate, with the California State Employees Association, with the Service Employees International Union, AFL-CIO, and with the American Association of University Professors.

The current chancellor of the CSU system is Dr. Barry Munitz. Since 1978, the president of San Diego State has been Dr. Thomas B. Day. President Day received his bachelor's degree from the University of Notre Dame and a Ph.D. in physics from Cornell University. Prior to assuming the presidency at San Diego State, he served in the administration of the University of Maryland. The current vice president for academic affairs, Dr. Ronald H. Hopkins, was appointed in 1991, shortly before the events under investigation occurred. His bachelor's degree is from Iowa State University, and he holds a Ph.D. in psychology from the University of Iowa. Much of his previous professional career had been at Washington State University, in which he served as department chair and later as vice provost.

* * *

The university's "Policy File" makes provision for a Senate . . . which, by its constitution, is "the delegate assembly of the faculty, through which the faculty shall normally exercise its powers." It has the power to act for the faculty in all matters (except student graduation) subject to a provision for review by a general meeting of the faculty, called upon petition of 10 percent of the general faculty. Paramount among the standing committees of the Senate is an Executive Committee, which has a very broad charge to consider all matters falling within the Senate's purview, to formulate recommendations on them for the Senate, and to act for the Senate on all matters that call for immediate action. Two other standing committees are of relevance here. First is the Committee on Academic Resources and Planning (CARP), which has recommendatory power over "all issues pertaining to . . . University budgets"—more particularly, the power "to review and recommend budget allocations, to review patterns of previous expenditures and propose changes as they may affect instructional programs, and to make general policy recommendations regarding present and future resource decisions." Second is the Committee on Academic Policy and Planning (CAPP), which has jurisdiction, *inter alia*, over "present and proposed programs."

Though the constitution speaks of the Senate as the "faculty's" delegate, it is not a faculty but rather a university body. Faculty senators are elected from each college, one senator per twenty-five faculty members; but these elected senators may include deans, associate deans, assistant deans, and department chairs. Moreover, six administrators sit *ex officio*, including the president and the vice president for academic affairs. Also included are four students and three staff members; the CFA has a non-voting delegate. The Executive Committee consists of three elected senators, with the remaining seats designated *ex officio* but expressly including three administrators, one of whom is the vice president for academic affairs. Similar administration participation is provided for on the CARP and CAPP.

The Senate, whose constituency thus transcends the core of full-time teaching faculty, co-exists with a collective bargaining agent which also has a broadened constituency, for the bargaining unit it represents includes the part-time and temporary faculty, lecturers, coaches, and additional persons holding a miscellany of other titles. . . . The "layoff" of faculty . . . is governed by Article 38 of the collective bargaining agreement. It provides in pertinent part:

> 38.1 The necessity for layoff of faculty unit employees shall be determined by the Employer on the basis of whether there exists, on a particular campus, a lack of work or lack of funds, or a programmatic change. Upon such a determination, the procedures of this Article shall apply.
> 38.2 Considerations in making such a determination shall include but not be limited to student enrollment data and projections, available funds, and scheduled curricular and program changes.

Consultation with the CFA is required after the administration has decided to invoke the provision; and notice of layoff "for lack of work or lack of funds" is required—ninety days for probationary faculty and 120 days for tenured faculty. Longer notice is required for layoff "in the event of programmatic change"—120 days for probationary faculty and one year for tenured faculty. The academic department is specified as the "unit" for layoff, and a specific order of layoff is mandated: (1) part-time temporary faculty; (2) full-time temporary faculty; (3) faculty on early retirement; (4) full-time probationary faculty; and last, (5) tenured faculty. A grievance procedure culminating in arbitration is contractually established as "the sole and exclusive method for the resolution of disputes arising out of issues covered by [the collective bargaining agreement]."

One recurring theme at San Diego State in the events to be recounted below is the insistence of the president and a large number of faculty members on the institution's "uniqueness" within the CSU system, by which they mean its extensive graduate programs and externally funded research, in contradistinction to what they take to be the less alloyed undergraduate teaching missions of its sister institutions. The graduate programs have been adverted to, in support of which a number of teaching assistantships are funded. In addition, a separate San Diego State Foundation is maintained, over which President Day presides, which serves as the conduit for externally funded research. (The foundation also has extensive real estate holdings, some of which it leases to the university; and it may disburse funds in support of other university activities or university-supported activities, such as public broadcasting.) In recent years, approximately $60 million in research contracts have been secured by San Diego State faculty members via the foundation, which receives indirect cost recovery; those overhead funds are later disbursed by the foundation in support of other projects or proposals within the discretion of the administration.

III. The Mass Layoff and Its Aftermath

A. The 1991 "Across-the-board" Reduction

The events in question have to be understood against the background of the 1991–92 academic year. The SDSU budget anticipated for 1991–92 was reduced in the spring of 1991, in advance of the budget year, because of a budgetary shortfall in the CSU system. According to a CARP report, issued in the fall of 1992, the budgetary shortfall at San Diego State was estimated at $18.7 million. This was calculated, however, on the basis of over $12 million in projected increases. Some were increases in mandatory costs, such as salaries and benefits, and others were increases in a variety of areas, such as leased space and an add-on of $1 million to the budget for utility costs (over the prior year's expenditure of about $4 million). The increases were to be taken against an actual reduction in direct state support of roughly $5.7 million below the prior year, from approximately $143,850,000 in 1991 to $138,160,000 in 1992. The "real" shortfall, in other words, was more than the actual drop in state support, but amounted to the $18 million figure given out at the time only by including the loss of every projected increase the prior budget contained. The latter may not have been fully realized by the faculty, however, until the audit of actual expenditures the following year.

To deal with what it described as a "financial crisis," the Senate Executive Committee recommended, in the words of a later Report of the Committee on University Restructuring, that

> [E]very effort should be made to preserve the "quality of the academic environment." Library, equipment, and supply budgets were to be spared if possible. [It recommended] (1) that every effort should be made to retain tenure and tenure-track faculty, and (2) that the budget reductions should be across the board.

These recommendations coincided with the administration's position. As a result, the SDSU administration terminated the services for the 1991–92 academic year of a substantial number of part-time faculty, of faculty members on early retirement, and of hundreds of full-time lecturers, all for "lack of funds." The loss of lecturers was to place the institution under considerable curricular and budgetary stress: the former because some departments were heavily dependent upon lecturers to teach their basic sections; the latter because lecturers taught on average a higher course load and for less money than the tenure-track faculty.

Various "infrastructure" accounts—which in SDSU parlance is taken to be virtually anything other than faculty salaries—were ostensibly frozen or reduced; but, as President Day reported in a memorandum of July 20, 1992, to the chair of the Senate, these were mostly restored by the year's end. "This was done," he wrote, "because for several previous years there were cuts in these items, and together with accumulating inflation they had fallen significantly below the level needed by the faculty."

The investigating committee has not deemed it necessary to pursue the history of the budgeting of "infrastructure" over time; but the committee did think it useful to capture a shorter-range picture of the university's overall budgetary history. Actual expenditures—not the sums budgeted—for the years 1989–90, 1990–91, and 1991–92 were roughly:

1989–90	1990–91	1991–92
$174,396,000	$175,831,000	$172,795,000

In other words, actual expenditures in 1990–91 were greater than those in 1989–90. And the actual decline in 1991–92 expenditures was actually less than the shortfall in state support alone of $5.7 million against the 1990–91 budget. The final expenditure figure is explained in part by an increase in student fees and other funds received as well as by faculty members availing themselves of early retirement. But in 1991–92, "infrastructure" was preserved as instructional lines were reduced. How this was accomplished is explored below.

First, Table 1 shows the 1991–92 anticipated budget in rounded figures—the budget in place before the reduction in state support—based upon the indicated proposed increases to the prior year's budget, allocated according to the institution's major programmatic areas (university-wide accounts omitted). Table II shows actual 1991–92 expenditures (in rounded figures) after the reductions and subsequent reallocations were made—compared to the same expenditures for 1990–91.

In fine, salaries for personnel in athletics, university telecommunications (the university's support for a public broadcasting station), and university relations actually experienced modest increases; salaries for personnel in business affairs and student affairs were reduced by 4 percent and 6 percent respectively—the latter, the investigating committee was informed, being taken at the president's direction largely from student health services. Operating expenses and equipment overall grew by $900,000, while salary lines in the academic component were reduced by more than $10 million, an 8.6 percent decrease.

In consequence of the reduction in the 1991–92 budget, and in expectation of future cuts—which were thought to be a virtual certainty and anticipated by many of those involved to be on an order of perhaps 3 percent to 5 percent—the chair of the Senate appointed an *Ad Hoc* Committee on University Restructuring to recommend the institution's future course of action. The committee surveyed the faculty (about 2 percent replied) and interviewed a number of faculty members and administrators. It decided that planning for a long-term readjustment was necessary and that any immediate—that is, midyear—additional reduction could not be addressed save by an attack upon the "infrastructure," given time constraints. But, the committee concluded,

> if the reductions come in the Governor's budget for the next fiscal year, then we will have a limited amount of time to respond. All agree that the highest priority is protection of our junior tenured and tenure-track faculty. Follow-

Table I

	Anticipated 1991–92	Proposed Increase Over 1990–91
Academic Affairs		
Salaries & Benefits (S&B)	$120,494,000	$3,328,000
Operating Expenses & Equipment (OE&E)	9,703,000	3,227,000*
Business Affairs		
S&B	18,574,000	654,000
OE&E	1,299,000	-0-
Student Affairs		
S&B	16,811,000	958,000
OE&E	1,727,000	13,000
University Relations		
S&B	1,222,000	17,000
OE&E	250,000	-0-
University Telecom		
S&B	877,000	35,000
OE&E	256,000	-0-
President's Office & Affirmative Action		
S&B	475,000	12,000
OE&E	38,000	-0-
Athletics		
S&B	2,642,000	80,000
OE&E	162,000	-0-

*Includes the transfer of approximately $2,100,000 from California lottery funds used for library purchases back to the prior system of direct state appropriations.

ing the budget reductions already absorbed, we recommend programmatic cuts.

The committee proposed "Policies and Procedures" for dealing with a future budgetary crisis: that the "Teacher-Scholar model" which character-ized SDSU's unique culture had to be preserved and was threatened by the impact of the "across the board" policy applied to the previous budget; that long-term restructuring ought to be pursued, gradually and especially through retirements; that the current budget reductions ought to be con-sidered permanent; and that the university was poorly positioned to re-

Table II

	Actual 1990–91	Actual 1991–92	% Change
Academic Affairs			
Salaries & Benefits (S&B)	$117,166,000	$107,057,000	− 8.6
Operating Expenses & Equipment (OE&E)	8,743,000	8,966,000	+ 2.6
Business Affairs			
S&B	17,920,000	17,218,000	− 3.9
OE&E	1,299,000	1,727,000	+ 32.9
Student Affairs			
S&B	15,853,000	14,897,000	− 6.0
OE&E	1,714,000	1,966,000	+ 14.7
University Relations			
S&B	1,205,000	1,232,000	+ 2.2
OE&E	250,000	229,000	− 8.4
University Telecom S&B	842,000	919,000	+ 9.1
OE&E	256,000	293,000	+ 14.5
President's Office & Affirmative Action			
S&B	463,000	467,000	+ 0.9
OE&E	38,000	44,000	+ 15.8
Athletics			
S&B	2,562,000	2,627,000	+ 2.6
OE&E	161,000	148,000	− 8.1

*The OE&E expenditure figure reported for 1990–91 was $6,643,000, but this omitted approximately $2,100,000 in California lottery funds that substituted for the regular state library funds that year. For the following year, the regular state funding was resumed.

spond to any further reduction beyond 1 percent. In terms of future action, it opined:

Any further permanent budget reductions should not be done by reducing positions across the board or by cutting into infrastructure. Further across-the-board reductions will probably result in wholesale layoff of some of our best and brightest newer faculty and will create serious long term hiring difficulties for the campus. Furthermore, across-the-board cuts will damage the efforts of the university to hold, recruit, and retain affirmative action hires.

Accordingly, the Committee on Restructuring recommended that any additional budgetary cuts be met by program elimination—a policy which came to be known on the campus as "narrow and deep." The committee explained that, although "the preservation of tenure track faculty is of utmost importance," program elimination was superior to the alternative—of "across-the-board" reductions—notwithstanding the impact upon tenured and probationary faculty. It set out six criteria to guide future decision-making:

Criteria

1. The overall quality of a program is an essential factor in decision making. Although quality is always ultimately a subjective value decision there are many forms of supporting evidence that lead to conclusions regarding overall quality. For example, evidence of excellence in teaching, academic reviews, accrediting agency reports, reputation within the discipline and reputation across the campus, evidence of faculty/student scholarship, timeliness of the curriculum, currency of the faculty, efforts to mentor students and involve students in intellectual and creative pursuits, and published evidence of quality through independent surveys attest to qualitative achievements.

2. Centrality of a program or department to the University is a second consideration. Although also ultimately subjective, this criterion basically addresses whether a university might exist within its mission were this program to be eliminated. Also, the contributions of the program to the education of other central programs is equally important in considering centrality.

3. Need is an important consideration. Both internal and external factors determine need. Internal considerations are related to the University's mission, its commitment to broad education and the overall commitment to a strong and balanced liberal arts and sciences curriculum which includes appreciation for applied and basic arts and sciences pursuits. External factors include the needs of our regional population, the traditional clientele we serve, the responsibility to educate for service professions important to our society, and to some extent, current student demand.

4. Our university is committed to fostering an appreciation of diversity that enriches our institution and creates an atmosphere that values all human potential. A curriculum and a faculty which embrace cultural diversity are essential. Because faculty and students who are themselves diverse contribute to our ability to create this environment and better model a changing population, we believe that faculty and student diversity are worthy criteria when considering program merit.

5. Program size is a consideration. To be effective a program must have a sufficient number of scholars to provide a reasonable exposure to the discipline. This may mean the elimination of smaller programs. It may also be that some relatively large programs might actually operate just as effectively

and certainly more efficiently with a narrower range of programs, activities, or with even fewer faculty.

6. When other factors are approximately the same, cost and resource generation are appropriate criteria. In determining cost the following factors are useful: S/F ratio, undergraduate/graduate education ratio, program administration costs, anticipated future outlays, and a judgment about maximum utilization of resources. When appropriate, the ability to generate outside revenue can be balanced against cost factors.

B. The 1992 "Narrow and Deep" Reductions

The Restructuring Report was approved by the Senate Executive Committee and by the full Senate respectively on January 28 and February 4, 1992. According to Professor Janis Andersen, who currently chairs the Senate and who served on both the Restructuring Committee and the Executive Committee at the time, the question was raised in the Executive Committee of how the particular decisions on termination would be made. The president offered to have the Senate make the decisions, but this met with little discussion and was declined. As Professor Andersen stated in the Senate minutes, "The committee was very strong in its position that it is up to administrators to administrate, but it is up to faculty to determine the values of the institution." The president, however, recalls having made the offer at a later date, when he presented his intentions for "narrow and deep" reductions to the Senate in May. We do not consider the discrepancy in recollection to be of significance, for reasons that will appear later.

Despite the Restructuring Report's reference to "Procedures for Meeting the Budgetary Crisis," no procedures, faculty or administrative, were put in place—or even discussed—at the time. More surprising, from the time the Senate approved the Restructuring Report in early February until the president's presentation of impending cuts to the Senate on May 12, neither the SDSU central administration nor the Senate developed plans to deal with any level of additional reductions beyond the "across-the-board" formula in the report for cuts not in excess of 1 percent: this despite the fact that the Restructuring Report was premised upon the prospect of additional budget reductions, and despite the general acknowledgment by all involved of the continuing prospect of a worsening budgetary situation for the State of California.

On Tuesday, May 12, President Day appeared before the Senate to announce that by facsimile transmission that morning Chancellor Munitz called on all campuses in the CSU system to take an 8 percent reduction in their 1992–93 budgets. The president announced that, while the prospect of enhanced early retirement incentives (a "golden handshake") was under consideration in the state legislature and would go far to ameliorate the situation, he had to implement the mandated reduction, which, because of an anticipated shrinkage in enrollment, meant about an $11 million reduction in the budget overall. The strategy he was prepared to follow, he stated, was that contained in the Restructuring Report:

> I have decided to go the "deep and narrow" way, with the strong advice of this group. It means that some areas will be cut deeply, and others may not be cut at all. I don't want to lower morale more than necessary, but once I have said that, I have said it all. This time we will be trying to save, in as many places as we can, the youngest members of our faculty and the expression of our commitment to reach out to underrepresented people. We do not mean in any way to belittle our long-time members, but in a very real sense we are seeking to protect the future of our institution.

He announced that he would review "the academic implications and consequences to students" and would "notify the Senate thereafter of particular areas." But he stated that he was anticipating the layoff of about one hundred tenured members of the faculty and the closing of ten to twelve departments, with others to be heavily reduced.

Six days later, on Monday, May 18, President Day reported his decisions to the Senate. He pointed out, as he had on May 12, that a policy to transfer funds from all available infrastructure counts for the year—to "burn the furniture"—would suspend the layoff of faculty for only one semester, at best. The president recounted the consultation he had had with the deans, the deans with department chairs "or faculty as necessary," and further consultation with the academic vice president, deans, students, and faculty. He "collected information from the vice president for study over the weekend" and was now prepared to announce his decisions. "There may be some particular changes as we look to alternatives," he observed, "but at this level of cut, I do not expect any deep areas."

Scheduled for "entire cuts"—that is, elimination—were:

College of Arts and Letters
  Anthropology
  German/Russian
  Religious Studies
College of Business Administration
  none
College of Education
  none

College of Engineering
   Aerospace Engineering
College of Health and Human Services
   Health Science
College of Professional Studies and Fine Arts
   Family Studies
   Industrial Technology
   Recreation
College of Sciences
   Natural Science

Scheduled for "deep cuts" were:

College of Arts and Letters
   French/Italian
   Sociology [Sociology was not listed in the written document President Day submitted to the Senate on May 18; but seven tenured members of the Sociology Department had been told on May 13 that their appointments would be terminated. It would appear that the department was slated for a deep cut at the time and that its omission from the written document was an oversight.]
College of Sciences
   Chemistry
College of Professional Studies and Fine Arts
   Art
   Telecommunications and Film

These decisions proceeded from the president's threshold decision to hold constant the existing proportion of the budget devoted to each of the major budget centers—academic affairs, student affairs, business affairs, and the like. By this reasoning, if academic affairs represented roughly 75 percent of the budget, he concluded that it ought to absorb roughly 75 percent of the reductions; but because "infrastructure" within academic affairs was considered sacrosanct, the decision actually placed an even heavier emphasis upon the reduction of teaching staff. There was no involvement in this decision by the Senate or its Executive Committee.

Once the sum that had to be saved from the academic side of the institution was roughly settled upon in this fashion, the president took it upon himself first to apportion reductions among the various colleges according to both the size of their budgets and to his sense of their importance to the university, and then to designate the departments for elimination within the colleges on the basis of the information and consultations he had had over the prior few days. Initially, he decided that every college ought to eliminate at least one department; but, after discussion with the deans of Education and Business, he was persuaded to exclude these colleges from that policy on the ground that their curricula and accreditation were such that they ought to be considered essentially as a single department in themselves, and so the choice, as he perceived it, was one of total elimination of the college or not. He chose the latter. The remainder of the "deep cuts" were left to the academic vice president to work out with the deans.

In the May 18 Senate meeting, the President noted that many details remained and that particular changes might be made as alternatives were explored. He told the investigating committee that he expected the Senate to engage with him in an exploration of these details and alternatives. But he confronted instead an outpouring of protest—of faculty anger and student demonstrations: in the president's words, of "theater" instead of discussion. He decided accordingly to proceed with his announced program without further Senate participation.

What ensued was a process of bargaining between the deans and Vice President Hopkins before the actual notices of layoff were mailed on June 9. The deans complained that the target figures kept changing. Dean Strand of the College of Arts and Letters stated that he and the vice president initially discussed twenty-five positions for elimination, but over time this increased to forty-five; Dean Short of the College of Sciences was told initially to plan for a reduction in anywhere from twenty to thirty positions, later more directly to thirty positions, and then eventually to forty positions. Vice President Hopkins agreed that such may have been the deans' perception, but he said that the numbers were merely refined as the targets were "narrowed."

The final list for elimination, deep cuts, less drastic cuts, and no cuts at all is set out . . . in Table III.

Table III   SDSU Teaching Faculty Placed on Notice for 1992–93 Layoff in Full-Time-Equivalent Faculty (FTEF)

	FTEF entering 1992	Proposed cuts in 1992	Proposed FTEF for 1993
Academic Skills	13.85		13.85
Accountancy	23.94	2	21.94

Administrative Rehabilitation & Postsecondary Education	10.12	1	9.12
Aerospace Engineering	11.729	12	-0-
Africana Studies	4.95		4.95
American Indian Studies	1.8		1.8
Anthropology	12.8	15	-0-
Art	34.71	5	29.71
Arts & Letters College	4.38		4.38
Astronomy	6.05		6.05
Athletics	34.35		34.35
Biology	79.03	3	76.03
Business Administration College	3.1		3.1
Chemistry	31.63	13	18.63
Civil Engineering	12.039		12.039
Classics & Humanities	4.9		4.9
Communication Disorders	16.58		16.58
Counseling & School Psychology	13.92	1	12.92
Drama	14.04		14.04
Economics	17.43	1	16.43
Education College	1.42		1.42
Education (Joint Doctorate)	5.15		5.15
Education Technology	7.36	1	6.36
Electrical Engineering	17.62		17.62
Engineering College	2.451		2.451
English & Composition	57.75		57.75
Family Studies & Consumer Sciences	20.52	21	-0-
Finance	26.02		26.02
French & Italian	10.03	4	6.03
Geography	20.96		20.96
Geology	17.71		17.71
German & Russian	6.4	8	-0-
Health & Human Services College	2.45		2.45
Health Science	10.08	14	-0-
History	35.18	1	34.18
Industrial Technology	6.7	9	-0-
Information & Decision Systems	20.58	2	18.58
Journalism	11.88		11.88
Linguistics & Oriental Languages	15.25	1	14.25
Management	15.7		15.7
Marketing	13.31	1	12.31

Math & Computer Science	62.337	11	51.337
Mechanical Engineering	13.129		13.129
Mexican American Studies	6.1		6.1
Music	23.49		23.49
Natural Science	10.67	15	-0-
Nursing	26.19		26.19
Philosophy	6.84	2	4.84
Physical Education & Dance	35.24	5	30.24
Physics	20.28	3	17.28
Policy Studies	7.43	1	6.43
Political Science	21.61	1	20.61
Professional Studies & Fine Arts	2.94		2.94
Psychology	53.511	5	48.511
Public Administration & Urban Studies	23.03		23.03
Public Health	21.77		21.77
Recreation	8.6	9	-0-
Religious Studies	6.7	8	-0-
Sciences College	5.79		5.79
Social Work	30.64		30.64
Sociology	23.48	7	16.48
Spanish & Portuguese	25.65		25.65
Special Education	7.67	2	5.67
Speech Communication	19.67		19.67
Teacher Education	46.42		46.42
Telecommunications & Film	14.29	4	10.29
Women's Studies	6.5		6.5

As noted earlier, the president took it upon himself to designate the departments for abolition, in which, he said, he was guided by the criteria adopted by the Senate: (1) quality, (2) centrality, (3) curricular and community need, (4) diversity, (5) program size, and (6) cost (and resource generation) when all else is equal. These criteria might have provided an adequate framework for a rigorous, systematic process of programmatic review by the San Diego State faculty. Their all-embracing character, however, allowed the freest play to justify almost any departmental termination decision. That is, unless one could find departments that fall afoul of virtually all of them—small, peripheral, unneeded, of poor quality, cost-ineffective, and composed of senior white male faculty members—any one criterion could be pointed to as justifying a decision, the others to the contrary notwithstanding, even as the same factor is discounted in a determination in another case.

Health Science, for example, had been slated by President Day for closure in 1979, in the wake of the anticipated consequences of that year's budgetary restraints. It was a small department, engaged in health education, a mission that would appear to have been eclipsed by SDSU's development as a research-oriented institution. But it had extensive community outreach programs—its mission in sex education alone would seem to meet the test of contemporary community need—and two of its six full-time faculty members (not scheduled for retirement) were female.

The various foreign language programs slated for termination (and reduction) were also small and had few majors in contrast to the various ethnic and women's studies departments which were more popular. These, however, were insulated under the rubric of "diversity," even as the Sociology Department's slated deep cuts included Hispanic and black faculty members and the closure of the German and Russian Department involved two junior female members of the faculty.

Astronomy, too, is small, but it suffered no cuts. President Day told the investigating committee that the department represented a heavy investment in equipment, and he felt it to be a "colorful" department, worth protecting on that ground. Aerospace Engineering was larger than Astronomy and, from the perspective of student need, arguably performing a more important function in terms of educating for professional training. It was selected for elimination, however, because the School of Engineering had only four departments, each separately accredited; and, under the policy of "narrow and deep," one had to go.

Anthropology had the misfortune of having recently undergone a regularly scheduled external review, which put the department under the president's eye, and which the president took to indicate an arguable lack of overall quality. That review, however, was not paired with any comparable external reviews of departments not slated for cuts. Nor was the review undertaken with elimination of the department in prospect; it was, rather, an evaluation made in expectation of institutional support and improvement. Far more important, however, the department was heavily staffed by senior faculty. And so it was slated for abolition, even though its offerings were part of the General Education distribution requirements—seemingly meeting the criteria of both centrality and need—and it had over 120 undergraduate majors and fifty graduate students at the time. It would, in other words, seem more central and needed than some smaller departments that were to be touched only lightly or not at all.

As a quick glance at Table III shows, a strict policy of "narrow and deep" had been considerably diluted, given the wide distribution of tenured and tenure-track layoffs. Because the decisions to reduce short of departmental elimination were the product of *ad hoc* bargains between the deans and the vice president for academic affairs, it is difficult to find a consistent rationale for the resulting display of terminations. To the extent that there is one, it can be found in the cost effectiveness of reducing senior faculty. As the president explained the department eliminations in a memorandum to the Senate chair on May 29:

> I have re-studied in detail the potential layoffs from the nine departments affected by the deep-cut strategy. There are two observations. First, of the roughly ninety tenured or probationary potential layoffs, about seventy could take advantage of a "golden handshake." Second, remember that the average annualized salary for a tenured faculty member is roughly 25 percent more than that of a probationary faculty member. If instead of narrowing the majority of the cuts to only nine departments, the same amount of money was spread across the entire campus, it would mean all (about 120) probationary faculty in the entire University would be laid off, plus still having to lay off about fifty tenured in all the departments, and fifty lecturers. If alternatively one were to try to protect the tenured faculty at all costs (i.e., the current across-the-board approach), because of the ratio of tenured to lecturer average salary, to meet this current 8–10 percent cut would remove essentially all remaining full-time and part-time lecturers, all probationary faculty, and still have some layoffs in tenured ranks.

In the words of the former Senate chair, the policy at work was "bodies for bucks," in which the more senior bodies represented the greater savings.

Inasmuch as tenure was to be disregarded—the senior faculty actually to be disfavored—the major constraints upon the administration were two: first, the collective bargaining agreement required that layoff occur by department in inverse order of seniority; second, the deans desired to retain those of the more recently appointed who were deemed especially valued because of research productivity or potential—putting aside the express desire for "diversity."[3] Consequently, deeper cuts in the senior faculty of some departments would protect the more desired junior faculty in others.

---

3. Dean Strand of the College of Arts and Letters, commenting on a draft text of this report that was shared with the principal parties prior to publication, wrote as follows: "I certainly did not 'desire to retain those of the more recently appointed who were deemed especially valued because of research productivity or potential . . .' I was ordered to participate in cuts that were deep and narrow. Under the circumstances, Sociology lost some of the people who the President indicated he was attempting to retain. My point to the committee was that these people would likely have been targeted in an approach that was not deep and narrow, assuming that forty-five positions were to be taken from the College of Arts and Letters. I also do not understand what is meant by '—putting aside the express desire for diversity' in the context in which it is used."

Sociology, for example, had three or four junior faculty members whom the dean determined to be especially valued; once these were cut, as they had to be if Sociology were reduced at all, it seemed only logical to cut much more deeply into that department's senior ranks. So, too, of Chemistry. Dean Short explained that the department had four very promising junior faculty members. But if they were laid off, as they would have to be under the seniority rule, he found it possible to continue them on non-state funds; at that point, it made sense to cut much deeply into the senior faculty of the department to save other more valued junior faculty members elsewhere, for example, the most recent appointee in Geology, who was female (and in consequence of which no reduction was made in that department).

Other decisions were even more questionable. According to Dean Short, Vice President Hopkins told him that because the Day, Hopkins, and Short disciplines were Physics, Psychology, and Mathematics respectively, each of these departments had to absorb at least one cut lest the faculty have the impression that the administration was protecting its own. Vice President Hopkins denied having made that statement, but he did recall telling Dean Short that he believed that cuts could be made in his own department. Those cuts resulted in the loss of two highly valued non-tenured faculty members, who accepted positions elsewhere after having been placed on notice; they represented virtually the entirety of the department's program in Industrial Psychology.

The issuance of the notices of layoff triggered continuing protests, demands for greater faculty consultation and for the institution of alternatives, in the face of which President Day continued to defend his decisions. On June 29, the Senate adopted a motion criticizing the president and his administration and calling for a policy affirming the importance of tenure. In that meeting, the president pledged to postpone the effective date of at least half the announced layoffs. But later that day he wrote to the chair of the Senate:

> Alternatives would: (1) miss the fall layoff needed for the high end; (2) result in doubling-up layoffs in the spring because of insufficient infrastructure at the high end; (3) require—possibly, depending on the kind of consultation—one-year instead of 120-day notices, counted from the end of consultation, instead of June 1992. Worst case, this could be notice not truly effective until June 1994. Again because of insufficient infrastructure at the high end, this would mean making the doubling-up essentially permanent, at least four semesters.

No one regrets the lack of time more than I. But, under time pressure, the prudent budgetary thing to do is always to plan so you can cover the reasonably foreseeable worst, then work back towards the best.

Events moved rapidly thereafter. On July 20, President Day sent a memorandum to the Senate that vigorously defended his decisions on the ground of preserving SDSU's uniqueness, but on August 4, his decision to postpone half the layoffs until January was extended to all the remaining announced layoffs of tenured and probationary faculty. Shortly thereafter the California legislature passed an early-retirement enhancement. More than one hundred SDSU faculty were to avail themselves of this early retirement package, well beyond the administration's estimate that perhaps sixty would do so, and the eventual result was considerably to relieve the 1992–93 budgetary stress.

A note on these early retirements is in order here. Many more senior members of the faculty applied for early retirement than had been expected. Although this was a "voluntary" action on their part, the investigating committee heard from several of these "volunteers" that it was not a positive career choice, but a surrender of tenure to save others in their departments. While the large number of early retirements allowed some departments or colleges to meet the "bills" imposed by President Day's initial budgetary directives, a combination of early retirements and layoffs negatively affected the instructional mission of specific departments as well as the ability to offer a full range of the general studies courses for undergraduates. As of late November, faculty members and department chairs who met with the investigating committee were uncertain if classes and programs affected by faculty losses from the early-retirement program would be continued or curtailed.

C. The September Rescission

As noted in the introduction of this report, an August 27 meeting of the general faculty was held at which a majority of the nearly nine hundred participants (constituting almost three-fourths of the constituency) voted to ask the trustees of the California State University system to declare President Day's position vacant and to select a new campus leader to confront the challenges of a reduced budget. A resolution adopted by the faculty asserted that the president had "irrevocably broken" the trust that must exist between SDSU's administrators and its faculty, staff, and students.

Chancellor Munitz reacted cautiously, saying that he wanted to find out why the process of consulting with SDSU's faculty had apparently broken down. This process, he said, "is in a sense more important than the product because you can't move forward at an academic institution without the faculty having a feel of participation." The chancellor urged the SDSU administration and faculty to discuss and debate the president's decision to give special protection to SDSU's graduate programs. "Do you let some tenured professors go in order to maintain more research-oriented graduate programs for those who remain?" He called on President Day to reestablish "traditional consensus building" on the campus and to base budgetary decisions on wide consultation.

In a major step, taken on September 14, Chancellor Munitz released special funds to SDSU permitting the rescission of all notices of layoff of tenured and probationary faculty members and the prevention of any such layoffs through June 1993. The chancellor stated that "I have encouraged Tom to pull all the [termination] letters." He said that he was doing this in order to cool tensions between President Day and the SDSU faculty: "Undoubtedly there will be layoffs . . . next spring which will be effective at the end of June, but they could be for different professors. That will all depend on a genuine consultative process with the faculty and the burden is now on the administration and the faculty to work together, for Tom to bring the critical core of faculty back into the decision-making process." He added that the rescissions would give President Day and the faculty a half year of "building this academic family . . . and hopefully will wind up with a more healthy sense of togetherness than we've had."

Presidents at other CSU campuses were reported in the press as having complained that the rescissions appeared to reward SDSU disproportionately. Other campuses had severely cut their administration, athletics, and student services in order to preserve faculty positions, and it seemed to them unfair that SDSU made lesser cuts in these areas and still had its senior faculty untouched for 1992–93. Chancellor Munitz commented that "my job is to make sure that the [SDSU] decision-making process has been healthy." At other campuses, he said, "it seems that the process has been healthy."

* * *

IV. An Assessment

* * *

A. The Faculty Role

The constitution of the Senate at San Diego State University recognizes the importance of faculty participation in the key areas of resource allocation and academic program. . . . Until President Day's report to the Senate of May 12, 1992, it could be argued that the spirit as well as the letter of faculty participation was being observed at San Diego State: a restructuring report had been adopted by the Senate as policy in anticipation of future reductions; the president claimed to be acting on the basis of that policy; and the Senate's Executive Committee had declined the president's invitation to undertake a more active role in designating departments for "narrow and deep" cuts. Even so, the faculty body is to be faulted for its failure to extend its work to the procedural aspects of the Restructuring Report and to assert its own role in that regard. That failure, however, is more than matched by the administration's failure to engage the faculty in planning for additional budgetary reductions, the likelihood of which was conceded to the investigating committee by faculty members and administrators alike. In the College of Education, for example, the dean asked the faculty to prepare exercises in how it might respond to reductions of 5 percent, 10 percent, and 15 percent in the college's budget. No similar effort was made on a university-wide basis. As a result of this inaction, SDSU was poorly positioned to respond when the call for further reductions in the budget was issued in May.

At that point, the president's frequently stated reliance on the Restructuring Report, as his asserted carrying out of the faculty's will, claims too much. By every account of those who were then serving on the Senate Executive Committee, including Vice President Hopkins, the reduction to which the Restructuring Report was intended to respond was anticipated on the order of perhaps 3 percent to 5 percent. The assumption was that such a reduction could be dealt with essentially by pruning some marginal programs. As the president put it to us, the assumption was that the pain could be confined to a limited area. The Executive Committee did not contemplate that the approach charted in the report would be taken to respond to a reduction in excess of 8 percent, estimated (with an attendant loss of student fees) at about $11 million.

Even were that not so, by May 18 President Day confronted a Senate squarely set against the application of the Restructuring Report to this changed budgetary situation and hostile to the cuts he planned. Rather than attempt to heal what was by then a rift with the faculty, by abandoning or at least postponing the "narrow and deep" policy and inviting the Senate to join with him in fashioning a short-term policy to deal with the immediate situation, he broke with the faculty and proceeded on his own. The Senate was thus left out of the process, at least until the chancellor's intervention in August.

Nor was the CFA able to fill the vacuum in faculty representation. Relations between President Day and the CFA had never been cordial. The CFA leadership stated to the investigating committee that since certification in 1983 President Day had never personally met with them in their representative capacity, and they pointed out that no formal union grievance had ever been settled at the campus level. However active on the state level—recently, especially in lobbying the legislature with the CSU central administration for an enhanced early retirement law—at the SDSU campus the CFA spoke from the sidelines, as critic and antagonist of the president.

Some members of the faculty stressed to the investigating committee that they did not perceive the local CFA unit as a fully representative body: they claimed that it enjoyed an active membership of less than half the faculty, including the most vocal element displeased with SDSU's development as a comprehensive university. President Day may share this perception, for he emphasized to the committee the need to maintain a strong Senate on a unionized campus. But he was presented with the choice of giving content to that need when the Senate rebuffed his plan on May 18. Rather than heal a rift with his faculty, President Day forced a rupture.

Part of the explanation for President Day's decision may lie in the fact that Vice President Hopkins was relatively new to his position. He lacked a firm base of support in the faculty or among the deans and, unlike his long-serving predecessor, had had no experience in mediating between them and President Day. In the investigating committee's estimation, there seems to have been no voice of influence and independence within the administration to save an insulated president from his own instincts.

The result, in the eyes of many of the faculty members we interviewed, was an effort by the president unilaterally to make (or remake) SDSU in his image. This explanation has superficial appeal, but it focuses too narrowly on the discrete layoff decisions. To be sure, some of the more teaching- and service-oriented programs that President Day scheduled for abolition—Health Science, Natural Science, and Industrial Studies—had been slated by him for elimination back in 1979. But the decisions to abolish other departments were driven, to the extent that one can find any driving factor, by savings pegged to the elimination of senior faculty or, in the case of Aerospace Engineering, by the need to sacrifice a department on the altar of a "narrow and deep" cut. These decisions were made over the period of a few days, largely on the basis of anecdotal evidence of programmatic quality and as the product of catch-as-catch-can consultation. And the decisions short of departmental elimination, those to cut tenured and probationary faculty members (deeply, lightly, or not at all), were the product of *ad hoc* bargains between the academic vice president and the deans. As late as the time of our visit, we encountered faculty members vainly striving to find some pattern, some rationale to explain these decisions, refusing to acknowledge the obvious—and compelling—explanation that they were in a fundamental sense arbitrary, that is, inherently lacking any rationale or coherent governing principle other than as an *ad hoc* response to budget reduction.

If there was a broad vision at work, it is not to be found in the decision to cut so many chemists as compared to astronomers, or so many sociologists as compared to political scientists, but in the larger decision, made unilaterally by the president, to apportion reductions among the various institutional areas according to their then-existing proportions of the budget. It seems to the investigating committee that what President Day strove to protect was less his personal curricular preferences than his image of . . . an institution in which university relations stood on a proportional footing with academic affairs, and which included public broadcasting and major-league collegiate football as part of its portfolio. That vision was seen by the president as not subject to faculty evaluation. As faculty hostility grew, he clung to it even more tenaciously.

*   *   *

B. The Role of Tenure

The 1940 *Statement of Principles on Academic Freedom and Tenure,* jointly drafted with the Association of American Colleges and now endorsed by over 150 educational and disciplinary societies, sets out the reasons for academic tenure:

> Tenure is a means to certain ends; specifically: (1) Freedom of teaching and research and extramural activities and (2) a sufficient degree of economic security to make the profession attractive to men and women of ability. Freedom and economic security, hence, are indispensable to the success of an institution in fulfilling its obligations to its students and to society.

Drafting against the background of the Great Depression, the presidential and faculty negotiators of the 1940 *Statement* were intimately familiar with the discharge of faculty members ostensibly justified on budgetary grounds. Termination of tenure was to be allowed in the case of "financial exigency," but the exigency had to be "demonstrably bona fide." The idea of "demonstrable bona fides" drew from the predecessor 1925 *Conference Statement on Academic Freedom and Tenure,* which allowed for the termination of tenured appointments because of "financial exigencies," but provided that such action should be taken "only as a last resort." A prime mover of the financial exigency clause of the 1940 *Statement,* President Henry C. Wriston of Brown University, explained the provision in similar terms to the Association of American Colleges in 1939: "The displacement of a teacher on continuous appointment should not be merely an 'economy move' but should be done only because of a genuine emergency involving serious general retrenchment. . . ." Consistent with this legislative history, the AAUP's own gloss on the 1940 *Statement,* contained in its *Recommended Institutional Regulations,* defines a "financial exigency" as an "imminent financial crisis which threatens the survival of the institution as a whole and which cannot be alleviated by less drastic means." Participation by the faculty is required, in part to ensure that "all feasible alternatives to termination of appointments have been pursued" and in part to determine the allocation of program reductions.

In May 1992, San Diego State University's financial condition could have been alleviated without the wholesale termination of the appointments of tenured members of the faculty. Nor did President Day claim that it could not. On the contrary, in the president's view adherence to tenure was feasible—as it had been on the other CSU campuses—but would have posed an obstacle to other institutional ends which to him were more deserving. "I am painfully aware," he said to the General Faculty on August 27, "of the meaning of tenure, and of its historical and symbolic importance." But he was even more painfully aware of the choice he claimed that the budget presented: "[M]aintain the traditional posture of defending tenured faculty—*in all parts of the University, at any and all costs*—or protect our SDSU unique programs, our personnel flexibility, our recent diverse hires." [Emphasis added.]

. . . A question that needs pursuing here is whether the operational significance of academic tenure, as the profession has long understood it, posed the stark dichotomies that President Day chose to put forth, and whether his policies achieved the more desired ends he stated.

President Day set tenure against SDSU's "unique programs," presenting his argument more fully in a memorandum to the Senate dated July 20:

> Protecting our infrastructure, and protecting our graduate programs, special lecturers and recent and diverse hires, has resulted in SDSU's response being quite different from most other CSU campuses, even though we got proportionate cuts. These differences have been made much of in the recent barrage of flyers over the past weeks, as if there were some mystery. But there is no mystery. We all have known what we are about here at SDSU. Other

campuses have stripped their library, and acquisitions, computers, equipment—not just temporarily, but permanently. And, they are now stripping all of their remaining lecturer and few graduate/teaching associate positions. Only SDSU, for twenty years or more, has supported its uniqueness in graduate programs and other special programs with a significant number of lecturer positions as graduate/teaching associates. We have been protecting these, and last year even had them removed from the bargaining unit for that very reason.

San Diego State University could easily be just like those other campuses. It would not have joint-doctoral, special master's degree, or other cutting-edge graduate programs; nor could it hope to keep the world-class recent and diverse tenured and probationary hires which work so closely with those graduate programs; nor attract, as in the fiscal year ended, more than $60 million in sponsored support of faculty scholarship and research—in a year which was one of the worst in Washington for such money, our faculty competed successfully to a record high, almost half of all CSU campuses combined. If we gave up these differences, and our carefully guarded infrastructure, we would no longer be the unique kind of teacher-scholar university it has taken so long to build. We would be a large collection of tenured departments, essentially a tenured-in university, with no special programs, nothing to attract new people, no significant support from federal, state or community sources, with a tiny Foundation just like other campuses. And, the only way to rebuild in the years of budget constraint still facing us, would be through retirements from a pool already significantly depleted prematurely, so no vibrant flow of different and new people would be possible; and those remaining would have no modern infrastructure.

The Association's *Recommended Institutional Regulations* (RIR) recognize that, subject to adequate safeguards, programs may be abandoned in consequence of a *bona fide* financial exigency, presumably including programs that are more tangential than others to the institution's particular (or "unique") mission. Before that is done, however, the faculty first must scrutinize all other sources of revenue (such as the manner in which the SDSU Foundation was utilized) and all other areas of expenditure—including athletics, public relations, public broadcasting, the salary lines accorded to other budget areas, and "infrastructure." It is well to remember that some non-instructional costs are necessary if an institution is to function at all—student records and fees must be processed, buildings and equipment have to be maintained at a minimally acceptable level, security must be afforded—and that at SDSU some cuts in the non-instructional budget were made. But the faculty at SDSU was never afforded opportunity to assess these larger choices. Because those areas were walled off by the president, it is impossible to say how much of SDSU's "uniqueness" would have been lost had the administration attempted to take the institution's tenure obligations seriously. The investigating committee sees it as far from obvious that a university needing to reduce a budget of $173 million by 8 percent must, as a consequence of tenure, abandon virtually every instructional and research program that makes the institution "unique."

Tenure under the 1940 *Statement* is not purchased "at any and all costs." Nothing in life, not even life itself, is saved at all costs. But tenure does impose a stringent review of all other areas of expenditure on the responsible belief that the highest priority in any serious general retrenchment is the preservation of the academic program. President Day foreclosed that review at San Diego State.

The President also set tenure against retaining "diversity," meaning not intellectual (or even disciplinary) diversity but primarily the retaining of faculty members on grounds of their race, ethnicity, or sex. This potentially presents some difficult questions: first because the Association's *Recommended Institutional Regulations* acknowledge "affirmative action" as a consideration of educational policy that an institution can take into account in determining where within the overall academic program terminations of appointments may occur; and second, because the elaboration of that acknowledgment seems to the investigating committee fraught with educational, moral, and even legal issues that the Association has not fully explored. But in this instance we need not teach the claim that "diversity" is a greater good which trumps tenure. We would have to deal with it had it been a governing principle at SDSU, but it was not. A significant number of women were in fact scheduled for termination of appointment as a result of the decision to terminate a female-intensive department such as Health Science and Family Studies, and there were a number of women and minority-group members scheduled for termination of services in consequence of other cuts, such as those in sociology. In the context of the fundamentally arbitrary nature of the discrete termination decisions, "diversity" served as an adventitious consideration: proclaimed as policy, but operational only on occasion. The consequence is reflected in a letter to the investigating committee from a professor of Mexican-American Studies, arguably "saved" by the policy: "[President Day's] reasoning about diversity," he wrote, "has created a climate of distrust and resentment toward ethnic studies and faculty of color which has divided the campus like never before."

President Day likewise set tenure against "recent hires," the "seed corn" of the institution. In a retrenchment, the tenured, those who have passed a probationary period and have been determined by the institution to warrant a presumption of continuing professional competence, are not to be displaced in favor of the nontenured, those who are on probation and who have not established any such continuing presumption. President Day, in seeking to displace the tenured in favor of retaining the non-tenured, inverted the presumptions. A policy driven by the same cost considerations, to terminate appointments of the most highly paid faculty as a response to a financial crisis, was condemned on educational grounds by the Association shortly after the 1940 *Statement* was adopted.² A similar approach would today implicate the additional civil concern for impermissible discrimination on grounds of age.

Finally, President Day set tenure against the catch-all claim of "flexibility." And here he had it exactly right. Tenure *is* a limit on the institution's ability to adjust to a reduced budget in any way it seeks. The presidents and faculty members who drafted the 1940 *Statement* thought the limit to be necessary to the other ends adverted to at the outset of this section. How the disregard of tenure requirements at SDSU affected those ends will be taken up at the close of this report, in our discussion of academic freedom.

*   *   *

C. Due Process

Under the Association's recommended standards, a faculty member whose appointment is terminated for reason of financial exigency is entitled to a hearing before a faculty committee. The issues to be heard might include:

> (i) The existence and extent of the condition of financial exigency. The burden will rest on the administration to prove the existence and extent of the condition. The findings of a faculty committee in a previous proceeding involving the same issue may be introduced. (ii) The validity of the educational judgments and the criteria for identification for termination; but the recommendations of a faculty body on these matters will be considered presumptively valid. (iii) Whether the criteria are being properly applied in the individual case.

The Association is not alone in recognizing the utility of such a hearing. In 1981 the United States Court of Appeals for the First Circuit observed with respect to the termination of faculty appointments because of program discontinuance, that the persons displaced should have an opportunity to be heard as to "the authenticity of the reasons asserted by the institution

5. "Academic Freedom and Tenure: Adelphi College," *AAUP Bulletin*, October 1941, pp. 491–517.

for the termination of the faculty member's position and as to the reasonableness of the standards employed to single his position out for elimination."[8]

At SDSU, the collective bargaining agreement supplies the sole and exclusive method for resolution of disputes arising out of "issues covered by" the agreement. Arbitration is afforded on the threshold question of "lack of fluids," but, for the reasons just discussed, the nature of that inquiry may be very different from the showing required to justify a termination on grounds of financial exigency. Moreover, under the bargaining agreement there seems to be no opportunity for a faculty member to be heard on the validity of the criteria utilized to single him or her out for termination of appointment on or whether the criteria were fairly applied. The need for such review is underlined by these events, for we have concluded that the actual decisions to designate the individuals for layoff could not meet a test of reasonable standards evenly applied.

* * *

E. Academic Freedom

The 1940 *Statement* advances tenure not as a special protection that attaches to the longer serving, as a species of seniority, but as an instrument that serves to secure academic freedom and to induce the most promising to the profession. . . .

It is unsurprising that in the wake of the disregard for the protections of tenure at SDSU charges of violation of academic freedom have been made: that intramural vendettas were settled, that departments were singled out for deeper cuts to reach outspoken critics of the administration. We have not attempted to assess these charges. We suspect, given the manner in which the decisions were made, that the allegations cannot be proved. Nor, for that same reason, can they be disproved. The disregard of tenure has placed the administration under a cloud of suspicion which, by the very methods it employed, cannot be dispelled; and that fact has contributed significantly to the atmosphere of distrust on the campus. We are concerned in consequence that it will be difficult to involve members of the faculty, in committees or in the Senate—to get the benefit of their candid views—when they sit with and are expected critically to analyze the positions advanced by an administration which claims and has exercised a largely unconstrained discretion to eliminate their positions.

8. Jiminez v. Almodover, 650 F.2d 363, 369 (1st Cir. 1981).

It is less easy to gauge the impact on would-be entrants to the profession or on the more junior among the faculty at SDSU, the "seed corn" for whom President Day professed solicitude, but among the communications directed to us subsequent to our visit is a letter from a nontenured faculty member that we found revealing:

> What is it like to work as a junior faculty member under . . . [existing] conditions? Here, at least, intentions speak louder than words. Of the half dozen or so junior faculty members across campus I know personally, virtually all of them are actively seeking employment elsewhere. One has already left academia (her case in particular represents the tragic and entirely preventable loss of a superlative teacher). For almost all of us, our primary motive for re-entering the job market is the feeling that SDSU is no longer a safe place to live one's academic life. We have all reached the painful conclusion that cultivating and maintaining a political stance harmonious with, or at least not antagonistic towards, the present administration will make a significant difference to our promotion, tenure, and ultimate retention as faculty members. . . . To be a junior faculty member at SDSU is to feel cheated of one's vocation as a teacher and researcher by an administration whose daily actions denigrate both.

The writer has permitted the investigating committee to publish this excerpt only upon an assurance of anonymity.

* * *

Comment: Bennington College Revisited

The San Diego State report explores the role of tenure (and of the faculty) in efforts to deal with financial stress. No more need be said here on its account. But reconsider the Bennington College case, set out in Chapter 1. Bennington's rules allowed the trustees to terminate the "presumptively tenured"—those on five-year renewable appointments—if "financial exigency or a change in educational policy requires the elimination" of the position. The investigating committee doubted that Bennington's financial condition, serious as it was, justified *all* the actions it took, which the investigating committee characterized as "abrupt, excessive, inhumane, and profoundly procedurally flawed." But the committee reserved separate criticism for the emphasized feature of the college's policy that allowed a "change in educational policy" to be a condition of discharge. Assume for the moment that the college's redefinition of the positions in dance (to "professionally active choreographers"), in the visual arts (to "professionally active visual artists"), and in literature (to "professionally active writers of fiction, nonfiction, poetry or drama whose creative work is ongoing, whose work is published and reviewed, and whose work is addressed to the public at large beyond professional colleagues") worked a defensible change in "educational policy." Even so, the redefinition was instituted without faculty participation; and those affected by it were denied any way intramurally to contest the policy. But more important, the pattern of decisions lent weight to the conclusion that what was claimed to be a "change in educational policy" was a thinly veiled purge of dissident faculty; that is, the very abuse tenure was designed to prevent.

Jimenez v. Almodovar

(United States Court of Appeals for the First Circuit, 1981)
Wyzanski, Senior District Judge

* * *

[Marcia L. Garcia-Feliciano, Raul E. Medina Jimenez, and Jorge H. Garofalo Pastrema were tenured professors in the University of Puerto Rico, teaching physical education at the university's Humacao University College.]

* * *

On July 19, 1978 the current president of the university—the defendant Ismael Almodovar—wrote to each of the aforesaid three persons identical letters having the following text:

At a meeting held on 11 July 1978, the Council on Higher Education decided to inactivate the Associate Degree Program in Physical Education of the Humacao University College. This decision results from a series of factors, among them, the slight enrollment which has been benefiting from the program, the evaluation of the program recently carried out and the recommendations of the Department's Director and of the College, Dr. Federico Matheu. As a result of the recent action, it is necessary to eliminate three of the five teaching positions of the Physical Education Department at the Humacao College, since the teaching activity in that Department will be reduced to one of services to the other teaching programs of the College.

I am sorry to inform you that, after taking various objective factors into consideration, one of the positions to be eliminated will be the one currently occupied by you. As a result of this programmatic reduction we must do without your services as part of our College's teaching staff as of 15 August 1978.

As was determined by the Council on Higher Education itself, we have

From 650 F.2d 363 (1st Cir. 1981).

communicated with the chancellors and directors of other institutional units with offerings in the field of physical education to explore the possibility of relocating in one of the units of the University System, with reference to those programs' needs, the professors harmed by this action. Should any such possibility turn up, we will communicate with you immediately. With the purpose of allowing us to offer the directors and chancellors information about you I would be obliged, if you think if convenient, that you send us your "curriculum vitae."

Each of the two teaching positions of the Physical Education Department which were not eliminated was held by a professor senior to the three recipients of the aforesaid letter.

The plaintiffs do not question that the university in reducing the number of professors in the Physical Education Department acted in good faith, exclusively for the reasons stated in the July 19, 1978 letter, and without any motive or intention to dismiss the plaintiffs on "personal grounds"—a term here used to include not only dismissals for cause, or for fault, or for deficiency of any kind, but also to include dismissals reflecting any superior's personal attitude toward a plaintiff or any other individual.

Nor do the plaintiffs question that if eliminations were justified, the university, in selecting for elimination the plaintiffs rather than the two professors who were not eliminated, acted in good faith, on the basis of an appropriate standard of seniority of service and not on "personal grounds," as above defined.

On July 26, 1978, the plaintiffs were given an informal hearing by Mr. Pedro Juan Barbosa, assistant to President Almodovar, whom the president, being ill, had designated as his representative for the hearing. Mr. Barbosa informed the plaintiffs that seniority was the only criterion on which the president had based his decision. He also invited them to set forth any grievances or challenges they might make against the decision under which their employment would terminate on August 15, 1978. None was raised by the plaintiffs at that time.

The plaintiffs have never appealed from the president's July 19, 1978 decision effective August 15, 1978 eliminating their positions and terminating their employment. It is inferable that they knew that such an appeal was available because, to the knowledge of plaintiff's counsel, their colleague Maria L. Garcia-Feliciano appealed . . . the decision against her to the Council on Higher Education. The Council has ordered a full evidentiary hearing of her appeal before a hearing examiner . . . but, in accordance with a stipulation of the parties, the Council stayed the hearing pending the outcome of the present action.

Meanwhile, President Almodovar had been seeking to secure positions within the university for the plaintiffs. On July 19, 1978, the very day he transmitted to the plaintiffs and Maria L. Garcia-Feliciano the termination letters, the president directed to each of the chancellors and directors of the other university colleges within the university an inquiry as to whether any position was available for any of the three professors being eliminated. The president pursued these inquiries by telegrams sent at a later date.

On August 2, 1978, the Aguadilla College of the University of Puerto Rico employed Maria L. Garcia-Feliciano, who was senior to the plaintiffs, at the same rank and salary she had enjoyed at Humacao University College.

On September 6, 1978, the president offered both the plaintiffs the only teaching position then available at the Carolina Regional College of the University of Puerto Rico. At the same time, the president offered to the plaintiff Medina Jimenez, and later offered to the other plaintiff, Garofalo, an administrative position at Humacao University College. Medina Jimenez accepted effective October 2, 1978 the teaching position at Carolina Regional College, with the same rank and salary he enjoyed at Humacao University College. He still holds that position. He has also received retroactively to August 15, 1978 his salary. The other plaintiff, Garofalo, did not accept any position then or later.

On April 5, 1979, the president of the university offered plaintiff Medina Jimenez a teaching position in Humacao University College—a position which was in every respect similar to the one had previously held in that college, including tenure and rank, plus an administrative, tenured position as the administrator of the new sports facilities in said college. The president offered plaintiff Garofalo the position occupied by plaintiff Medina Jimenez in the Carolina Regional College "that will be left vacant by the latter in case he accepts the offer made to him." Both positions were to be occupied immediately, retroactively as of April 1, 1979. On August 11, 1979, Medina Jimenez declined the offer made to him, so the Carolina position did not become available to Garofalo.

On July 28, 1978, the plaintiffs filed in the district court a complaint alleging that the defendants had taken their property without due process of law . . . and seeking an injunction ordering the defendants "to continue the plaintiffs in their posts as tenured teaching staff of the University of Puerto Rico" and a payment of "their back salaries in full." Without a jury, the district judge heard the evidence, made findings, and dismissing the complaint, entered judgment for the defendants.

The plaintiffs appealed. Inasmuch as there is no significant difference in the status of the plaintiff Medina Jimenez and the plaintiff Garofalo, we shall, for convenience, hereafter address the opinion principally to Medina Jimenez's case and to his claim that the defendants deprived him of his property. . . .

Medina Jimenez's principal contention is that the defendants deprived him of his *property* rights under Puerto Rican law, including his right under 18 LPRA §613(c) not to be deprived of his position without a hearing in which charges are preferred and he has an opportunity to defend himself. We do best to reach that contention against a broad background.

Such property rights as Medina Jimenez has were created by the law of Puerto Rico, not by the United States Constitution. *Board of Regents v. Roth,* 408 U.S. 564, 577, 92 S.Ct. 2701, 2709, 33 L.Ed.2d 548 (1972); *Perry v. Sindermann,* 408 U.S. 593, 601, 92 S.Ct. 2694, 2699, 33 L.Ed.2d 570 (1972). It having been stipulated that he is a "tenured professor of the University of Puerto Rico," we shall assume that he had property rights of which he cannot be deprived without the process of law. *Perry v. Sindermann, supra.* But those property rights were only sketchily outlined by the express terms of the July 1, 1977 contract letter. . . . There is an obvious need to fill in this outline with implied terms and conditions of employment.

*   *   *

American courts[5] and secondary authorities[6] uniformly recognize that, unless otherwise provided in the agreement of the parties, or in the regula-

5. Members of faculties of *private* universities who have been dismissed because of an elimination of positions on account of *bona fide* changes of academic program, or on account of financial exigency, or both, were denied *contractual* claims in *Krotkoff v. Goucher College,* 585 F.2d 675 (4th Cir. 1978); *Browzin v. Catholic University of America,* 527 F.2d 843 (D.C. Cir. 1975); and *Scheuer v. Creighton University,* 199 Neb. 618, 260 N.W.2d 595 (1977). Members of faculties of *public* universities dismissed on similar grounds were denied both their contractual and their constitutional claims in *Bignall v. North Idaho College,* 538 F.2d 243, 246 (9th Cir. 1976) and *Johnson v. Board of Regents,* 377 F.Supp. 227 (W.D. Wis. 1974), aff'd without opinion, 510 F.2d 975 (7th Cir. 1975).

6. A comprehensive and carefully analyzed treatise containing leading cases and other relevant material has been recently published. H. T. Edwards and V. D. Nordin, *Higher Education and The Law* (Institute for Educational Management, Harvard University 1979), see particularly pp. 220–288. *See also* Commission on Academic Tenure in Higher Education, *Faculty Tenure: A Report and Recommendations* (1973); C. Byse and L. Joughin, *Tenure in American Higher Education: Plans, Practices and the Law* (1959), pp. 49–57; authorities collected in *Beitzell v. Jeffrey,* 643 F.2d 870, footnote 8; (1st Cir. 1981); Developments In The Law—Academic Freedom, 81 Harv.L.Rev. 1045 (1968); Matheson, *Judicial Enforcement of Academic Tenure:* An Examination, *50 Wash. U.L.Rev. 597 (1975);* Financial Exigency as Cause For Termination of Tenure of Faculty Members in Private Post Secondary Education Institutions, *62 Iowa L.Rev. 481 (1976);* Peterson, The Dismissal of Tenured Faculty for Reasons of Financial Exigency, *51 Indiana L.J. 417 (1976).*

tions of the institution, or in a statute, an institution of higher education has an implied contractual right to make in good faith an *unavoidable* termination of right to the employment of a tenured member of the faculty when his position is being eliminated as part of a change in academic program. The American court decisions are consistent with the 1940 *Statement of Principles on Academic Freedom and Tenure* widely adopted by institutions of higher education and professional organizations of faculty members. 60 AAUP Bulletin 269–272 (1974). See *Bignall v. North Idaho College, Browzin v. American Catholic University,* and *Scheuer v. Creighton University, supra.* That the institution has an implied right of *bona fide* unavoidable termination due to changes in academic program is wholly different from its right of termination for cause or on other personal grounds is plainly recognized in the following definition of tenure of the Commission on Academic Tenure in Higher Education, *Faculty Tenure: A Report and Recommendations* (1973):

> [A]n arrangement under which faculty appointments in an institution of higher education are continued until retirement for age or disability, subject to dismissal for adequate cause or unavoidable termination on account of financial exigency or change of institutional program. [Emphasis in original omitted.]

The foregoing authorities lead to the conclusion that, unless a Puerto Rican statute or a university regulation otherwise provides, the instant contracts should be interpreted as giving the University of Puerto Rico an implied right of *bona fide* unavoidable termination on the ground of change of academic program.

There are no preclusive Puerto Rican statutes. The plaintiff's reliance on 18 LPRA § 613(c) is misplaced. Section 613(c) provides that:

> "No member of the University personnel whose appointment is of a permanent character may be removed without the previous preferment of charges and an opportunity to defend himself."

The text and the underlying purpose of § 613(c) make it evident that, like comparable state statutes governing the removal of faculty members for cause, § 613(c) is limited to removals based on *ad hominem* or personal grounds which "touch the qualifications or performance of the professor's duties, showing that he is not a fit or proper person to hold the position." *State ex rel Richardson v. Board of Regents,* 70 Nev. 144, 261 P.2d 515 (1953); *Ziegler v. City Manager,* 115 N.J.L. 328, 180 A. 225, 226 (1925). *See* Brown, *Tenure Rights in Contractual and Constitutional Context,* 6 J. Law & Ed. 280, 281–282 (1977). By itself, the use of the word "removed" strongly suggests

that the statute is addressed to a movement of a person out of a position
rather than to the elimination of a position. Of greater significance is the
fact that the procedure prescribed by § 613(c) with its reference to the "pre-
ferment of charges" and the "opportunity to defend" is tailored to the
removal of a person on account of his personal fault or deficiency and is
unsuitable for the resolution of a controversy as to the authenticity of the
reasons asserted by an institution for the termination of a faculty member's
position and as to the reasonableness of the standards employed to single
out his position for elimination. *See Browzin v. Catholic University of
America,* 527 F.2d 843, 847 (D.C. Cir. 1975); Finkin, *The Limits of Majority
Rule in Collective Bargaining,* 64 Minn.L.Rev. 183, 244 (1980). Moreover, it
is a reasonable inference that when the Puerto Rican legislature enacted §
16 of Act No. 135, Laws of Puerto Rico, 1942, and Act No. 334, Laws of
Puerto Rico, 1949, which are the source of § 613 of 18 LPRA, the legislature,
being aware of and intending to preserve the distinction drawn by the
1940 *Statement of Principles on Academic Freedom and Tenure* between a dismissal for impersonal institutional reasons, had a purpose to limit what is
now § 613(c) to *ad hominem* dismissals for cause, or other personal
grounds.[7]

* * *

Having concluded that the university had an implied right of *bona fide*
unavoidable termination of the contracts of the tenured members of the
faculty on the ground of change of academic program, and that such right
could be exercised by a procedure different from the one set forth in 18
LPRA § 613(c), we now consider what procedure the university did afford
the plaintiffs and examine it in the light of the *procedural* aspects of the due
process clause. The plaintiffs, as they presumably knew, had the right to a
hearing by an intramural administrative tribunal[9] which was empowered
to receive evidence, to direct that the university give the plaintiffs employment substantially equivalent to their last employment, and probably to

7. Nothing that we have said implies that § 613(c) does not apply where a faculty member alleges that in bad faith the institution terminated his employment ostensibly because
of a change in program which eliminated his position, but with the real purpose of removing him on personal grounds.

9. The plaintiffs have not suggested that the Council on Higher Education, because it
authorized the termination of the pilot program, was not a disinterested tribunal. If they
had wished to make that point, they could have done so before the Council and, if that
point had merit and did not prevail, the point could have been preserved for adjudication
by a reviewing court. *Bignall v. North Idaho College, supra,* 249.

award damages. . . . The decision of the tribunal was subject to review by a Puerto Rican court which had even greater powers.

That procedure fully satisfied the *procedural* requirements of the due process clause. . . .

*   *   *

A Comment on Program Termination

In terminating the appointments of Medina Jimenez and his colleagues, the University of Puerto Rico did not decide to reallocate resources—less for physical education, more for something else. It decided to do away with a degree in physical education, and in consequence of that decision, fewer faculty would be needed. That decision was not a dismissal for cause requiring a hearing. But because the adversely affected faculty had tenure, the court held due process to be required nevertheless. The same considerations of fairness and accuracy that undergird the need for due process, set out in Chapter 3, apply here as well. The issue to be decided is not just cause for dismissal but rather "the authenticity of the reasons asserted by an institution for the termination of a faculty member's position and . . . the reasonableness of the standards employed to single out his position for elimination." For the need for a hearing on the latter account, see "Academic Freedom and Tenure: Sonoma State University (California)," *Academe* 69 (May–June 1983), treating an effort to manipulate outcomes in a retrenchment by assigning faculty to administratively created "teaching service areas." Such a hearing was available to Medina Jimenez, but neither he nor the other terminated faculty members availed themselves of it or challenged its fairness.

Comments on "Market-Mediated" Tenure

Richard Chait has observed that "even the most sympathetic supporters of higher education will be hard-pressed to defend lifetime appointments that are virtually impervious to dismissal irrespective of economic conditions, revenue shortfalls, or market demand." He has speculated accordingly on the prospect of a closer linkage of tenure to "institutional needs and enrollment levels." What is needed, he believes, is a means to enhance an institution's ability to discontinue select areas *and individuals,* and reallocate positions and resources to accommodate change in student demand.

It also is possible that subsequent to the award of tenure, employment might be contingent on a stipulated student-to-faculty ratio or certain enrollment levels (no layoffs unless enrollments drop 10 percent or more over two years, for example). But some enrollment or capacity measure would trigger dismissals rather than a declaration of financial exigency or program discontinuation *because these concepts have little application to subtler shifts in markets."* [Richard Chait, "The Future of Academic Tenure," *AGB Priorities* (Spring 1995): 11 (emphasis added)]

The proposal could not be taken seriously at any liberal arts college or research university; but it is useful to examine it for that very reason, as well as for what it tells us of the contemporary antagonism toward tenure. First, note the reasoning: Chait sets up tenured faculty as "virtually impervious to dismissal *irrespective"* of revenue. But then he acknowledges that that is not so. A tenured professor *can* be terminated in the event of financial exigency.

He sets up tenured faculty as impervious to "market demand." But then he acknowledges that tenure can be terminated in the event of a bona fide abrogation of a department or a program of instruction, a decision that may well be made in consequence of responsible projections of student interests or societal needs, including long-term shifts in "market demand."

In the third instance only is Chait accurate. Tenure is (and was meant to be) impervious—not "virtually" but actually—to the kind of short-term (or "subtle") shifts in student interest to which Chait adverts. The market is a marvelous mechanism for distributing fish; but the analogy of the student as a consumer of instruction to a consumer of fish will not work.

The imperfections of the market analogy have been laid out from the perspective of the market as a means of maintaining institutional accountability: "A market performs satisfactorily only when customers are well informed." A variety of nonacademic conditions—geographic location, athletic programs, social prestige—play a role in student choice. "Furthermore, it is not condescending to point out that making discriminating judgments concerning the quality and relevance of academic programs is beyond the capacity of most consumers" (Patricia Albjerg Graham, Richard W. Lyman, and Martin Trow, *Accountability of Colleges and Universities: An Essay* [New York: Accountability Study at Columbia University, October 1995], p. 7).

Apropos of the latter observation, a student may not know precisely what courses will and will not prove more or less beneficial in respect to either a general or a specialized education, even after matriculation. Hence the heated faculty debates on the core curriculum, on distribution and degree requirements—debates from which future "consumers" are excluded. No doubt these curricular decisions will affect the prospective student's choice of institution and concentration; but the analogy to the market could not drive a curriculum at the level the proposal requires, of a "spot market" in an individual instructor's offerings, save perhaps in adult or continuing education programs of the kind offered in community colleges.

Putting aside the proposal's mechanical obliviousness of quality (for one would think smaller classes offer a better education than larger ones), and momentarily putting aside the fact that accreditation and licensure requirements as well as the demands of other constituencies affect institutional offerings, we may observe that even an intensely cost-driven institution may have certain centers of excellence it wishes to maintain despite the cost, such as graduate or highly specialized programs that draw few students but that add luster and distinctiveness. In other words, variances from the hypothetical micro-market-managed policy would inevitably be required, lest the institution jeopardize some specialized accreditation, anger important constituents, and terminate some distinguished scholars it wishes to retain. Inasmuch as some faculty with small enrollments would be kept while others with equally small enrollments would be let go, and assuming that those in charge had acted in utmost good faith, the cloud of favoritism—or worse—resulting from these choices would be impossible to dispel. And consider as well the kinds of faculty behavior such a policy would encourage, for if a professor's relation to her institution is to be micro-market-mediated, why should a professor not take the cue and behave accordingly vis-à-vis students, colleagues, and the administration? (See George Stigler, "An Academic Episode," *AAUP Bulletin* 33 [Winter 1947]: 661–665, for a parable on point.)

More important, recall McPherson and Winston's analysis of the economics of tenure in Chapter 4. Why would a person spend years in graduate education, acquiring a specialty in art history, cell biology, welfare economics, or Scandinavian literature, if the prospect of an academic future is to hinge on short-term, possibly evanescent shifts in student interest? If one's academic post is to be micro-market-mediated in that fashion, what would attract the intellectually gifted to the academic life in contrast to a career in business, medicine, or law?

Machlup argued that institutions would have to pay higher salaries in return for the privilege to dismiss faculty more freely; and research suggests that he is right (Ronald Ehrenberg, Paul Pieper, and Rachel Willis, *Would Reducing Tenure Probabilities Increase Faculty Salaries?* National Bureau of Economic Research Working Paper no. 5150) [1995]). But the point here is not what best serves the individual or even the institution; it is rather what best serves society's interest in creating conditions most conducive to scholarship. A 1939 report by a joint investigating committee of the Association of American Law Schools (AALS) and the AAUP observed:

> The concept of academic tenure is an integral part of our academic system and forms one of the main inducements to the pursuit of an academic career. . . . This tradition embodies the conviction commonly held in higher educational circles that scholarship and a high grade of instruction which can only be nurtured by scholarship can best thrive in an atmosphere free from those fears and pressures used to promote production in the business world. This tradition embodies a faith that love of learning and love of teaching thrive under these conditions to such an extent that pressures commonly used in the commercial world are unnecessary as well as harmful. The appreciation of this tradition is so widespread that it affords one of the elementary considerations that justify an academic life. ["Academic Freedom and Tenure: John B. Stetson University," *AAUP Bulletin* 25 (1939): 383–384]

This consideration, however, brings up yet another point of criticism: that tenure contributes to an undue career rigidity, a "one-dimensional vision of excellence" that the joint committee's observation could be taken to exemplify. By adhering to the practice of tenure-track appointments, it has been argued, institutions "have denied themselves ways to make full use of available faculty talent and limited the faculty in exercising their full potential" (American Association for Higher Education [AAHE], "New Pathways: Faculty Careers and Employment in the 21st Century," project description [March 21, 1995], pp. 6, 7). "The idea that a scholar could move to another field and back, or a non-academic setting and back, or switch from a non-tenure-track to a tenure-track appointment, or work as part of an instructional group as doctors do in an HMO . . . these possibilities go against the grain of the dominant cultural assumption of what an academic career should be" (p. 11).

The criticism is congruent with McPherson and Winston's analysis of why, in economic terms, tenure exists: if less specialization were required, more flexibility could be afforded. But if they are right, the AAHE's critique has it back to front: tenure is the consequence, not the cause, of the "dominant cultural assumption" governing an academic career.

George Stigler's "trite as water" observation that specialization is "the royal road to efficiency in intellectual as in economic life" has only been underlined by the exponential growth of specialties since those words were penned in 1950. Nor are teachers distinct from researchers in this regard. The traits of a good teacher, Stigler argued, are competence and intellectual vitality.

> These traits may be acquired by wide reading and deep reflection, without engaging in research and becoming a specialist. But it is an improbable event. It is improbable psychologically: it asks a man to have the energy to read widely and the intellectual power to think freshly, and yet to do no research. He is to acquire knowledge and construct ideas—and keep them a secret. It is improbable scientifically: it asks a man to be competent in his understanding of work that he has had no part in constructing. At least in economics, this is almost impossible. There is no book that states the consensus of the profession on the ideas that are changing—and these are naturally the most interesting ideas. Only the man who has tried to improve the ideas will know their strengths and weaknesses. Scholarship is not a spectator sport. [George Stigler, *The Intellectual and the Market Place*, enl. ed. (Cambridge: Harvard University Press, 1984), p. 16]

For the rare polymath, as adept in musicology as in medicine, the tenure system would not seem to pose an obstacle to "exercising [his or her] full potential." Jonathan Lear, Professor of Philosophy at Yale (and author of two books on Aristotle), is also a clinical associate of the Western New England Institute of Psychoanalysis. Martha Nussbaum, previously Professor of Philosophy, Classics, and Comparative Literature at Brown University, is now Professor of Law, Literature, and Ethics at the University of Chicago. David Epstein, Professor of Music at MIT and an accomplished symphonic conductor (on two continents), works jointly in the brain sciences; his latest book is *Shaping Time: Music, the Brain, and Performance*. And joint appointment in two academic departments is not terribly unusual. What tenure should require in any chosen field is excellence, which is difficult enough to achieve in one.

Nevertheless, the AAHE's suggestion that the academic profession could learn from the way HMOs organize medical professionals is engaging. The analogy is interesting because here, too, the practitioners are often highly specialized, the "consumers" are inexpert and must get the permission of another—the HMO or an insurer—to secure the professional services they seek, and the containment of cost has driven a mechanical policy much like Chait's proposal. The AAHE acknowledges that employment in HMOs has led to an erosion of professional autonomy, but it neglects to explain how it has done so. Marc A. Rodwin has provided an explanation:

> Most health maintenance organizations and a few preferred-provider organizations increase or decrease a physician's compensation depending on the cost implications of his or her clinical choices or the organization's profitability. For example, they may reduce a physician's income if the number of referrals, tests ordered, or other medical choices cost more than the threshold the organization sets. . . . In addition, managed-care organizations simply may not renew a contract with physicians who practice medicine in a manner they consider unnecessarily costly. [Marc A. Rodwin, "Conflicts in Managed Care," *New England Journal of Medicine* 332 (March 2, 1995), pp. 604–605 (references omitted)]

It is altogether possible for professors to learn from employed physicians. But it is also possible that employed physicians could learn from the professoriate. Under these HMO policies, the conscientious physician may be penalized—even discharged—for disregarding her employer's cost-driven commands when they conflict with her best medical judgment of the patient's interests. Because these employed physicians lack tenure with their employing HMOs and, if terminated, may find themselves frozen out of the practice of medicine by insurers, one wonders how free they may be vigorously to question the cost caps set or their application to any significant number of individual patients. Lacking tenure, how willing are these physicians to be outspoken critics of their HMO's policy, or even to be seen as "troublemakers"?

6

Tenure and Retirement

The idea of mandatory retirement at a late but fixed age was long considered compatible with academic tenure; indeed, some people would argue it was an inextricable component of the tenure system. Accordingly, when Congress considered and later enacted an amendment to the Age Discrimination in Employment Act (ADEA) that prohibits mandatory age-based retirement, alarms sounded. Would the prospect of aged faculty clinging to their academic positions until death not inevitably threaten tenure itself? (Judge Richard A. Posner continues to believe that it does, "though probably only at elite universities": Posner, *Aging and Old Age* [Chicago: University of Chicago Press, 1995], p. 357). That question has become a subject of professional scrutiny.

Ending Mandatory Retirement for Tenured Faculty

National Research Council

*   *   *

As a part of the 1986 amendments, Congress directed the Equal Employment Opportunity Commission to ask the National Academy of Sciences to conduct a study analyzing "the potential consequences of the elimination of mandatory retirement in institutions of higher education" (ADEA, 1986, Section 12[c]). The committee's central task—the subject of this report—is to establish whether the special circumstances of tenured faculty in higher education justify a continued exception to the national policy prohibiting age discrimination in employment. . . .

From Committee on Mandatory Retirement in Higher Education, Commission on Behavioral and Social Sciences and Education, National Research Council, *Ending Mandatory Retirement for Tenured Faculty: The Consequences for Higher Education,* ed. P. Brett Hammond and Harriet P. Morgan (Washington, D.C.: National Academy Press, 1991), pp. 1–3.

Although the committee could not avoid the exercise of its judgment in a matter of this complexity, it based that judgment on all the available relevant data it could obtain. The committee reviewed current faculty retirement patterns as well as studies projecting future patterns. The committee also examined college and university tenure, evaluation, and retirement policies. Institutional policies affect faculty retirement patterns, and changes in those policies could provide a basis for responding to the elimination of mandatory retirement. Thus, in order to estimate the costs and benefits of the potential elimination of mandatory retirement, the committee considered whether policies—both institutional and congressional—exist that would mitigate the potential adverse effects of uncapping.

We base two key conclusions on our review of the evidence:

• *At most colleges and universities, few tenured faculty would continue working past age 70 if mandatory retirement is eliminated.* Most faculty retire before age 70. The few uncapped colleges and universities with data report that the proportion of faculty over age 70 is no more than 1.6 percent.

• *At some research universities, a high proportion of faculty would choose to work past age 70 if mandatory retirement is eliminated.* At a small number of research universities, more than 40 percent of the faculty who retire each year have done so at the current mandatory retirement age of 70. Evidence suggests that faculty who are research oriented, enjoy inspiring students, have light teaching loads, and are covered by pension plans that reward later retirement are more likely to work past age 70.

These two conclusions underlie the rest of our conclusions and our recommendations. If mandatory retirement is eliminated, *some research universities are likely to suffer adverse effects* from low faculty turnover: increased costs and limited flexibility to respond to changing needs and to provide support for new fields by hiring new faculty.

An increase in the number of faculty over age 70 or, more generally, an increase in the average age of faculty does not by itself, as distinct from reduced turnover, affect institutional quality. Available evidence does not show significant declines in faculty performance caused by age.

At most colleges and universities, few faculty are likely to work past age 70. *Therefore, eliminating mandatory retirement would not pose a threat to tenure.* Colleges and universities can dismiss tenured faculty, provided they afford due process in a clearly defined and understood dismissal procedure, with the burden of proving cause resting with the institution; however, dismissal of faculty members for poor performance is rare now and likely to remain rare.

In response to larger concerns about faculty performance, the committee recommends that faculty and administrators work to develop ways to offer faculty feedback on their performance. Colleges and universities hoping to hire scholars in new fields or to change the balance of faculty research and teaching interests will need to encourage turnover using mechanisms other than performance evaluation and dismissal.

Retirement incentive programs are clearly an important tool for increasing turnover. They should be considered by any college or university concerned about the effects of faculty working past age 70, including reduced faculty turnover and increased costs. Colleges and universities can target such programs to fields or disciplines in which turnover is most needed, and they can limit participation to control both turnover and costs.

The committee emphasizes that retirement incentive programs and individual retirement incentive contracts must be entered into freely and without coercion, when seen by both the institution and the individual as beneficial. . . .

_____

Faculty Retirement in the Arts and Sciences

Albert Rees and Sharon Smith

*   *   *

The passage of the 1986 amendments was viewed by the higher education community with considerable alarm. Shortly before their passage, the prestigious Commission on College Retirement wrote, "Government intervention to 'uncap' the retirement age would imperil academic freedom since regular performance evaluations of all tenured faculty would become inevitable." Similar statements of concern were made by a number of leading university administrators after the passage of the amendments.

Our principal conclusion is that these statements of alarm and concern have surprisingly little basis in fact. If professors in the future behave as do those in institutions already uncapped under state law, the impact of uncapping will be much smaller than has been anticipated. It is possible that the impact will increase over time, but it should be noted that some of our data come from institutions that have been uncapped for more than a decade. A return to double-digit inflation could magnify the effect of uncapping by raising new fears about the decline of real income in retirement, as could a sustained decline in the stock market, by reducing the value of accumulations in the College Retirement Equities Fund.

In any event, we do not mean to say that the end of mandatory retirement will cause no problems. A single incompetent professor is a severe problem for his or her students, colleagues, and institution. But we find no evidence to suggest that any considerable number of those who choose to stay on beyond age 70 will in fact be incompetent. More important, we believe that the large majority of professors whose work is unsatisfactory will be below age 70, simply because the number choosing to stay beyond 70 will be so small. This conclusion is based largely on the evidence . . . that there is no significant difference in mean retirement age between capped and uncapped public universities or capped and uncapped liberal arts colleges.

This conclusion should hold for most of the institutions in the groups we have studied: doctorate-granting universities and selective liberal arts colleges. It should hold still more strongly for those we have not studied—comprehensive institutions and less selective colleges, where evidence from other studies indicates that retirement ages will be even lower. Nevertheless, there are a few institutions that will have substantial problems: those whose faculty now generally choose to retire at the mandatory age of 70. In our sample, all of these are private research universities. Within this group, they are some of the most prestigious and selective, and are among the few that have not had generous incentive early retirement plans. . . .

One of the sources of concern about uncapping is that it will reduce institutional vitality by producing an aging tenured faculty with less room for new blood. Somewhat to our surprise, we find no support for this concern. In Chapter Three, we have made projections of the age distributions of tenured faculty in the arts and sciences to the year 2004. Making the extremely conservative assumption that there is no growth in the size of the tenured faculty and that the retention rate in the oldest cohorts is 50 percent higher than we now observe in uncapped institutions, we still project a higher proportion of tenured faculty under age 40 in every class of institution. The effects of delayed retirement for part of the oldest cohorts is simply outweighed by other aspects of faculty demography.

Underlying the concern about uncapping is the belief that faculty productivity declines with age after midcareer. In Chapter Four, we have reviewed and extended the evidence on the relationship between age and research productivity, and have for the first time furnished some statistical evidence on the relationship between age and teaching effectiveness. The evidence that research productivity in general decreases after midcareer is very consistent. But research output does not disappear completely late in an academic career. Professors in their sixties still publish, although less than they did before. All this implies that an increase in the number of faculty members in their 70s could lead to some overall reduction in research productivity. It is not clear, however, that this poses serious problems for the universities that employ older faculty members. It is, of course, an important part of the mission of a university to add to knowledge. But individual universities are also greatly concerned with enhancing their prestige as institutions. From this perspective, a faculty member's lifetime research output may be more important than his or her current output. Lifetime output is the basis of reputation, which lags behind achievement, and it is reputation that helps in recruiting graduate students and junior colleagues. A faculty member who is no longer active in research may also still be productively involved in teaching and administration.

The real specter that haunts college and university administrators is that of the incompetent teacher—the aging professor who totters up to the podium and delivers a soporific lecture from notes that have not been revised in twenty years. Our evidence on the relationship between age and teaching effectiveness is much more mixed than that on research productivity. First, age does not seem to be a very large factor in student evaluations of teaching effectiveness. Moreover, the patterns are not the same for different disciplines. Although teaching effectiveness seems to decline after midcareer for scientists, the evidence is mixed for humanists, while for social scientists teaching effectiveness seems to rise in their 60s. This evidence tends to support our view that the number of ineffective elderly faculty members will not be large.

We turn now to some of the specific proposals that have been made for coping with problems that may be created by uncapping. One of these is the suggestion for formal posttenure review. We know of one large university system—the University of California—that uses periodic posttenure review, using much the same standards and procedures that are used for the initial granting of tenure. On one campus where a backlog of reviews had accumulated, sixty faculty members were reviewed in one year, and five of these, all over age 55, were determined to be "grossly incompetent."

Of these, three retired and the possibility of dismissal was being considered for the others.

The California experience makes clear that formal posttenure review can be used to identify incompetent faculty members. However, it also makes clear that the process, if conducted rigorously, is enormously costly in terms of faculty and administrative time. Many institutions will decide that the benefits do not outweigh these costs. In smaller institutions, it seems likely that chairs and deans know who the incompetent faculty members are without going through a formal review process. Although incompetence has always been a ground for revoking tenure, very few dismissals have been attempted. In part this is because the process of dismissal is inherently distasteful, and in part it is because affording the faculty member due process, involving careful documentation of all charges, can be lengthy and costly. The end of mandatory retirement may increase the number of such cases, even absent formal posttenure review. At present, the realization that a 66-year-old professor is incompetent may not precipitate any action by the administration, since he or she will retire anyway in four more years. The prospect that he or she might choose to stay six or eight more years could lead administrators to face the problem earlier.

A step beyond the concept of posttenure review is the proposal to replace lifetime tenure with a series of fixed-term contracts. If the term of these contracts is short, the protection afforded to faculty members by tenure would be seriously eroded, and even long contracts would not fully protect the freedoms protected by tenure. Oscar M. Reubhausen proposes a long-term contract, from twenty to thirty-five years at the option of the faculty member.* But if a faculty member appointed to a tenured position at age 35 is allowed to select a contract of thirty-five years, will the same option be offered to a faculty member appointed to a tenured position at age 50? If not, does not the arrangement itself on its face violate the Age Discrimination in Employment Act?

We are not lawyers, and others more qualified than we are exploring these issues. Our point is a different one. The number of faculty members likely to teach beyond age 70 after uncapping and the number of years beyond age 70 that they are likely to continue teaching do not seem to us

---

*The proposal of Oscar Ruebhausen, a distinguished member of the New York bar and chairman of the Commission on College Retirement, appeared as "The Age Discrimination in Employment Act Amendments of 1986: Implications for Tenure and Retirement," *Journal of College and University Law* 14 (Winter 1988): 561–574. It was replied to by Matthew Finkin, "Tenure after an Uncapped ADEA: A Different View," *Journal of College and University Law* 15 (Summer 1988): 43–60. [Ed. Note.].

to be large enough to warrant in themselves making substantial changes in tenure arrangements developed over a long period of years for an important purpose, protecting academic freedom, and widely accepted in the higher education community. It is not our intention to review here the whole debate over whether or not there should be academic tenure, although we personally favor it. But if tenure arrangements should be changed, it should not be because of the 1986 amendments to ADEA, but for some more fundamental reason.

A third policy suggestion for coping with the 1986 amendments is to replace defined-contribution pension plans with defined-benefit plans, on the ground that absent mandatory retirement, defined-contribution plans offer too large a financial incentive to delay retirement. We noted in Chapter Two that the advocates of this position seem to underestimate the extent to which the defined-benefit plans in present use in higher education offer similar incentives. It is nevertheless true that at moderate rates of salary increase (6 percent or less), defined-contribution plans offer a larger reward for teaching an additional year. We therefore compared the mean age of retirement at public universities with defined-contribution plans and found almost no difference between the two groups. This suggests that the existence of incentives does not always mean that large numbers of people will respond to them. It is true that our results are based on a small sample of institutions. However, we know of no other results that hold the type of institution constant, and unless this is done, no valid conclusion can be drawn from the comparison. We should also note that we did find a defined-contribution pension plan increases the age at which senior faculty say they plan to retire (see Chapter Five).

Defined-contribution plans offer very important advantages both to the faculty member and to the institution. To the faculty member, the advantages include immediate vesting of all contributions and complete portability. Neither of these benefits is available in existing defined-benefit plans, although better ones could no doubt be devised. For the institution, the defined-contribution plan offers the great advantage that the faculty member bears all the investment risk. There can be no such thing as an underfunded defined-contribution plan, while there are large numbers of severely underfunded defined-benefit plans in American industry.

Given our estimates of the probable effects of the 1986 ADEA amendments, we cannot recommend that institutions that currently have defined-contribution plans should terminate them and replace them with defined-benefit plans. We do not see some evidence from our surveys of retirees that defined-contribution plans in some institutions have provided higher retirement benefits than was originally intended. This, of course, can be corrected by reducing the rate of contribution without shifting to a defined-benefit plan. However, to make the plans less generous now could increase the number of faculty members who choose to teach beyond 70.

Let us now return to the case of the few institutions that will confront the possibility that many faculty members will choose to teach beyond age 70. The extreme case in our sample is a private research university where 73 percent of retiring faculty members in the arts and sciences retire at the mandatory age. What can such an institution do if it prefers not to have many of these teach three or four more years We have three suggestions.

The first is that such institutions review the benefits offered to retired faculty and see whether they can be improved at reasonable cost. For example, can the institution afford to guarantee that these professors can keep offices in close proximity to their departments? We can think of nothing more likely to delay retirement for a scholar than the prospect of being relocated to some remote academic Siberia. Do all retired faculty have access to secretarial help and to computing facilities? If not, would better provisions be advisable?

Our second suggestion is that these institutions consider an incentive early retirement plan or a partial retirement plan if they do not already have one, and consider improving these plans if they do. The evidence presented in Chapter Two suggests, though not decisively, that on average such plans reduce mean age at retirement by about a year. We are aware that such plans can be very expensive, and for many colleges and universities they are not worth what they cost. The universities under discussion here may be the exceptions to the rule. . . .

Third, it is our impression, which we cannot document, that the institutions with the highest rates of retirement at the mandatory age are those in which the most senior faculty have the lightest teaching duties, both because a large part of their duties consist of research and because the teaching they do consists largely of graduate seminars or small upper-division course in their fields of specialization. These institutions may want to make sure that teaching duties are equitably shared among faculty members of all ages, with the most senior faculty teaching their fair share of introductory courses. Among its other virtues, such a distribution of duties might improve teaching, since the youngest faculty members, who are the most recently trained, are often the most qualified to teach the most advanced courses, while the most senior faculty have the broad perspectives of their fields and that enrich introductory courses.

* * *

A Comment on Tenure and Teaching Responsibilities

Rees and Smith argue for a more equitable distribution of teaching responsibilities to senior faculty. Indeed, a significant source of dissatisfaction with public higher education has been the assignment of large sections of introductory courses to teaching assistants, some of whom are not fluent in English. Academic tenure limits an institution's ability to assign to a specific individual work that is so demeaning or disproportionate as to effect a "constructive discharge." (See *Patterson v. Portch*, 853 F.2d 1399 [7th Cir. 1988].) But tenure is otherwise unaffected by a general policy of distributing teaching more equitably. As Van Alstyne observed in Chapter 1, an institution is free to decide on its norms for performance and productivity. The "Study on the Accountability of Colleges and Universities" has made just such a recommendation:

> The relatively light teaching obligations of teachers in research universities are meant to provide research scholars and scientists the time they need to pursue knowledge. For academics actively engaged in research, there is never enough time, and their hours free from teaching are fully engaged. Indeed, these academics ordinarily spend more than 60 hours a week on teaching, research, and the myriad activities that go with a distinguished academic career. But even in the best research universities, many faculty are not doing research or pursuing serious scholarship. Most universities provide people who are not doing much research the same light teaching obligations that are properly accorded active researchers. Academics in such universities do not accept—or are not asked to accept—a balance of teaching and research that reflects what they are actually doing. Universities need to develop a more differentiated distribution of labor that reflects the actual work of its academic staff, one that can vary over time as their interests and energies change. [Patricia Albjerg Graham, Richard W. Lyman, and Martin Trow, *Accountability of Colleges and Universities: An Essay* (New York: Accountability Study at Columbia University, October 1995), p. 13]

No mention is made here of tenure because tenure poses no obstacle to such a policy; and some institutions do distribute teaching in proportion to individual research demands.

7

Posttenure Review

Rees and Smith's study in Chapter 6 pointed out that there has been a good deal of discussion and some experimentation with systems of post-tenure review. In 1982 the National Commission on Higher Educational Issues, established by ten presidential associations of higher education, recommended the development of a system of "posttenure evaluation." As a result, a conference was sponsored jointly by the American Council on Education (ACE) and the AAUP at Wingspread, Wisconsin, in which administrators from a variety of colleges and universities, faculty members, and representatives of higher education organizations and foundations took part. Its consensus statement concludes this chapter.

As will be seen, the refinement of precisely what such a system entails requires a good deal of attention; but at the outset, the apparent assumption behind the recommendation—that once tenure is accorded, all further evaluation ceases—was addressed by Bryant Kearl, then Vice Chancellor for Academic Affairs at the University of Wisconsin at Madison.

Remarks

Bryant Kearl

* * *

I consider it unfortunate that the Commission worded its recommendation on this subject as it did. To advise that universities "should develop a system of posttenure evaluation" is uncomfortably close to asking "when did you stop beating your wife?" If we accept such a recommendation in unedited form, it seems to me that we go much too far toward suggesting that nothing is now being done.

But the fact that the question was posed at all indicates that we have work to do. The question will not go away. Universities cannot afford the

From *Academe* 69 (November–December 1983): 8a–9a.

cost of a public perception that tenure is a shelter for laziness and incompetence and that we are unable or unwilling to correct its abuses.

What kinds of posttenure evaluation do we have in place? I don't believe there is a global answer to that question. Each institution must ask itself what measures it uses and how effective they are. And there will be as many patterns as there are universities.

First, of course, every tenured professor must present himself or herself in public regularly, in the classroom or on the lecture platform or in scholarly or general writing. This is certainly a powerful reviewing force. It may, in fact, be the source of much of our problem, since there are few occupations that involve such extensive and continuing public scrutiny of what a person says and how he says it.

What the critics refer to are more formal types of evaluation, though, and I believe that here, in particular, many of us are doing more than we realize.

At my university (the University of Wisconsin, Madison), we will begin in September the process of allocating a limited number of sabbatical leaves. Provisions of our sabbatical system are legislatively established, and the awards are limited to tenured faculty. Individuals will apply or be nominated at the department level, and departmental executive committees (made up of all tenured faculty) will make selections for submission to the dean. On the assumption that nominations will outnumber the slots available, a faculty committee at the school or college level will make a further screening and the dean, in consultation with that committee, will submit names to the chancellor. Here a final list will be established, giving as much attention to the integrity of departmental and college priorities as possible.

Since all tenured faculty are eligible for such awards, and since faculty members and administration work together at all levels in reviewing the nominations or applications, this is surely a valuable method of posttenure evaluation. True, it takes into account departmental needs as well as faculty desires, but that may give it special additional value.

In October, a similar process is undertaken for faculty development grants. Again the number of awards is small. Departmental and university needs are given more consideration, but the process of shared faculty and administration review is quite similar.

In November, the Graduate School begins the allocation of a relatively large number of grants in support of research. These provide for research assistants, computer time, equipment purchases, data acquisition, released time, and other forms of help. The selection process depends on decisions of a faculty research committee which has organized itself into two subcommittees (social science/humanities and physical/biological science). Administrative input is quite limited, and neither departmental nor college endorsement is necessary for the individual to make application or receive support.

In December, at semester's end, a large share of tenured faculty members get the results of anonymous student evaluations of their teaching. Untenured faculty are subject to student evaluations only every third year, although most do so more often.

In January, most departments require that their faculty members submit some form of "annual activity report," to put on record each person's teaching program, research activities, publications, and public service contributions.

Beginning about in February, departments consider promotions in rank. For tenured faculty, only one promotion takes place, from associate professor to professor. Although most tenured faculty members receive this promotion, the promotional review is taken seriously both within the department and by the dean.

It is the promotion that I think points out most clearly the fallacy in a recommendation that universities "develop" a "system" of posttenure evaluation. One element of such a system is obviously in place at every university; where it is being used casually or perfunctorily, I do not see why anyone would hope that some new form of evaluation will be taken more seriously.

Between February and April, the tenured faculty members in each department review the performance of all faculty members and make recommendations as to merit salary allocations. The initiative is with the department, although there is considerable consultation between faculty and administration.

In mid-March, selections are made for ten to fifteen teaching awards granted annually in May. A few of these are at the departmental or college level. Most are university-wide. Selections are made by a committee established jointly by the executive committee of our faculty senate and the chancellor. This committee usually includes student representation, and the student contribution has been uniformly constructive and valuable. There is no administrative input into or review of the decisions of the committee; hence this represents still another kind of evaluation with different forms of feedback.

In late spring, each department submits an advisory vote as to its preference for department chairman for the coming year. This evaluation is by written ballot, and each "voter" may use different criteria, but somewhere in the voting is an evaluation of past and potential administrative ability and of departmental expectations.

Throughout the year, but most often towards spring, selections are made for a limited number of named professorships or chairs which have been vacated or are newly established. The process will differ, depending on the field to which the chair is assigned and the terms of its establishment, but another careful review process occurs.

Between April and June, selections are made for a wide range of all-university committees. Some of these are elective, some are filled by appointment by the Faculty Senate Executive Committee in consultation with the chancellor, some are chancellor-appointed in consultation with relevant faculty groups. Whatever the mechanism, these, too, represent part of an evaluation process.

In May, at the end of another semester, more student evaluations of teaching are made.

Meanwhile, of course, most faculty members also encounter external evaluation through actions on grant applications they have submitted, response to manuscripts sent off for publication, recognition by or participation in professional societies, response to requests for Fulbright or Guggenheim or similar awards, and even election to such bodies as NAS, NAE, or NAM.

Finally, we do have a regular cycle of five-year reviews of all academic programs, and these shed some light on individual performance of tenured faculty members. Because of the overlap with accreditation visits and other external reviews, the five-year cycle is not followed as carefully as we might wish, but these other reviews, too, offer an evaluation of faculty members.

It is obvious that this mixture of evaluations leans more heavily on the carrot than the stick, although an award withheld has some of the same consequences as other kinds of sanctions.

The strength of such a pluralistic system is the variety of sources of feedback to the individual. There are independent messages—from departmental colleagues, from other faculty members inside and outside the department, from administrators, from students, and from colleagues at other universities. I would be the first to acknowledge that this is not a "system" of evaluation. It is more a program or a process. But I do not like being told that it is vague and unspecific, or that I am unable to describe it in detail. It may not be perfect, but it is not accidental or haphazard, and the person who proposes additions or alternatives must surely accept the burden of proving their usefulness and desirability.

*   *   *

[Consequently, Kearl wondered whether the costs of such a system would be too great.]

First, it requires an inordinate amount of paperwork at the department and college levels and of administrative time further along.

Second, it unquestionably would have a chilling effect on the activities and behavior of faculty. Particularly on top of existing reviews, the imposition of an arbitrary and potentially menacing new evaluation mechanism could not help being resented, doubted, and challenged. My personal opinion is that unless such a scheme were nationwide in its application (a manifest impossibility), it would certainly drive many able faculty members from institutions that demand it to those that do not.

Finally, the more monolithic and formal the review mechanism the less value it is likely to have for self-improvement. There is a great deal to be said for a system that lets a faculty member get frank advice from colleagues, friends, and students without feeling defensive and threatened. This may be particularly true for mature and senior faculty members who have achieved tenure long before; mechanisms that encourage self-improvement are likely to be better in every way than those that seem to be designed as accusation and defense. A formal and legalistic evaluation must be organized with potential legal challenge in mind. Faculty member and administrator became adversaries. The mood is much less likely to be one of "How can I help" than one of "What can I prove—in court if necessary?" Standards and expectations will need to be quantifiable, a difficult process if we are also to promote the creativity that depends on faculty members defining their own problems, setting their own priorities, and working out their own time schedules.

[Kearl also wondered whether the call for posttenure review was a consequence of a degree of laxity in decisions on tenure and promotion. But if so, if these decisions were not made carefully, "what makes us think we would do a better job with formal annual or periodic reviews?" If these reviews were conducted as mechanisms of improvement, however, he admonished the institution to be aware of consequence of their own.]

A university that wants its faculty members to keep abreast of their fields and to upgrade their skills should surely share in that cost. A faculty member who has not used development grants or sabbatical opportunities may deserve censure, but what about a university that has failed to provide them? Surely the cost should not rest on the faculty member alone.

* * *

A Comment on Posttenure Review

Kearl's concluding thought was echoed in an appraisal of the system of posttenure review instituted at the University of Colorado:

> The most useful aspect of post-tenure review at the University of Colorado is, paradoxically, that which has been most neglected. The original purpose of the process was the identification of faculty members whose flagging efforts might be reinvigorated by thoughtfully designed and delivered assistance. The capacity to identify those faculty members is clearly present in the process, but resources have seldom been forthcoming. The potential of the process remains, but specific actions and resources must be implemented for its fulfillment.
>
> Approximately one hundred faculty members undergo post-tenure review each year on all campuses. We estimate that roughly half of those faculty members are, by virtue of promise or need, appropriate candidates for resource commitments for faculty development in such areas as staff assistance, and equipment purchases. Based on the experience of the Boulder campus, which has in the past set aside funds for this use, a mean of $5,000 per faculty member may be predicted, thus suggesting a faculty development fund of $250,000 per year.
>
> Accordingly, we submit the following recommendations:
>
> 1. If post-tenure review is to be pursued, it should be with its original purpose—faculty development—clearly in mind. The process should be revitalized as a tool for continued faculty development, consistent with the academic needs and goals of the university and the most effective use of institutional resources.
>
> 2. In order to achieve this purpose, a resource base of no less than $250,000 should be set aside annually.
>
> 3. Universal and thorough feedback of the results of post-tenure review should be provided faculty members through conferences with their dean and/or review committee, and by a written report and recommendations in every case.
>
> 4. Consistent with the original policy statement, external reviews should be permitted in any case, and required when there is a difference of opinion or when the faculty member or a member of the review committee requests them.
>
> 5. The Office of the Vice President for Academic Affairs should continue its efforts to develop and sustain a clear definition of excellence in faculty performance. Any such definition should take into account teaching, research, creative work, and service, and consider the different characters and missions of various campuses and departments. In this way, faculty members will come to understand more clearly the university's expectations of them, and the criteria that their periodic review will employ. [Marianne Wesson (Associate Vice President for Academic Affairs) and Sandra Johnson (Director of Policy and Planning), "A Study of Post-Tenure Per Review at the University of Colorado" (1989), pp. 17–18.]

A system of posttenure review designed to identify tenured faculty members whose work could be better advanced—or, as the University of Colorado report put it, "whose flagging efforts might be reinvigo-rated"—is compatible with tenure. However, some people have pro-posed a system of periodic evaluation, which perforce must be tenure-like in rigor, to weed out the incompetent of indolent, as a kind of academic search-and-destroy mission. (See Christine Licata, *Post-Tenure Faculty Evaluation,* ASHE-ERIC Higher Education Reports [1986].) This was the kind of review to which Rees and Smith referred: if "conducted rigorously"—and how else should it be conducted?—it would be "enor-mously costly in terms of faculty and administrative time." And as McPherson and Winston observe in Chapter 4, "it is far from obvious that intensive hierarchical efforts to evaluate and motivate senior fac-ulty in fact make much sense." (It might pay the reader to revisit their assessment.) Rees and Smith's observation may need just a bit of elabo-ration.

Return to the discussion of probation in Chapter 2 and assume that a process that looks much like the one employed in a tenure decision must be undergone by the tenured faculty at, say, five-year intervals, the reviews necessarily being staggered. As a result, four-fifths of the tenured faculty of a department, school, or college (for who else would be competent to conduct such an evaluation?) will be evaluating rigor-ously one-fifth of their colleagues every year for the remainder of their professional lives. Is the cohort of the incompetent or indolent so large, and so difficult otherwise to discern, that such a system would be worth the effort? Ralph Brown and Jordan Kurland observe in a slightly differ-ent context:

> All the handwringing over deadwood is itself remarkably devoid of anything resembling data about the extent of the blight. The present writers have been paying attention for thirty years to controversies about the value of tenure; they cannot recall ever seeing anything resembling a statistic. In fact, the only numerical estimate that they can summon is from Dean Rosovsky's genial appraisal of tenure, based chiefly on his long experience at Harvard. He opines that "the label deadwood would apply only to under 2 percent of a major uni-versity faculty; that is my totally unscientific conclusion." If that is a plausible guess, how many more could be labeled deadwood at universities and four-year colleges that make less demanding re-quirements for tenure? Might we guess 5 percent? The issue whether any small number, 2 percent or 5 percent, justifies undoing the ten-ure system leads to further questions. [Ralph Brown and Jordan Kur-land, "Academic Tenure and Academic Freedom," in *Freedom and Tenure in the Academy,* ed. William Van Alstyne (Durham, N.C.: Duke University Press, 1993), p. 332, quoting Henry Rosovsky, *The Univer-sity: An Owner's Manual* (New York: Norton, 1990)]

"Many institutions will decide, "Rees and Smith observe, "that the benefits do not outweigh the costs."

Kenneth Mortimer and his colleagues also noted several "practical drawbacks" to the use of posttenure review as a means of removing faculty, including "ethical dissonance"—that is, the conflict that results when a review seemingly conducted as a means of stimulating faculty improvement is actually used "summatively as grounds for termination." (In law, that kind of "ethical dissonance" is called "deceit.") They commended the "summative" use of posttenure review nevertheless to increase "the rate of departure of currently tenured faculty." Institutions' reluctance to institute such systems, they concluded, stems from faculty resistance: "The apparent reluctance of institutions to use posttenure review for dismissal on grounds of incompetence underscores the relatively privileged position of the individual tenured faculty member when institutions seek to reduce expenditures or reallocate resources." (Kenneth Mortimer et al., *Flexibility in Academic Staffing,* ASHE-ERIC Higher Education Reports [1985], pp. 42, 41). But the proposal has less to do with resource allocation than with making it easy to dismiss tenured faculty without a hearing, to increase their "rate of departure."

The picture of resistance by entrenched privilege to a beneficial policy change, unbecoming though it be, would be understandable if it were accurate. But the ethical basis of resistance has to be measured by what is being resisted. Not any further evaluation after tenure is awarded, for, as Bryant Kearl's remarks make clear, evaluation is the very stuff of academic life. Nor is "ethical dissonance" the crucial problem, for the institution could readily remove that difficulty by making it perfectly clear that the purpose of the periodic evaluations was to search out and eliminate incompetent faculty. What tenured faculty members resist is the "summative use" of periodic evaluations for that purpose. Mortimer and his colleagues think that use beneficial. But one is hard pressed to square such a "summative use" with the very idea of tenure, which, as William Van Alstyne explained, works a shift in the presumption of competence.

Recall that in a termination of a tenured professor for cause the burden of proof rests with the administration to show that the faculty member is unfit for office. In such a case, the "evidence" accumulated in the periodic reevaluation process (student testimony, reviews of published work by external referees, and the like) would presumably be relevant to the incumbent's fitness or competence, to be decided in a hearing. But "the fact of a negative evaluation could not itself be 'cause' to discharge. Were a system of posttenure review devised to make a negative evaluation 'cause' for dismissal, it would, in practical effect, substitute periodic evaluation for a dismissal hearing and would be indistinguishable from the abolition of tenure and the adoption in its stead of a system of periodic appointments" (Matthew W. Finkin, "The Tenure System," in *The Academic's Handbook,* ed. A. Leigh DeNeef and Crawford D. Goodwin [Durham, N.C.: Duke University Press, 1988], pp. 97–98). Would not a system of "summative use" pose the same potential threat to academic freedom that a lack of a firm tenure system implicates? Consider whether Kingman Brewster's observation, made in a different context, takes on added significance in this one:

> I think that even with their privileges and immunities our academic communities are often too timid in their explorations. The fear of failure in the peerage inhibits some of our colleagues, even when they do have tenure. Too many seek the safe road of detailed elaboration of accepted truth rather than the riskier paths of true exploration, which might defy conventional assumptions. Boldness would suffer if the research and scholarship of a mature faculty were to be subject to periodic scorekeeping, on pain of dismissal if they did not score well. Then what should be a venture in creative discovery would for almost everyone degenerate into a safe-side devotion to riskless footnote gathering. ["Report of the President," Yale University, 1972]

Statement of the Wingspread Conference on Evaluation of Tenured Faculty

* * *

1. Along with the Commission, we reaffirm our commitment to academic tenure and the protections of academic freedom it provides. No system of faculty evaluation should be permitted to weaken or undermine those principles.

2. Institutional assessments of the teaching, research, and service programs of departments, schools and other academic units should be made at regular intervals.

3. The performance of tenured faculty members is evaluated on a continuing basis, formal and informal, by their colleagues and students, by their peers in their disciplines at other institutions, and by potential fund-

From *Academe* 69 (November–December 1983): 14a.

ing agencies both public and private; we regard this continuing evaluation as healthy and indeed valuable.

4. The performance of tenured faculty members should be and normally is regularly evaluated by their institutions for some or all of the following purposes: distribution of merit salary increases, promotion, and institutional academic awards such as sabbaticals, research support, and teaching awards. Written descriptions of the purposes, criteria, and methods by which these evaluations are made should be provided to the faculty.

5. Decisions made as a result of these approaches to the evaluation and improvement of faculty performance should not be used as a ground to dismiss tenured faculty. Where grounds for dismissal are believed to exist, informal resolutions of the problem should be pursued first. If these fail, then existing due process procedures can be employed.

8

The New Criticism

The case for tenure rests on two grounds. In the words of the 1940 *Statement,* "Freedom and economic security, hence, tenure, are indispensable to the success of an institution in fulfilling its obligations to its students and to society." The importance of economic security is discussed by McPherson and Winston, and at various points elsewhere in this book. But as Machlup argued, the case for tenure rests equally on the necessity of freedom. The early critics of tenure saw this connection clearly: the AAC resisted tenure in 1917 because of the claim to academic freedom it buttressed. Recent criticism has been more discriminating. It is captured rather nicely by Richard Chait in "The Future of Tenure," *AGB Priorities* 1 (Spring 1995).

Pointing to "high-profile controversies about 'political correctness' " on campus, Chait argues, first, that the "forcefulness of the academic freedom argument has been weakened by the habitual and often successful resort to litigation by faculty who contend their right to unfettered expression has been abridged"; and second, that the connection (at least in the public eye) claims too much: "Especially with respect to matters of 'political correctness,' many trustees, legislators, and citizens believe academic freedom actually *enables* faculty to offer unsubstantiated conclusions and pernicious perspectives with utter impunity. In other words, were it not for academic tenure, professors would have to be *more* intellectually rigorous and *more* professionally responsible" (p. 3; emphases in original).

To modern critics tenure is at once unnecessary to ensure freedom and too protective of its exercise. Let us examine each claim in turn.

"Tenure is unnecessary because the law adequately protects academic freedom"

In support of this proposition, Chait cites the court-ordered reinstatement of Leonard Jeffries (removed as a department chairman because of remarks on Jews in a public speech) at the City University of New York (CUNY). He cites also a "professor at the University of New Hampshire, whose language in the classroom was regarded by some women to be offensive and tantamount to sexual harassment," and who likewise was "awarded reinstatement and damages" by a federal court. "Decisions such as these," Chait argues, "persuade the public that to ensure academic freedom, professors do not need an additional layer of protection above and beyond the judicial system."

What is claimed is that inasmuch as the First Amendment adequately protects academic freedom, no additional protection is needed. It is a "new" argument in the sense that it postdates the 1940 *Statement,* for it was not until 1968 that the United States Supreme Court held that public employees can claim the protection of the First Amendment at all. Putting aside the fact that the First Amendment is inapplicable to private institutions, the arguments rests on the assumption that the First Amendment is coextensive with academic freedom. It isn't.[1]

The refinement of First Amendment doctrine by the U.S. Supreme Court makes clear that in order for a public employee's speech to come within constitutional coverage, it must be on a matter of "public concern"—it must fairly be considered to relate to a matter of "political, social, or other concern to the community" at large (*Connick v. Myers,* 461 U.S. 138 [1983]). If it is not speech of that kind, it is unprotected, and so can be a permissible ground for sanction or discharge. But even if it is speech of that kind, it may still be unprotected if the threat to the maintenance of discipline by superiors or to "harmony among coworkers" is sufficiently great. In *Waters v. Churchill* (114 S.Ct. 1878 [1994]), a plurality of the justices made clear that a public employer could fire an employee for speech on the basis of the employer's "reasonable *belief* of what the employee said, regardless of what was *actually* said." And on this ground the removal of Professor Jeffries from his department chairmanship at CUNY, as a sanction for his public utterance, was more recently sustained (*Jeffries v. Harleston,* 52 F.3d 9 [2nd Cir. 1995]).

What constitution standards apply—whether these or others—to

---

1. The differences were rather fully explored in Walter P. Metzger, "Profession and Constitution: Two Definitions of Academic Freedom in America," *Texas Law Review* 66 (1988): 1265–1322; Matthew W. Finkin, "Intramural Speech, Academic Freedom, and the First Amendment," ibid., pp. 1323–1399; and William W. Van Alstyne, "Academic Freedom and the First Amendment in the Supreme Court of the United States: An Unhurried Historical Review," in *Freedom and Tenure in the Academy,* ed. Van Alstyne (Durham, N.C.: Duke University Press, 1993), pp. 79–154. What follows is a brief rehearsal of these studies.

professional publications or to classroom speech is not yet resolved. Professor Silva was disciplined by the University of New Hampshire for "sexual harassment," in presenting the idea of "focus" in a technical writing class in graphic sexual terms. He sought relief in federal court under the First Amendment and secured a preliminary injunction at the trial court level—not a final judgment, not an award of damages (*Silva v. The University of New Hampshire,* 888 F. Supp. 293 [D.N.H. 1994]). (His case was later settled.) The district court's opinion is altogether congenial to the assimilation of the profession's conception of academic freedom by the First Amendment, drawing on lower court decisions that antedate the Supreme Court's more recent holdings; but another trial court flatly rejected that approach on similar facts, applying the *Connick* test to classroom speech (*Cohen v. San Bernardino Valley College,* 883 F. Supp. 1407 [C.D. Cal. 1995]; now on appeal). Thus the case law is too sparse and conflicting to permit us to conclude that insofar as freedom of teaching in the classroom is concerned, the First Amendment is coextensive with academic freedom; nor is there any case law on professional publications.

But in another area, freedom of intramural criticism of the sort for which Professor Rice and his colleagues were discharged at Rollins College, the law has a well-developed texture: "Courts have held that speech concerning departmental administration and curriculum, the denial of tenure to a colleague, personnel actions, and the reorganization of an academic program, including its accreditation separate from that of the department . . . are unprotected" (Finkin, "Intramural Speech," p. 1326). Note, for example, the reasoning of the U.S. Court of Appeals for the Seventh Circuit sustaining the grant of summary judgment against two faculty members at Indiana University who claimed they were denied tenure because they had written letters to the dean arguing that interpersonal relations in the Sociology Department had so deteriorated as to require an external review of the department:

> In the present case, the employee speech was in the form of letters addressed to University officials. The letters requested an examination of the review process within the Department of Sociology by another committee within the University. The requests were made in the context of a faculty feud. Plaintiffs alleged that the Sociology Department was so divided that individuals' careers, and the effective functioning of the Department, were being threatened. Given these facts, we agree with the district court that plaintiffs' statements are not properly characterized as matters of public concern.
> Plaintiffs contend that their letters were not simply an internal

matter, but revealed that the integrity of the University was being threatened. Exposing wrongdoing within a public entity may be a matter of public concern. . . . However, the record shows that although members of the Sociology Department may have "done wrong" in the sense they had evaluated professors based on their personal affiliations, plaintiffs' letters were principally in an attempt to seek intervention in a clash of hostile personalities. No doubt the public would be displeased to learn that faculty members at a public university were evaluating their colleagues based on personal biases. Nonetheless, the fact that the issue could be "interesting" to the community does not make it an issue of public concern. Plaintiffs' statements reveal that individual biases within the Sociology Department's peer review process may have been present to excess, but they did not attempt to expose some malfeasance that would directly affect the community at large. [*Colburn v. Trustees of Indiana University*, 973 F.2d 581, 586 (7th Cir. 1992) (citations omitted]

It appears from the court's recitation that the academic profession would consider these letters to be well within the scope of academic freedom even though they were not constitutionally protected.

Neither Professor Rice at Rollins College nor the dissident faculty at Bennington could today secure constitution protection—not only because the Constitution is inapplicable to private institutions but because, even if it were, their underlying disputes do not appear to implicate an issue of sufficient "public interest," and because, even if they did, their administrations believed, rightly or not, that they posed a risk of "disharmony." Such are the constitutional tests. Such are not the contours of academic freedom.

Further, it is doubtful, to say the very least, that a trial on a free speech claim long after the faculty member has been dismissed will serve as an adequate deterrent to speech-based reprisals. "[R]etaliation," Cynthia Estlund has pointed out, "is readily cloaked in the guise of arbitrariness, and uncloaking it is likely to be too difficult, too time-consuming, and too costly to offer much reassurance to the typical employee" ("Free Speech and Due Process in the Workplace," *Indiana Law Journal* 71 [Winter 1995]: 102–151).

Her observation highlights the fact that in the absence of tenure there is no prohibition against arbitrary dismissal; without tenure there is no constitutional right to a prior (and proper) hearing on the cause alleged to justify the dismissal. As William Van Alstyne cautioned in Chapter 1:

Even supposing that in many instances a particular charge of professional irresponsibility is neither stated in terms which anyone would claim to raise a question of academic freedom . . . nor that the charge is otherwise suspected of having been brought forward solely

from an ulterior reason which itself relates to academic freedom, still
the need would remain to protect the individual from unreasonable
risks of error and prejudice in the resolution of that charge.

Recall the case of Professor King at the University of Minnesota, set
out in Chapter 3. The administration asserted that he should be dismissed for inadequate performance, a charge he contested. That dispute could not be considered to be a matter of "public concern" under
the Constitution; his case involved no issue of constitutional free
speech. But tenure required the administration to demonstrate the accuracy of its assertions before a fair forum. And recall further the proposed wholesale terminations at San Diego State University set out in
Chapter 5. The tenured faculty, because they had tenure, could have
required the administration to demonstrate in a hearing the "reasonableness of the standards" used to eliminate their departments; that, at
least, is the judicial teaching in the *Jimenez* case (also in Chapter 5). In
the absence of tenure, no such showing would be required; and according to the ad hoc committee of investigation, it is doubtful that any
such showing could have been made. The power to fire without a fair
hearing, Van Alstyne observed, "deserves to be called 'arbitrary' and to
be despised."

"Tenure enables too much freedom"

It is asserted that professors have been allowed to become less intellectually rigorous, less professionally responsible, ostensibly because they
cannot be dismissed save for adequate cause demonstrated in a hearing;
in Richard Chait's words, they "offer unsubstantiated conclusions and
pernicious perspectives with utter impunity."

Have professors departed from the canons of responsible scholarship
in disciplinary discourse, if not by falsifying the evidence, then by dis-
torting it or ignoring relevant evidence to the contrary? Have they
abused the classroom by using it for political proselytizing? We are
given no suggestion how widespread such alleged derelictions are. And
we ought to be cautious, for whether a scholar's publications or teach-
ings are adequately grounded may not be easily determined. (See Edward Shils, "Do We Still Need Academic Freedom?" *American Scholar* 62
[1993]: 194–195.) It is well here also to recall Edward Kirkland's admonition that in the search for truth, much that is false must be assayed:
the miasmic theory of contagious disease was the prevailing wisdom—
with much explanatory power—until transmission by bacteria was
proved. As he observed, "Colleges and universities do not possess or

teach the whole truth. They are engaged in the quest for truth. For that reason their scholars must be free to examine and test all facts and ideas, the unpleasant, the distasteful, and dangerous ones, and even those regarded as erroneous by a majority of their learned colleagues" (Edward C. Kirkland, "Academic Freedom in the Community," in Edgar N. Johnson et al., *Freedom and the University* [Ithaca: Cornell University Press, 1950], p. 119). In sum, this part of the claim implicates professional ethics; and given the need for accuracy and fairness, how should such questions be determined save upon a hearing before a competent and impartial panel?

A larger part of the claim is directed less to acts of academic dishonesty than to conclusions derived through the exercise of professional care that the reader or listener finds profoundly offensive. But the purveying of what to influential groups are "pernicious perspectives"—in religion, economics, morality, or on any of the other issues that fire the passions of the moment—*is* what academic freedom and tenure were designed to protect. If today some professors of "critical legal studies" (CLS) argue that the law's distinction between the public and private works a reification of a capitalist hegemony, or if some feminist professors of philosophy argue that logic—the *modus ponens* and the Aristotelian syllogism—are patriarchal creations that oppress women, the corrective is not dismissal for purveying "pernicious perspectives" but analysis and refutation. (See, e.g., Louis B. Schwartz, "With Gun and Camera through Darkest CLS-Land," *Stanford Law Review* 36 [1984]: 413 and Martha Nussbaum, "Feminists in Philosophy," *New York Review of Books,* October 20, 1994.)

In much larger measure, however, the invocation of "political correctness" is unconcerned with disciplinary debates played out in the literature. It is concerned with the role of politically committed faculty in campus affairs; with efforts to place a certain ideological cast on the curriculum or to proscribe certain forms of utterance. Professors' speech has been constrained at the behest of aggrieved groups of "homosexuals, feminists, blacks and Hispanics in the student body" (Edward Shils, "Do We Still Need Academic Freedom?" *American Scholar* 62 [1933]: 197–198). These constraints are often instigated, encouraged, and abetted by "postmodern," "feminist," or "communitarian" faculty. (Cf. William Van Alstyne, "The University in the Manner of Tiananmen Square," *Hastings Constitutional Law Quarterly* 21 [1993]: 1–4.) Indeed, Professor Silva's brush with those forces has been noted, and others—a veritable parade of horribles—have been compiled. (See Neil Hamilton,

Zealotry and Academic Freedom [New Brunswick, N.J.: Transaction, 1995], chap. 2.)

In all these cases, however, official sanctions have been sought (and can only be sought) by administrations, often against tenured faculty whose very tenure serves as a partial brake on precipitate action, as in Professor Silva's case. Thus it is difficult to see what tenure has to do with the claim of "too much" freedom unless the critics of correctness wish to have the power summarily to dismiss faculty for advocating policies they, the critics, find "pernicious," much as President Holt dismissed Professor Rice and colleagues who supported him.

The suppression of speech on the campus—even in the name of a more sensitive, open, welcoming environment—is an evil, antithetical to the essence of the university as a place where all ideas may be expressed, no matter how distasteful, offensive, or repugnant they may be. The evil, however, lies in the act of suppression, not in its advocacy.

Thus it is curious that the critics direct their attack at tenure, which protects the advocate from summary dismissal, rather than at the governing boards that have the power to ensure "that continued and fearless sifting and winnowing by which the truth can be found," as the Regents of the University of Wisconsin declared in the wake of the Ely case in 1894. To the extent that trustees and regents fail in that duty and administrators of public universities act on the impulse to suppress speech, succor may have to come from the courts, now as in the suppression of utterances thought to be communistic in the 1950s. But it should suffice here to say that if tenure protects from summary dismissal those faculty members who would have their institutions suppress speech, it protects as well those who oppose those efforts; and the highly charged contemporary campus climate seems to signal the need for more protection, not less.

As both Machlup and Shils observed, most academics find little occasion to do the sorts of things that call their exercise of academic freedom into question. That is why, as Machlup pointed out, many professors would be happy to "sell" their tenure for higher salaries. And that is why, as Shils noted, most faculty have been indifferent when sanctions have been imposed on others or have even been resentful of the trouble they have stirred up. But, as Machlup explained:

> Since the temptation to go after the "abuser" of freedom may be irresistible to the powers that be, the protection of freedom may depend on the strength of the defense. Hence we need and want teachers and scholars who would unhesitatingly come to the defense of

the "odd ball," the heretic, the dissenter, the troublemaker, whose freedom to speak and to write is under *some threat from colleagues,* administrators, governing board, government, *or pressure groups.* The impulse to take up the cudgels for the "odd ball" is all too easily suppressed if unpleasant consequences must be feared by those who defend him. [Emphases added.]

In sum, the need to protect free speech extends to advocates of all stripes; and the summary dismissal of radical faculty, even those who would deny free speech to others, must have a chilling effect on the ground of its having been exercised at all. Note the experiences of an ad hoc committee in 1942 when it investigated the summary dismissal of a faculty member (of fourteen years' service) at an institution that lacked tenure:

> From several sources within the faculty came expressions of doubt that anyone would be bold enough to talk to the Committee when it arrived. This prediction was not entirely accurate, but it led the Committee to send a questionnaire to the members of the faculty before its visit to Rock Hill. Many of the replies to the questionnaire were brought to the Committee at night. Only a small proportion of the replies was transmitted by mail. Faculty members expressed distrust of the College post office. Some indicated that they had not submitted their answers previously lest they be made available to the College authorities. ["Academic Freedom and Tenure: Winthrop College," *AAUP Bulletin* 28 (April 1942): 190]

and of another committee called upon in 1975 to investigate the Oklahoma College of Liberal Arts, (OCLA), which had abolished tenure and summarily dismissed fourteen dissident faculty, seven of whom had tenure under the college's previous rule:

> No true institution of higher education can function successfully in an atmosphere of suspicion and fear even remotely similar to what the investigating committee encountered at OCLA. Many faculty members expressed fear to the investigating committee that their services might be terminated if they associated with the "wrong" people or expressed unacceptable ideas or even if it became known that they were talking to the committee. Conditions at OCLA, unfortunate as they are, stand witness to the wisdom of the tenure system as essential to the protection of academic freedom. ["Academic Freedom and Tenure: University of Science and Arts of Oklahoma," *AAUP Bulletin* 61 (Spring 1975): 44]

and of yet another committee investigating in 1991 the dismissal of dissident faculty without the safeguards of academic due process:

> Evidence of the ongoing state of affairs at Wesley College was revealed to the members of the investigating committee while they

were in Dover. Faculty members reported that they are afraid to be seen in the presence of their friends who are among those dismissed. One current faculty member reported going out of town to meet one of the dismissed professors. Another current faculty member reported coming to the meeting with the investigating committee through alleyways in the hope of not being seen. ["Academic Freedom and Tenure: Wesley College (Delaware)," *AAUP Bulletin* 78 (May–June, 1992): 35]

It does not appear that human nature, even the nature of academics, has changed very much in this regard.

Postscript

Editorial opinion on tenure has long been divided. An editorial writer for the *Washington Post* provided an example of the critical kind on January 11, 1995:

> Tenure's current status dates from the post-McCarthy era and was based on fears that professors were uniquely vulnerable to job pressure because of their political views—and uniquely in need of protection so as to be able to pursue their teaching and research free of political interference or reprisal. This idea, in turn, harks back to a much older image, that of the cloistered, monkish scholar pursuing his labors for decades, safely insulated from the pressures of the outside world. The image has its nostalgic appeal, but it is a long way from reality on most campuses these days.

The editorial drew a reply from Professor Robert M. O'Neil, former president of the University of Wisconsin system and later of the University of Virginia. It is well to close the case for tenure on that note:

> However one may feel about the departure of Dr. Joycelyn Elders as surgeon general, she remains free as professor of medicine at the University of Arkansas to speak of sex and drugs and other issues the nation needs to discuss candidly. Similarly, it is vital that Prof. Lani Guinier remain free to speak and write about racial injustice as tenured professor at Pennsylvania, if not as assistant attorney general.
>
> Most recently, I hope the same will be true for Prof. Christina Jeffrey. Though perhaps misguided in her views of the Holocaust (dearly has she paid for those views) and whatever the merits of Speaker Gingrich's dismissal of her as House historian, I assume that as tenured professor at Kennesaw State College she will remain free to express her views about how history should be taught.
>
> The Post may treat McCarthyism as "nostalgia" and assume that most academics are free to speak and write these days—though both assumptions are much frailer than the editorial implies. It's the Elderses, the Guiniers and the Jeffreys I worry about here and now. As long as their freedom to speak is buttressed by tenure, it seems to me well worth keeping the old system intact for a good while longer.

Supplemental Notes and References

Introduction

Some of the prior discussion of tenure can be found in Commission on Academic Tenure, *Faculty Tenure* (San Francisco: Jossey-Bass, 1973) and *The Tenure Debate* (San Francisco: Jossey-Bass, 1973). A fuller bibliography is supplied in Howard R. Bowen and Jack H. Schuster, *American Professors: A National Resource Imperiled* (New York: Oxford University Press, 1986), pp. 301–316.

On tenure "refuseniks" see David Helfand, "Tenure or No Tenure? I Turned Down Tenure," *Current,* October 1986, p. 33, and "Tenure: Thanks but No Thanks," *Chronicle of Higher Education,* December 15, 1995, p. B1; James O'Toole, "Tenure: A Conscientious Objection," and a rebuttal by William Van Alstyne, "Tenure: A Conscientious Objective," both in *Change* 26 (May/June 1994) (reprinted from 1978).

Not all op-ed commentary in tenure has been critical. See Louis Morrell, "Let's Not Do Away with Tenure," *Boston Sunday Globe,* July 17, 1994; and "Tenure Can't Be Tenuous," *St. Louis Post Dispatch,* July 6, 1994.

The "dragon of tenure" reference is from Richard P. Chait and Andrew T. Ford, *Beyond Traditional Tenure* (San Francisco: Jossey-Bass, 1982), p. 143; reviewed by Matthew W. Finkin in *Journal of College and University Law* 10 (1983–84): 105.

1. The Meaning of Tenure

The standard history is still Richard Hofstadter and Walter P. Metzger, *The Development of Academic Freedom in the United States* (New York: Columbia University Press, 1955). Metzger has more recently explored the history of the 1940 *Statement* in "The 1940 Statement of Principles on Academic Freedom and Tenure," in *Freedom and Tenure in the Academy,* ed. William W. Van Alstyne (Durham, N.C.: Duke University Press, 1993). That volume also contains a thorough bibliography on tenure and academic freedom.

Wigmore's statement on the "judicial" character of the AAUP's investigative reports was made in his "President's Report," *AAUP Bulletin* 21 (1916): 9.

3. *Dismissal and Due Process*

The requirement of an impartial hearing body in the academic setting is best (and most commonly) served by a faculty committee, as in Professor King's case. Such a body is, as William Van Alstyne put it earlier, the "least dangerous" branch to be entrusted with that responsibility. (That faculty role was not well received by college and university presidents when it was first broached at the turn of the century [see Walter P. Metzger, "Academic Tenure in America: A Historical Essay" in Commission on Academic Tenure in Higher Education, *Faculty Tenure*, p. 145]. But it has become the norm.) However, two prominent students of higher education, while strongly endorsing academic tenure, are critical of the role of faculty members as adjudicators and are even more critical of the procedures required, which, they argue, "take on the flavor of a trial for murder": Bowen and Schuster, *American Professors*, p. 243. No doubt the procedural rules of some institutions are unnecessarily complex. No doubt some faculties are reluctant to police themselves aggressively. The former difficulty, however, is the consequence of institutional choice and not of anything inherent in the element of due process outlined in the *King* case. The latter problem raises the question who is better positioned and better qualified to adjudicate professional incompetence or misconduct than a body of peers. Bowen and Schuster suggest that a body of specialized arbitrators be used, and the AAUP has given the suggestion its qualified endorsement. We ought to note, however, that under no tenure regime is the decision of a faculty hearing body final and binding: as in Professor King's case, the faculty hearing committee submits its findings and recommendations to the governing board, though one would expect them to have weight. To that extent, tenure is only a limited brake on precipitate action. The *King* case is discussed more fully in Brian Brooks, "Adequate Cause for Dismissal: The Missing Element in Academic Freedom," *Journal of College and University Law* 22 (Fall 1995): 331–358.

4. *The Economics of Tenure*

For more of the debate on how "anachronistic" job security really is in the American economy, compare Kenneth Swinnerton and Howard Wial, "Is Job Security Declining in the U.S. Economy?" *Industrial and*

Labor Relations Review 48 (1995): 293, with Francis Diebold, David Neumark, and Daniel Polsky, "Comment on Swinnerton and Wial," ibid. 49 (1996): 348, followed by Swinnerton and Wial's reply, p. 352.

The demands of corporate employee "loyalty" may be eroding as a result of legislative and judicial action, but that is well beyond the scope of this work. For a comparison of the industrial and academic settings see Matthew W. Finkin, "A Higher Order of Liberty in the Workplace": Academic Freedom and Tenure in the Vortex of Employment Practices and Law," in Van Alstyne, *Freedom and Tenure in the Academy,* pp. 357–380.

Bowen and Schuster's conclusion, referred to in the text, is worth noting in full:

> The weakening of tenure would be certain to reduce the power of academe to attract and retain staff. Furthermore, because it would undermine security and collegiality, it would impair morale even in the short run. The tactless references to "dead wood" and "new blood," the unconcealed glee sometimes shown over arranging an early retirement, and the operation of a revolving door policy in the recruitment and probation of young faculty are all unnecessary and ultimately counter-productive departures from well-understood tradition and are viewed by some, morally, if not legally, as breaches of contract. The accumulation of these events across the country simply makes the academic profession less attractive and bids up the price of recruiting new talent in the future. We think this is short-sighted policy.

The fullest account of the Loring episode is supplied in *Centennial History of the Harvard Law School, 1817–1917* (Cambridge: Harvard University Press, 1918), pp. 236–239.

5. *Tenure and Resource Allocation*

A reprise of the neoclassical argument against tenure is essayed by Robert McGee and Walter Block, "Academic Tenure: An Economic Critique," *Harvard Journal of Law and Public Policy* 14 (Spring 1991): 545–563. For the purpose of their critique, they conflate tenure in secondary schools with tenure in higher education, though one would think the respective settings (and resulting analyses) would be quite different.

On the roots of the "financial exigency" clause in the Great Depression, see *Depression Recovery and Higher Education* (New York: McGraw-Hill, 1937). On a survey of institutional practice see "Retrenchment Practices in Higher Education: A Technical Report," *Journal of the College and University Personnel Association* 31, nos. 3–4 (1980). It should be noted that Bowen and Schuster are critical of the content of the "financial exigency" clause, though not of its purpose: *American Professors,* pp. 241–242.

For a study of how traditional liberal arts colleges have adapted to long-term "market demand" by adding preprofessional or vocation curricula, see Matthew S. Kraatz and Edward J. Zajac, "Exploring the Limits of the New Institutionalism: The Cause and Consequences of Illegitimate Organizational Change," forthcoming in *American Sociological Review.*

With respect to physicians employed by HMOs, it has been reported that the employment contracts of some HMOs include "gag clauses" that limit physicians' ability to discuss the quality of the care they provide. A "typical clause" is open-ended with regard to those to whom such utterance is prohibited: "Physician shall take no action nor make any communication which undermines or could undermine the confidence of enrollees, potential enrollees, their employers, plan sponsors or the public in . . . [the HMO], or in the quality of care which . . . [the HMO's] enrollees receive" ("Doctors Say H.M.O.'s Limit What They Can Tell Patients," *New York Times,* December 21, 1995, p. A14).

7. *Posttenure Review*

The Sonoma State investigation was conducted by Henry Mason (Political Science, Tulane University) and George Schatzki (Law, University of Washington). The Stetson investigation was conducted by Lon Fuller (Duke Law School), James A. McLaughlin (Harvard Law School), and William M. Hepburn (University of Alabama Law School).

The papers (in addition to Bryant Kearl's) presented at the Wingspread Conference as well as a list of the conferees is published in *Academe* 69 (November–December 1983): 1a–14a. For an essay explaining the workings of a system at the University of Kentucky akin to the one discussed at the University of Colorado, see Richard Edwards, "Toward Constructive Review of Disengaged Faculty," *AAHE Bulletin,* October 1994, p. 6. It supplies an updated bibliography on the question of posttenure review. For a review of the plan instituted at the University of Hawaii see Madeleine Goodman, "The Review of Tenured Faculty at a Research University: Outcomes and Appraisals," *Review of Higher Education,* Fall 1994, pp. 83–94.

8. *The New Criticism*

On the "too much freedom" claim, it is odd that critics of political correctness have seized upon tenure as an evil, for it would seem otherwise obvious that on a campus captured by correctness, the most likely victims are those who have spoken "incorrectly"—who have been charged, for example, with harassing speech—and whom tenure could no longer protect.

The Winthrop College investigation was conducted by Newman White (English, Duke University) and William M. Hepburn (Law, University of Alabama). The OCLA investigation was conducted by Robert Bogomolny (Law, Southern Methodist University) and Marilyn Stokstad (Art History, University of Kansas). The Wesley College investigation was conducted by C. William Heywood (History, Cornell College) and Sterling Delano (English, Villanova University).

Postscript

After Professor O'Neil's reply, Professor Joycelyn Elders addressed the annual meeting of the American Association of University Professors to report that Arkansas legislators had made a serious effort to prevent her return to the University of Arkansas School of Medicine. "The thing that allows me to be here," she said, "is your 1940 *Statement of Principles on Academic Freedom and Tenure*" (*Academe* 81 [July–August 1995]: 52).

Index